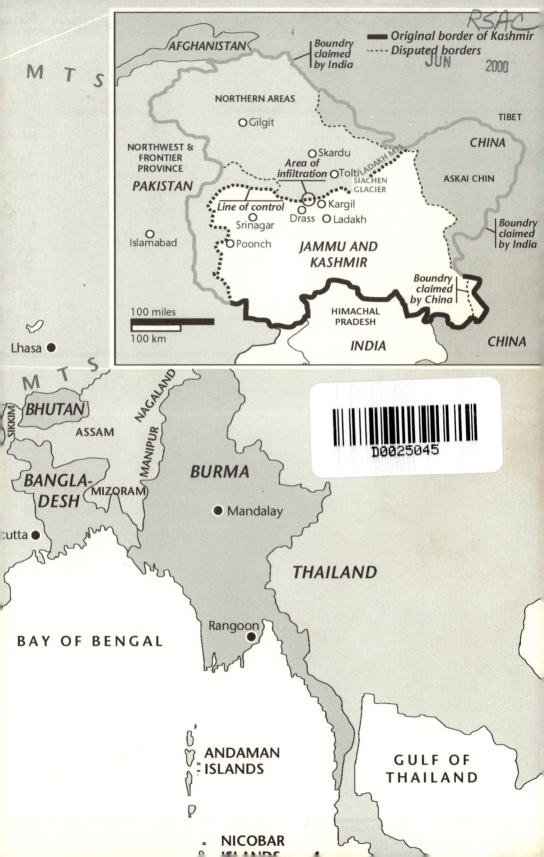

M T S

RSAC

AFGHANISTAN

━━━ Original border of Kashmir
····· Disputed borders

JUN 2000

Boundry claimed by India

NORTHERN AREAS

○ Gilgit

TIBET

NORTHWEST & FRONTIER PROVINCE

○ Skardu

Area of infiltration ○ Tolti

CHINA

LADAKH MTS

SIACHEN GLACIER

ASKAI CHIN

PAKISTAN

Line of control

○ Kargil

Drass ○ Ladakh

Boundry claimed by India

○ Islamabad

Srinagar ○

○ Poonch

JAMMU AND KASHMIR

Boundry claimed by China

100 miles

100 km

HIMACHAL PRADESH

CHINA

INDIA

M T S

Lhasa ●

NAGALAND

SIKKIM

BHUTAN

ASSAM

MANIPUR

BURMA

D0025045

BANGLA-DESH

MIZORAM

● Mandalay

cutta ●

THAILAND

● Rangoon

BAY OF BENGAL

ANDAMAN ISLANDS

GULF OF THAILAND

NICOBAR ISLANDS

WAR *at* *the* TOP OF THE WORLD

The Struggle for

Afghanistan, Kashmir,

and Tibet

WAR *at*
the TOP OF THE WORLD

The Struggle for

Afghanistan, Kashmir,

and Tibet

Eric S. Margolis

ROUTLEDGE

New York

Published in 2000 by
Routledge
29 West 35th Street
New York, NY 10001

First published in Canada in 1999 by Key Porter Books Limited,
and reprinted by arrangement with Key Porter Books Limited.
First Routledge hardback edition, 2000
Copyright © 1999, 2000 by Eric Margolis

Printed in the United States of America on acid-free paper.

Library of Congress Cataloging-in-Publication Data

Margolis, Eric S.
    War at the top of the world : the struggle for Afghanistan, Kashmir, and Tibet /
Eric S. Margolis.
        p. cm.
    Includes index.
    ISBN 0-415-92712-9 (hb)
    1. Afghanistan—Politics and government—1973-. 2. Jammu and Kashmir
(India)—Politics and government. 3. Tibet (China)—Politics and government. 4.
China—Foreign relations—India. 5. India—Foreign relations—China. I. Title.

DS371.3 .M37 2000
950—dc21
                                                                    99-056853

10 9 8 7 6 5 4 3 2 1

Contents

To Nexhmie Zaimi,
my mother,
to Henry Margolis,
my father,
and to LC

Introduction

In the nineteenth century the British Empire and the expanding power of Czarist Russia came into conflict as the Russians moved south toward India. The rivalry was fierce and hard fought. Kipling called it the "Great Game."

A new Great Game is afoot at the top of the world. The chain of mountain ranges, plateaus, and valleys that begins in Afghanistan and Kashmir, and then sweeps 2,500 miles (4,000 km) across the Indian subcontinent to Burma (now Myanmar), is fast becoming one of the globe's most volatile and dangerous geopolitical fault zones. Along that line four nuclear-armed powers—China, India, Pakistan, and Russia—are locked in a long-term rivalry that may erupt into the first major international conflict of the twenty-first century.

This assertion may come as a surprise, since most people are accustomed to regarding South-Central Asia and the Himalayas as an exotic, remote, backward part of the world, whose unstable societies and bitter disputes are of little concern to the rest of mankind.

Such may have been the case a century ago, when the first Great Game was played out on India's wild Northwest Frontier and in Central Asia between the British and Russian Empires. Today, however, the region known as South Asia, which contains a full quarter of humanity, is being shaken by a confluence of strategic, political, and economic tensions that threatens to ignite a series of interlocking conflicts whose effects may be felt around the globe.

According to a 1993 U.S. Central Intelligence Agency (CIA) study, the border of disputed Jammu and Kashmir, along which Indian and Pakistani forces have skirmished almost daily for the last half-century, is now considered the most likely place for a nuclear war to begin. Studies conducted by the Rand Corporation estimate such a nuclear exchange between India and Pakistan would initially kill 2 million people, cause 100 million casualties, and contaminate South and Central Asia, as well as much of the globe, with radioactive fallout.

In May 1998, India shocked the world by detonating five nuclear devices, and testing intermediate-range missiles in an unmistakable assertion of its new, self-proclaimed status as a superpower. India's scimitar-rattling was aimed at cowing old foe Pakistan, and, even more significantly, as a clear warning to its new and now principal enemy, China.

Pakistan riposted by testing its own nuclear-capable missiles. China accelerated its numerous intermediate-missile programs and warned India against any aggressive actions. Russia, in spite of ostensible bankruptcy, sharply accelerated delivery of high-tech arms to India, its old Soviet-era strategic ally, while increasingly funneling weapons, military advisors, and intelligence agents into Afghanistan and Central Asia.

Clearly, a new Great Game is under way, but this time one played for the very highest stakes by nuclear-armed rivals across a vast region of growing political and social instability, at a time when Asia's giants, India and China, haunted by the memory of the collapsed Soviet Union, are being shaken by deepening uncertainty over their continued viability as unitary states.

I have covered or explored South Asia as a political journalist, war correspondent, and old-fashioned adventurer for the past twenty-five years. My many journeys across the subcontinent have taken me to the great Holy War in Afghanistan against the Soviets; to conflicts in Kashmir and atop the Siachen Glacier at 18,000 feet (5,486 m); and to insurgencies in Punjab, Sri Lanka, and Burma. Frequent contacts with intelligence agencies and senior military figures in the region have afforded me particular insight into the tensions and rivalries beneath the surface of Asian geopolitics.

There is no other region on Earth, in my view—not even the murderous Balkans or the ever-seething Middle East—that presents such a toxic stew of boiling religious, ethnic, political, strategic, and historical animosities, made all the more volatile by endemic poverty, illiteracy, and the sheer agony of daily existence. Two powerful and energetic new forces, Islamic and Hindu political religious fundamentalism, have fanned the already flaring fires of South Asia. Both movements, a reaction to centuries of colonialism and backwardness, have released pent-up passions that are shaking the subcontinent.

The prospect of nuclear-armed states ruled by aggressive nationalists, religious extremists, or unsteady governments is extremely disturbing. Old foes Pakistan and India have fought three major wars in the past 50 years and could blunder into a fourth at any time. This danger was dramatically illustrated by a series of violent clashes in the Ladakh Valley of northern Kashmir that began in May 1999, the heaviest fighting between India and Pakistan in three decades.

Eight hundred Kashmiri Islamic insurgents, or mujihadin, crossed the northern sector of the Line of Control in one of its remotest regions. They seized commanding positions on the 16,000-ft-high northern flank of Ladakh overlooking the valley below, the city of Kargil, and the vital Indian military road running from Srinagar through Ladakh and Leh to the Siachen Glacier.

Caught totally unprepared and badly shaken, India claimed the intruders were 'Islamic mercenaries' or Pakistani army regulars, not 'Kashmiri freedom fighters' as Pakistan maintained. India threw 30,000 troops into the battle for the towering heights above Kargil and the town of Drass. Indian warplanes, helicopter gunships, and heavy artillery launched intensive attacks against the insurgent positions: two Indian warplanes and a helicopter were downed.

Heavy fighting raged for two months as Indian mountain troops fought an uphill battle at extremely high altitudes to dislodge the Islamic attackers, who were well dug in and amply provisioned. India suffered at least 1,000 casualties in the fighting. During the battles in Ladakh, senior Indian commanders put intensive pressure on the government in New Delhi to launch a major land offensive in the south against Pakistan — in other words, an all-out war involving 1.5 million soldiers.

Ominously, in June, U.S. satellites showed two Indian 'strike corps,' armor-heavy, multi-division offensive formations designed to slice through Pakistan's narrow waist, were preparing to launch a major invasion of Pakistan from Rajastan and Punjab. Powerful units of the Indian Navy took up station within striking range of Karachi, through which 90 percent of Pakistan's trade passes, ready to impose a maritime blockade and attack the smaller Pakistani fleet.

Intelligence sources in Washington and Islamabad told this author that in late May and June, 1999, Pakistan and India were 'within hours' of a massive war. Both sides put their nuclear strike forces on the highest alert and, reportedly, began inserting fissionable cores into their nuclear weapons. This crisis, whose full gravity was largely concealed from the international public, was the most dangerous direct confrontation between nuclear armed powers since the 1962 Cuban missile crisis.

Threats by the United States to impose a cut-off of international aid to Pakistan forced Prime Minister Nawaz Sharif to rush to Washington, where he received a public dressing down by President Clinton. Nawaz, who had until then maintained he had no control over the 'mujihadin' intruders, was compelled to order them to fully withdraw.

Compounding this national and personal humiliation, Nawaz told the Americans that he had known nothing about the Kargil operation, claiming 'rogue' Pakistani generals had staged the 'coup de main' without his knowledge. In fact, Nawaz had sanctioned the intrusion as a handy way of dramatically internationalizing the long-forgotten Kashmir issue. In this, Nawaz succeeded brilliantly, but at the cost of a stinging defeat for Pakistan, which was widely blamed and rebuked for bringing the world close to nuclear war.

Ironically, the Pakistani-instigated Kargil fighting created a surge of nationalist passion in India, producing a decisive electoral victory in September, 1999 elections for Pakistans' sworn enemy, the Hindu chauvinist Bharatiya Janata Party.

While India crowed with victory, and Pakistan's generals growled in fury, Nawaz attempted to impose his direct control on the restive military by sacking the army's chief of staff, Gen. Pervez Musharraf. The military, which had long chaffed under Nawaz's increasingly corrupt and dictatorial rule, rallied around Musharraf, and arrested the prime minister and his senior supporters.

In spite of worldwide criticism, the bloodless military coup was acclaimed by most Pakistanis. By the time the generals struck, Pakistan was plagued by growing internal chaos and open civil war in certain regions that may have tempted India to intervene, just as Delhi did in crumbling East Pakistan during 1971. Intervention by India in Pakistan would very likely have triggered a nuclear war. Though a full-scale war that could have resulted in a nuclear exchange had been averted, heavy fighting along the Kashmir border continues to the present, while Delhi and Islamabad continue to rattle their missiles.

Adding a final element of danger to this already perilous situation, India and Pakistan have repeatedly traded threats to attack one another's civilian and military nuclear reactors and missile sites. Reactors producing weapons-grade uranium or plutonium would likely be primary targets in any strategic level war, whether conventional or nuclear.

A war between India and Pakistan could very well draw China into the fray. Pakistan, which is constantly menaced by attack from India, is China's closest and most important ally. A full-scale war between Pakistan and India would most likely result in a major Pakistani defeat, unless China intervened in the Himalayas and Karakorams to support Pakistan. In fact, China has made clear it will not easily allow Pakistan, its sole "window on the West," to be defeated and, possibly, broken up or reabsorbed by India.

The festering problem of Tibet, and growing rivalry between India and China over Burma and the Indian Ocean, are other likely sources of potential conflict.

The collapse of the Soviet Union reminds us that China and India are also susceptible to a similar process of political and regional dissolution. Disintegration of either great nation-state seems almost unimaginable, yet so did the Soviet Union's stunningly sudden collapse. National instability in China or India would produce a geopolitical earthquake of enormous magnitude across Asia.

Even more ominous, India and China appear set on a collision course, as their regional interests and strategic ambitions come increasingly into conflict. Each superpower sees itself as the rightful dominant political and economic power in Asia. Both nations are developing intermediate-range nuclear arsenals clearly designed to fight a tactical or sub-strategic war. China and India are rapidly modernizing their huge ground forces, respectively the world's largest and second-largest, and making them more mobile, as well as expanding their air and naval arms. Naval rivalry between India and China is already under way in the eastern approaches of the Indian Ocean.

Any weakening of China's central government produced by the eventual decline or collapse of the ruling Communist party would almost certainly encourage secessionist movements and regionalism in China, most notably in Tibet and Sinkiang. Such a development would tempt India to seize the opportunity to intervene in Tibet, thus rectifying its disastrous strategic error in the 1950s when Delhi allowed China to annex and militarize the highly strategic Tibetan Plateau, which looms over North India and controls the headwaters of most of India's major rivers.

China and India's rivalry over Burma is also increasing. Burma's important strategic location and rich resources are coveted by both neighboring powers. Delhi accuses China of seeking to forge a "strategic encirclement" of India through Pakistan, Tibet, Burma, and by naval expansion in the eastern reaches of the Indian Ocean. China, by contrast, sees itself encircled and challenged by an aggressive India, a resurgent Russia, and a hostile Vietnam, possibly joined at some later date by Japan or the United States.

Both China and India have long demonstrated hegemonistic behavior toward their smaller Asian neighbors by demanding acceptance of their strategic diktat. As China and India continue to grow stronger militarily and economically, their demands for compliance and cooperation from their smaller neighbors are certain to grow apace. This, in turn, will bring China and India increasingly into contention as they vie to dominate South and Central Asia. Both powers will also increasingly compete for Asian oil, water, food, and mineral resources to fuel their expanding economies and sustain growing, increasingly urbanized populations.

History demonstrates that new powers, or resurgent older ones, invariably challenge the status quo, which we euphemistically term "stability." As new powers expand and flex their strategic muscles, they must clash with the old powers of the status quo, and, inevitably, destabilize the existing world order. In Asia, we see the unique spectacle of two ancient nations that are fast emerging as the newest superpowers in the midst of a fragmented, unstable region composed of small, weak states and a wounded, revanchist Russia.

This, and the fact that the two Asian superpowers are also uneasy neighbors sharing a long, disputed border, is a recipe for future conflict. War between China and India is not inevitable. But there are so many dangerous points of contention between them—a nuclear-weapons race, Pakistan, Kashmir, Tibet, India's eastern hill states, their disputed Himalayan borders, Burma, and the Indian Ocean—that a major military clash between China and India within the next decade thus appears highly likely. There can be only one master of Asia.

When this clash finally occurs, when Asia's two titans, the world's newest superpowers, meet, the world will shake.

• • •

To understand the origins of this coming conflict at the top of the world, we must turn the clock back two decades to the remote mountains of Afghanistan, where a little-known tribal people who valued liberty more than their lives or fortunes joined battle in a seemingly hopeless struggle against the world's most powerful army. . . .

PART ONE

The

Great Jihad

1
Soldiers of Allah

Oh, Lord Shiva, save us from the claw of the tiger, the fang of the cobra,
and the vengeance of the Afghan.
OLD HINDU PRAYER

Speak not of those who are slain in the way of God as
dead; for they are alive.
HOLY KORAN

JALALABAD, AFGHANISTAN, May 1992

The first 107mm rocket arced across a flat, arid plain of scrub and rock toward the enemy position, a high, flat-topped hill, about half a mile (1 km) distant from where we stood. The rocket's fiery backblast produced a cloud of swirling black smoke and a thunderous roar that seemed to advertise our exposed position to everyone within the great amphitheater-shaped valley surrounding the besieged city of Jalalabad.

The missile hit the Communist position at its center. First came an elongated puff of gray-black smoke. Then, a few seconds later, there was a loud explosion whose deep roar echoed off the dark mountains towering over the Jalalabad plain. It seemed to me a good time to take cover, but our leader, the venerable Hadji Ajab, and his nine men continued to stand proudly upright, and in full view of the enemy position, unconcerned that we offered a splendid target to the now aroused Communist garrison.

Curiously, the enemy remained silent. Hadji Ajab suggested in strongly flavored Pushtun that the Communist dogs were too frightened of the *mujahedin* to fight. The Hadji was a grandfatherly seventy-two, a tiny, frail-looking man with a gentle smile and a wispy white beard that curled upward at the end. He had commanded mujahedin bands in battle against the Afghan Communists and the Soviets for the past eleven years; he was also the *imam* (prayer leader) of his small village, which was located some 9 miles (15 km) south of our position. Somehow, the ancient mountain warrior had twice found time during the long struggle to make the *hadj*—or pilgrimage—to distant Mecca. Hence his much-respected title, Hadji, which gave him the right to wear a green turban and to lead his men both in prayer and in battle.

Hadji Ajab ordered another round to be fired. Selim, a skinny youth of eighteen who had been appointed our band's military technician on the basis of once having briefly worked in a Kabul garage, fiddled with the leads of a battered red car battery that he had wired up to the Chinese 107mm multibarrel rocket launcher.

A second rocket roared off, producing the usual dramatic pyrotechnics. As it arced toward the enemy position, the mujahedin cried out, in unison, "Allah Akbar!"—God is great—the ancient Muslim war cry first heard in AD 622 when the Prophet Mohammed and his tiny band of companions were fighting for their lives against superior forces.

When the second rocket hit the Communist position and exploded, the old Hadji cried out, "Al-hamdililah!"—Allah be praised. We joined him lustily, waving our arms, shaking our fists at the foe, yelling, "Al-hamdililah!" Thirteen hundred years seemed to vanish. The alchemy of battle had magically returned us to the time of the Prophet, as the holy warriors called upon the one, true God like the embattled Companions of the Prophet Mohammed, to give their arms strength to smite the idolaters.

We fired off ten more rounds in rapid succession, alternating more cries of "Allah Akbar" when they were loosed, and "Al-hamdililah" when they exploded. The Islamic barrage finally produced an angry response from the Communist garrison. They opened up on us with mortars. White puffs of smoke burst around our position, but none of the shells caused injury. Then two T-55 tanks, dug in atop the enemy redoubt, opened rapid fire. The flat-trajectory tank shells made a sharp crack. While we could usually observe the mortar shells flying lazily through the air toward our position, the flat-trajectory, high-explosive tank shells came in too fast and level to be seen. Their explosions threw up big clumps of dirt, produced clouds of gray-black smoke, and sent red-hot shrapnel ricocheting off the rocks and boulders that lay scattered about us.

To my very great relief, Hadji Ajab finally ordered his men to squat down and take shelter behind the rocks. The blizzard of steel was becoming too much even for them. Adding to the danger, more enemy mortars took our position under fire. I crouched down and watched the explosions mushroom around us. Taking incoming artillery fire is one of life's more disagreeable, nerve-racking experiences. I attempted a Chinese meditation technique that I had recently learned in an effort to distance my inner self from the explosive outer reality around me. My meditation abruptly ended when a piece of hot shrapnel whistled by my right ear and ricocheted off a boulder.

After a half-hour that seemed to last for three days, the Communist barrage let up. Selim and two other gaunt mujahedin jumped up and began reloading the Chinese rocket launcher. The Hadji stood erect and peered at the enemy position through his aged, watery eyes, thoughtfully stroking his beard in the manner of Islamic wise men. "Fire," he ordered. Once again, we jumped up and chorused, "Allah Akbar," as a ripple-fire of rockets flew toward the enemy redoubt.

There was a huge detonation that must have been audible in Kabul, 70 miles (113 km) away. One of the rockets had hit and penetrated the redoubt's ammunition bunker. The entire Communist position was swathed in thick, billowing smoke, from whose center bright orange flames shot skyward. It was an enormously satisfying spectacle. We hugged and kissed one another, laughing joyously and yelling, "Al-hamdililah! Al-hamdililah!" until we were hoarse and exhausted. There was no return fire from the Communist position: its garrison had probably fled for their lives from exploding shells in the ammunition bunker.

For the rest of the afternoon, we kept firing rockets at the smoldering Communist position and at supply depots located behind it. Our little victory must finally have galvanized the Afghan army command at Jalalabad, because, around 4 p.m. concentrated fire from two different batteries of highly accurate, Soviet-built D30 122mm howitzers began to bracket our position. At the same time, we saw three T-54/55 tanks and four BTR armored personnel carriers moving toward us about 2 miles (3 km) away. The Hadji's men had no antitank weapons. We were also down to our last wooden case of Chinese rockets.

"Mr. Eric," the Hadji politely asked me through his son Jamal, who spoke some English, "would you like to stay and fight some more?" I didn't want to appear timid before these intrepid warriors, but I had to go back through the Khyber Pass that night to get to Peshawar, from where I was due to take a plane to Lahore next morning to interview Pakistan's prime minister, Nawaz Sharif.

"Please inform his Hadjiness that I think it would be better to go home now since I still have a long trip tonight." All this seemed very surreal, as if I were declining another cup of tea. Two 122mm shells exploded just to our right, showering us with dirt.

Almost reluctantly, Hadji Ajab and his band of holy warriors packed up their gear and manhandled the rocket launcher into the back of one of the white Toyota Land Cruisers—the favored vehicle of all Third World warriors—that had brought us to the battle. The investment of Jalalabad was a commuter's siege. The besiegers got up in the morning, drove or walked to the front lines, fought for four to six hours, and then often returned home for the night. The Hadji's men had been blessed with jeeps, thanks to the grace of Allah, and Saudi largesse.

This, however, was an exception. Many of the less fortunate mujahedin in other parts of the war zone were so poor they didn't even possess coats or shoes. Against the stabbing cold of the Afghan mountains they had only thin wool shawls. The mujahedin would walk to battle barefoot, through deep snow, sometimes for two days and nights, carrying 90 pounds (40 kg) of mortar shells or rockets on their backs. Then they would trudge home, dodging inevitable counterattacks by Communist artillery, or the far more fearsome Hind helicopter gunships, which hunted the mujahedin across the open plains of Afghanistan, where the only cover was an occasional boulder or gully.

Off we drove, out of the depression in which the jeeps had been hidden like so many docile ponies from an earlier age of war, and up into full view of the by now very angry Communist forces, who reopened a furious fire on us. Our drivers zigged and zagged across the rough ground as shells exploded around the racing jeeps. Death from a broken neck in the violently jolting vehicle seemed as real a peril as being shredded by red-hot shrapnel. The Afghan warriors, however, seemed to find the death-defying ride a romp: they laughed with glee as the jeeps careened perilously or hung on two wheels, as lethal white puffs of smoke from exploding shells blossomed around us. Finally, after what seemed hours, but was probably no more than five minutes, we rounded a knoll and moved out of the enemy's direct line of fire.

Ninety minutes later we arrived at the Hadji's mud-walled village, which bore the scars of frequent enemy bombing and shelling. He invited me to stay for evening prayers and dinner, but I insisted that I must press on to Peshawar. I slowly embraced each member of the muja-

hedin band. One, named Gul Khan, a great strapping man with a fero-
cious-looking black beard, held my hand in both of his, Afghan style,
and said, "Mr Eric, please do not forget us." A knife twisted inside me. I
felt a coward, a deserter, leaving these splendid fighters, my comrades-
in-arms, to their holy war, while I returned, the satiated voyeur, to the
relative security of Pakistan and then to my distant home.

Two jeeploads of mujahedin bodyguards belonging to the
renowned Commander Abdul Haq met me at the Hadji's village and
escorted me on a long drive through blooming poppy fields to the border post at Torkham. This part of eastern Afghanistan was chaotic and
extremely dangerous: bands of fighters from the seven different mujahedin factions roamed the countryside, sometimes clashing with one
another; the Communist Afghan regime still had garrisons in the area
and occasionally mounted offensive patrols; banditry and kidnapping
were common, particularly among the wild, lawless tribes around the
Khyber Pass.

The bodyguards had been arranged through the long arm of my
friend, Lt. Gen. Javid Nasser, director general of Pakistani intelligence.
Two jeeps are necessary to protect one vehicle in between: an ambush
often knocks out the lead or tailing jeep. The minute that firing begins,
the men in the second jeep can cover those in the first and the center
vehicles, with their fire.

Some miles outside of Torkham, I stopped to pay my respects to
Abdul Haq, the senior mujahedin leader of the region. We sat, Afghan-
style, on delicate carpets in a long room without any furniture save bolster cushions placed along the wall, where the commander and his
lieutenants reclined. The mujahedin sipped sweet tea and discussed
the day's fighting, which had gone well.

Abdul Haq told me his forces were steadily outflanking the thick
Communist defense lines around Jalalabad, which had for so long
resisted their assaults. This heavily fortified city was the gateway to
Kabul. Once it fell, the road to the Afghan capital would be open. The
hated Afghan Communists were on their last legs. Now that their godless Soviet masters had fled Afghanistan, it was only a matter of time
before the holy warriors would break the last enemy lines of resistance,
march on Kabul, and hang Najibullah, the Afghan Marxist leader, from
a lamppost, Allah willing.

We headed off for the Khyber Pass, which begins at Torkham. From there, I had to go on without my mujahedin bodyguards: they were banned from all Pathan tribal territory, including the Khyber Pass. So, too, were all Pakistani troops, except for the Khyber Rifles and the South Waziristan Scouts, who policed the turbulent Northwest Frontier from their high-walled medieval forts. An agent of Pakistani intelligence had warned me that Najibullah's Communist regime in Kabul had put a price on my head and had alerted tribal relatives among the Afridi to watch for my coming.

The Khyber Pass is a very narrow, twisting defile between 3,300-foot (1,006-m) peaks that begins, at its southern terminus, outside Peshawar, Pakistan. The pass then snakes north for 28 tortuous miles (45 km) over countless switchbacks and sharp curves to its northern end at Torkham, the first town one reaches in Afghanistan. Khyber is barren and bleak: its steep brown, gray, and black walls of broken rock and shale are devoid of vegetation or human habitation. The only sign of life on the pass is the large, rectangular fort of the Khyber Rifles, whose high, brown, crenelated walls and flag-surmounted towers lent it a wonderfully medieval flavor.

Though the pass seems uninhabited, Afridi tribesmen live atop the flat plateau on either side of the defile, and have made life miserable since the beginning of recorded history for merchants and armies seeking to transit Khyber. Alexander the Great and his Macedonian hoplites battled the Afridi when crossing Khyber in 327 BC, on their way to invading the rich plains of Punjab. Every invading army since then has pushed south through the fabled pass, from the early Aryan invaders of India; the Turkic-Afghan army of Mahmud of Gazni; the Mongol "tumans" of Timur the Lame; to the horse armies of Babur, the Mogul conqueror.

The armies of India's last invader, Britain, marched north through Khyber on their way to seize Afghanistan, battling the Afridi every bloodstained foot of the way. During the ferocious Afghan Wars of 1838–42 and 1878–80, battles between British forces and Pathans— mainly Afridis—raged the length of the pass, as well as at its southern and northern entrances. Afridis became rightly known by their British foes as among the bravest, and certainly the cruelest, of the notoriously cruel Pathan tribes.

The steel barrier gate at Torkham swung open to allow our jeep to pass. I looked back out the window and, with a sinking feeling, waved farewell to my bodyguards. The Torkham gate shut behind us: we had now left the manifold dangers of Afghanistan for the even greater danger of the Khyber Pass.

My driver, a young Afghan named Ahmed, extinguished the Toyota's headlamps. It was necessary to make the run down Khyber in darkness: otherwise the lights of our jeep would be visible for miles as we twisted and turned down the serpentine pass. Pakistani regulations did not allow us to carry automatic weapons, or, for that matter, even rifles—certainly a curious prohibition in a region where even twelve-year-old boys went heavily armed and Afghans treasured their guns, placing a higher value on them than on their wives. Our protection consisted of one revolver and two automatic pistols. I cocked my 9mm, made sure I had a second clip handy, and wished mightily for an AK-47 and some grenades. We felt naked, and terribly vulnerable.

Ahmed accelerated to 70 miles per hour (113 km/h). Speed would have to be our main protection. The jeep roared around the treacherous hairpin turns of the grim Khyber Pass, illuminated only by the weak moonlight, which was often obscured by thick, low-lying clouds. We swerved with neck-breaking force to avoid rocks that had fallen onto the road. The steep black walls of the pass seemed to be closing around us. One turn taken too quickly and the jeep would go into a fatal skid, plunging off the cliff into the dark abyss below.

After what seemed hours of death-defying driving, which was probably only about fifteen minutes, we heard bursts of automatic gunfire. We kept up our headlong descent of the pass. Once, at a particular sharp turn, we came within inches of driving off the road. Falling rocks crashed into the top of the hurtling jeep. We paid them no attention.

As we rounded a curve, we saw a cluster of shadowy figures standing on the black-topped road and along its shoulders. They were holding rifles and AK-47s and were very likely preparing to ambush us, but our speed was such that the jeep was on them before they could even aim their weapons. The surprised ambushers scattered out of our way; we may have hit one or two, for I felt a strong jolt as we passed them, accompanied by cries. Shots rang out behind us, as the angry tribesmen opened fire at our jeep, but by then we were rounding another bend in the road, and soon lost sight of the Afridis—if that is what they were. It was impossible to know whether these were the tribesmen Najibullah had sent to kidnap me or simply ordinary bandits—local tribesmen attempting to collect an impromptu road tax from whatever passing vehicle they might manage to stop.

I told Ahmed to slow down somewhat: better to shoot our way through another roadblock than go off the road into oblivion. If only we had our bodyguards, I mused, and a few RPG-7 antitank rockets—they are so handy for blasting one's way through roadblocks.

We hurtled through the night. The jeep jolted violently, throwing us around the inside. I kept one hand on the dashboard and the other braced against the roof. I was afraid the shaking might make the pistol tucked into my belt accidentally go off. The Toyota skidded over a wet section of the road, lost traction, nearly rolled over, then righted itself.

Only the thought of falling into the hands of the vicious Afridis kept me from agonizing over the multiple dangers of our wild plunge down the winding pass. A relatively quick death caused by flying off the road or hitting a fallen boulder seemed much preferable to ending up an involuntary guest of the Afridis and then the Afghan secret police, both of whom had an unrivaled reputation for cruelty and sadism. My companions clearly shared my views. We hung on grimly, flying down the curves of the pass, tires smoking and squealing, pistols cocked, ready at each new corner for another ambuscade.

About an hour later we saw a bare light bulb ahead of us in the darkness, then a wooden barrier across the road, then a uniformed, turbaned sentry. We had reached the first checkpoint of the renowned Khyber Rifles. The guard saluted smartly as we drove through.

A little while later we rounded a corner and saw, spread gloriously below us, the twinkling lights of the frontier city of Peshawar—and safety. Armies since the beginning of time had marched down the Khyber Pass, but we may well have been the first to race through the pass in the dark of night. Ahmed looked at the city lights of Peshawar, gazed back at the dark mouth of the sinister pass, and spoke for all of us: "Allah be praised. Truly, it was His hand that guided us this night."

2
The Bravest Men on Earth

The warlike Afghan tribes were well known to ancient Greek historians, and even more intimately by the soldiers of Alexander the Great, who fought many bitter battles with them. Yet Afghanistan remained a geographical abstraction until the mid-eighteenth century, when a local warlord, Ahmad Shah Durrani, imposed a rough, transitory form of order over the nebulous region, and it began its gradual transformation into a coherent political entity.

Before that time, the Afghans had lived in splendid isolation, feuding among themselves, exacting tolls from caravans plying the trade routes to and from India, and joyfully launching bloody raids into neighboring kingdoms. They acquired a reputation for cruelty, military prowess, and extreme unpredictability.

Afghan society has always been deeply divided by tribal, linguistic, religious, and regional loyalties, and so it remains today. Four principal ethnic groups dominated the country. South of the great natural divide formed by the Hindu Kush mountains—a name that means "crusher of Hindus"—dwell the mighty Pathans, the world's largest tribal group. Their lands extended as far west as Kandahar and the Iranian border, and as far south as the border of what is today Pakistan's Northwest Frontier Province.

The Hindu term "Pathan" is actually a misnomer. A Pathan is very likely to take deep and violent offense at the term if you address him as such. I will continue to use "Pathan" because that is the name most familiar to Western readers. These fierce tribesmen call themselves "Pakhtun" or "Pushtun," and their lands "Pushtunistan." Pathans are deeply religious Sunni Muslims, who regard Muslims from farther south as godless infidels, or *kufir*. They hold a special animosity for the Shia Muslims, who are a minority in parts of Afghanistan and Pakistan.

The Pathans are divided into many tribes of varying sizes, of which four predominate: the nomadic Ghilzai, also known as 'Kuchi, who roam the sweeping central plains of Afghanistan with their flocks; the imperial Durranis, traditionally the source of Afghanistan's royalty; the "free tribes" who are found straddling both sides of the Durand Line that separates Pakistan from Afghanistan; and the "settled" tribes who have been largely absorbed into Pakistani life, providing many of the army's senior officers and fiercest fighters.

Under the British Raj, Pathans were held to be one of India's six martial races, along with Sikhs, Gurkhas, Rajputs, Mahrattas, and Punjabi Muslims. All fit the British ideal of "grenadierism"—namely, admiration and preference for tall, sturdy soldiers of markedly aggressive nature who would form the army's élite offensive units. The Pathans embodied this ideal perfectly: they were tall, fair-skinned, and extremely warlike. These bellicose upland peoples formed the fighting core and finest units of the imperial armies of the Queen Empress of India.

The principal Pathan tribes are again divided into far more important subtribes, and then subdivided into powerful clans, known as *khels*. The most famous, or infamous, are the cruel, rapacious Afridis, guardians of the Khyber Pass, who inspired Kipling's admonition to British officers that, should they fall wounded on the Northwest Frontier, to save a last bullet for themselves lest they fall into the hands of Afridi and their women, whose exquisite sexual cruelties to prisoners were legendary on the frontier.

Best known of the khels are the proud Yusufzais; the cunning Shinwaris; those masters of raiding, Orakzais and Mahsuds; the clever Bangash, ferocious Wazirs, and arrogant Mohmands. Beneath the khels are a bewildering, fragmented galaxy of clans and subclans linked by blood, though often divided by vendettas and bitter rivalries over water, pastures, booty, and women.

All of the many peoples of the northern Indian subcontinent know one thing as surely as they know not to touch fire: never cross an Afghan, for he, or his heirs, will surely exact revenge, even if it takes five hundred years.

In the lands of the Pathan, there is no law save the tribal code of Pushtunwali. This ancient code deals with disputes over "*zar, zan,* and *zamin*": gold, women, and land. At the heart of Pushtunwali is Badal—the Afghan's fearsome code of revenge. Pushtunwali, and the medieval code of Lek Dukajin of the Gheg tribesmen of northern Albania, are remarkably similar. Under both codes, you can be shot dead for a disrespectful look, any slight to one's honor or female relatives, or simply because some gunman does not like the color of your hat. But you must kill with care, since the right and duty of vengeance is enshrined in both groups of mountaineers' laws. However, women, children, and, above all, guests must be protected, and spared violence.

Highland Scots, and Gheg tribesmen of northern Albania, would feel quite at home in an Afghan raiding party, where the badge of Afghan manhood is the ubiquitous AK-47 automatic rifle. Feuding bands of Pathans often fight out their vendettas with heavy weapons, and even armored vehicles. Pakistani authorities have learned not to interfere in these affairs of honor lest they provoke a general uprising among the hot-blooded Pathans.

North of the snow-capped Hindu Kush are Afghanistan's other main ethnic groups: the elegant, fine-featured Tajiks, whose ethnic roots, language (Dari), and culture are Persian; the nomadic, Shia Muslim, Hazara, a people of Tibetan-Mongol origin with pronounced Asiatic features; and the warlike Uzbeks of the northwest, a people of Turkic-Mongol origin who glory in the conquests of their great chieftain, Timur the Lame, or Tamerlane.

Tajiks traditionally formed Afghanistan's intellectual class and look down on the rustic Pathans as backward and uncouth. Add to this ethnic cocktail smaller numbers of Baluchis, Turkomen, and Nuristanis.

Fifty-seven years after the revelation of Islam in AD 622, its followers split over the succession to the caliphate, which combined the powers spiritual and temporal of the Muslim *ummah*, or society. A group of Muslims broke away, insisting the mantle of leadership should have passed to the Prophet Muhammad's son-in-law Ali, and to his son Hussein, who were subsequently killed in battle at Kerbala, and are venerated by all Shia as martyrs and virtual saints. Iran, which had been conquered by Islamic armies and converted to the Muslim religion, but which detested Arabs as desert primitives, quickly adopted Shiism as an expression of its nationalist spirit and individuality. In Iran, Shiism incorporated ancient Zoroastrian customs, the worship of saints, and mysticism, to produce a faith that was very different from the austere Sunni Islam of the Arabian desert.

The Shia, who make up about 12 percent of the world's one billion Muslims, are regarded as dangerous heretics by most orthodox Sunni Muslims. Today, Shia believers are concentrated in Iran, Lebanon, and Iraq, where they form the majority, and in Pakistan and parts of

Afghanistan, where they are a marginalized, widely disliked minority subject to occasional violent spasms of persecution. The Shia passion for martyrdom and self-sacrifice, and their deep sense of oppression, make them formidable fighters, as the Israelis learned to their dismay in southern Lebanon, where the Shia Hizbullah may become the first Arab force ever to defeat the Israeli Army in battle.

Imperial Britain attempted to invade and annex Afghanistan to its Indian empire, beginning in 1838. This ill-starred venture led to the First and Second Afghan Wars, which resulted in a series of bloody British defeats, or Pyrrhic victories, that shocked Victorian England. The annihilation, in 1842, of an entire British expeditionary force of 16,000 men by the Ghilzai Pathans, immortalized by Lady Jane Butler's famed painting, *The Retreat from Kabul*, was one of the worst disasters in British military history, compelling the Raj to forsake its ambitions to conquer Afghanistan. On a wild mountain ridge, a loner rider, his head bandaged and bloody, struggles to stay astride his exhausted horse. Vultures wheel in the cold, blue sky above them. This was Dr. Charles Grant, one of the only survivors of the British army that had marched off from Peshawar, India, two months earlier to conquer Afghanistan. Having failed to hold Kabul, the defeated British had withdrawn south through the Khyber Pass, where the waiting Afridi had fallen upon them like wolves, and slaughtered the Queen's army almost to a man, inflicting unspeakable tortures upon those unlucky enough to be captured alive.

After this debacle, Britain contented itself with meddling, rather than intervening, in Afghan affairs, discreetly supporting the pro-British royal dynasty in Kabul. After Britain and Russia nearly went to war in northern Afghanistan in the 1870s, they agreed to leave it as a buffer zone between their two expanding empires. They also tacitly agreed, after some intrigues, to do the same with the remote Himalayan kingdoms of Tibet and Bhutan.

In 1885, Afghan rulers and Imperial Russia signed an agreement that defined Afghanistan's northern border as running along the Oxus River (the modern Amu Darya). Eight years later, Sir Mortimer Durand, representing the British Raj, signed an agreement in Kabul defining the border between British India and Afghanistan. The 1,200-mile (1,930-km) border from the Pamir Mountains to Baluchistan, known hence-forth as the Durand Line, became the *de facto* and *de jure* southern border of Afghanistan. For the first time, the land between the Durand Line and the Oxus came to be called "Afghanistan," rather than its previous names, "Afghan territory" or "Afghan region."

The *modus vivendi* between Afghanistan's chiefs and the Raj did not stop incessant clashes between British forces and various Pathan tribes on the northwest frontier, nor prevent a third Anglo-Afghan War in 1919. Fighting continued to flare along the border until the late 1930s. Nevertheless, Afghanistan was more or less left to its own devices. Remarkably, it was the only independent Muslim nation left on Earth: all others had been conquered, or absorbed, by Western imperialist powers.

Afghanistan thus remained in splendid isolation from the 1930s until the early 1970s, a *terra incognita* and geopolitical lacuna on the map of Asia. However, the world's new superpowers, the Soviet Union and the United States, both recognized Afghanistan's strategic importance, and, as part of their global rivalry, steadily increased efforts to spread their influence in the kingdom. The USSR assumed an important role in arming and training the Afghan army, building roads and infrastructure, and in educational programs, which served as a vehicle for expanding the operations of the growing Afghan Communist party.

Afghanistan's royal family continued a tenuous, largely ceremonial rule over the fractious nation until 1973. In that year King Zahir Shah, a feeble and much-disrespected monarch, was overthrown, while on a visit to Italy, by his scheming cousin Prince Mohammed Daoud, who proclaimed himself president. Daoud received powerful support from the underground Communist party, which the Soviets had been building up since 1965 in an effort to undermine the Afghan monarchy.

A period of growing instability ensued, during which the Soviet Union intensified its intrigues in Afghanistan to further the Russian historical grand strategy of eventually pushing south over the Hindu Kush, and then through Pakistan, down to the warm waters of the Arabian Sea. Communist organizers infiltrated the Afghan armed forces, urban intelligentsia, and the many urban radical groups clamoring for various degrees of modernization. Soviet military and civilian technicians poured into Afghanistan.

In April 1978, two militant Afghan Communist leaders, Mohammed Taraki and Hafizullah Amin, mounted a coup in Kabul with planning and support from the Soviet KGB. Daoud was killed;

Communist forces seized power. Thousands of anti-state opponents were liquidated in the notorious Poli Charki prison outside Kabul.

But in typical Afghan style, the Communist leadership, made up of intellectuals, journalists, teachers, and some mid-level army officers, immediately became locked in bitter ideological feuds and personal rivalries. Two powerful Communist factions—the Khalq, which was dominated by Pathans, and the Parchem, in which Uzbeks, Tajiks, and Hazaras were prominent—waged ferocious ideological battles that often led to outright combat.

Hafizullah Amin, Taraki's deputy, argued furiously with his nominal boss, who was a homicidal maniac. Their feuding deputies, Babrak Karmal and Najibullah, were packed off to Moscow.

In September 1979, Hafizullah Amin organized the murder of Mohammed Taraki, seized power, and began executing supporters of his late rival. In the finest tradition of baroque Soviet lies, and with delicious understatement, Radio Kabul announced the bullet-riddled Taraki had "resigned for health reasons." One version of events held that Amin had drawn a revolver in the course of a heated cabinet meeting and emptied it into Taraki. Another, that Taraki had been hustled from the meeting room and gunned down in the hall by Amin's guards.

Amin quickly proved to be an even more dangerous lunatic than Taraki. Completely misjudging his nation—as only an intellectual ideologue can—he embarked on a radical modernization and bloody Sovietization of the country that immediately provoked armed resistance from traditional, rural Afghans. Amin managed to combine the most vicious aspects of totalitarian Stalinism with Afghan ferocity, and an inability to compromise over the most minor issues. He instituted a reign of terror against all opponents, including the more moderate Communist Khalq faction, torturing and killing thousands of his victims by electrocution, burning, castration, impalement, slow freezing in giant refrigerators, acid baths, or by burying them alive.

The increasing turmoil and Amin's unspeakable cruelties were too much even for Moscow, which feared that its new socialist ally was about to collapse in chaos. The KGB warned the Kremlin that the Marxist regime in Kabul was drowning in a factional bloodbath.

In early December 1979, a seriously ailing Leonid Brezhnev, KGB boss Yuri Andropov, Defense Minister Dimitri Ustinov, and a single Central Committee official decided, without consulting the rest of the

Communist party or the government, to invade Afghanistan. This was a venture that was to have unforeseen, unimaginable, and ultimately catastrophic consequences for the Soviet Empire. Whether these aged Communist leaders embarked on war as a reflex action, in response to the disorder in Afghanistan, or as the first step in a grand geopolitical drive to the Arabian Sea will be the subject of debate until the Kremlin archives are opened—if they ever are.

On a frigid, snowy December night, a Soviet special forces unit from the élite Alpha group, which had covertly infiltrated Afghanistan on military cargo aircraft, raced into Kabul. The Soviet commandos stormed President Amin's palace, killed his surprised guards, burst into Amin's bedroom, and executed the cowering Afghan Communist leader with a burst of AK-47 fire.

Three Soviet motor rifle divisions immediately moved south across the border from Termez, quickly occupying most of Afghanistan. The Soviet mechanized units took advantage of the modern trans-Afghan highway that the Soviet Union had thoughtfully constructed as part of its "fraternal friendship assistance" to Afghanistan. Ironically, in the spirit of benevolent coexistence, Washington had supplied most of the cash for the project, Moscow the materials and labor. The Americans failed to note that the highway was being built to support tanks and heavy armored vehicles.

A more compliant Communist satrap, the ineffectual Babrak Karmal, was hustled back from Moscow and appointed president. The menacing Najibullah, known as "The Bull," was named his deputy. The United States and its NATO allies protested loudly but without effect.

Far from settling the political imbroglio in Afghanistan, or assuring Communist domination, the brutal Soviet coup and subsequent invasion only made matters worse. The intervention was supposed to be a bloodless *coup de main*, like the highly successful 1968 invasion of Czechoslovakia. But the Russians, who should have known better, disastrously miscalculated the response of their Afghan neighbors, who were nothing like the docile Czechs.

The arrival of Soviet troops suddenly diverted the natural bellicosity of the Afghans away from their usual feuds and focused it, full force, on a far more appealing target, a foreign invader. Religious leaders and local mullahs proclaimed a *jihad* (holy war) against the godless Soviet infidels from the north and their local Communist allies.

At first, the Soviets shrugged off the occasional guerrilla raids mounted by the poorly armed, hopelessly disorganized Afghan tribesmen, who were mostly equipped with antique, World War I British Lee-Enfield .303 rifles, but as resistance to the Soviet occupation forces and their Afghan Communist allies intensified, it became increasingly clear the insurgency was taking root and would not be easily extinguished.

However, few nations outside Afghanistan, except for its immediate neighbors Pakistan, Iran, and India, cared in the least about this obscure conflict. In fact, in the newspaper business, an "Afghanistan story" was an editor's dismissive term for utterly unimportant, boring news that no one would ever want to read. The Soviets encouraged this obscurity by keeping journalists out of the parts of Afghanistan controlled by Communist forces—and by hunting down and trying to kill the tiny number of reporters bold enough to sneak in with the *mujahedin* from Pakistan. After all, the world had forgotten Tibetan resistance to Chinese invasion in the early 1950s; Moscow reckoned the same creeping amnesia would happen with Afghanistan, which, after a time, would simply vanish from the world's consciousness, and be absorbed, like the old Muslim emirates of Central Asia, into the Soviet Empire.

Besides, Afghanistan was a most inconvenient, difficult war for journalists. Places like South Africa or the Mideast had decent accommodation and good telecommunications. You could cover a battle, or the latest bloody outrage, and be back in your Intercontinental Hotel in time for a hot bath and dinner. Getting into Afghanistan usually meant trekking in from Pakistan through the mountains, an arduous and dangerous trip that could take weeks, during which hepatitis and food poisoning were as much a danger as Soviet bullets, rockets, or mines. And every step deeper into Afghanistan meant a longer, more perilous return voyage to the safety of Pakistan.

Equally discouraging, TV teams were far too expensive to send on lengthy, dangerous missions into a remote war in the mountains of the Hindu Kush. Besides, most Americans couldn't find Afghanistan on a map if their lives depended on it, nor could they register exotic foreign names in their minds. Afghanistan was a media-unfriendly war. The few Western news teams that ventured into Afghanistan usually penetrated no more than a few miles, had themselves filmed in Afghan garb beside a knocked-out Soviet tank, and then returned before dark to

Pakistan. One prominent American TV newscaster, decked out in Afghan garb, even had a small fake battle staged for his benefit.

I followed this terrible war for three years, beginning in 1980, and tried to publish stories about the conflict in North American newspapers, but with infrequent success. Other journalists fared no better. Afghanistan's remoteness and the West's desire to avoid disturbing supposed détente with the USSR for the sake of what one newspaper described as "a few Afghan mountain bandits" made people deaf and blind to the industrial-scale butchery in Afghanistan. Nevertheless, the Afghans fought on, heedless of the seemingly hopeless odds against them.

As Afghan resistance spread, the Soviets and their Afghan allies, unseen by the outside world, embarked on a ferocious scorched-earth campaign that combined the merciless destructiveness of Genghis Khan's Mongols with the calculated terrorism of Stalin. Villages that had sheltered mujahedin were razed. Crops were burned; farm animals machine-gunned. Tiny butterfly mines, no bigger than a tea saucer, but capable of blowing off a man's foot, were strewn by the millions. Booby-trapped toys were dropped from the air; Afghan children picked them up and had their hands blown off. Irrigation systems that had provided water for eight hundred years were destroyed; wells were poisoned. The dreaded Afghan KHAD secret police, trained and led by the KGB, imprisoned, tortured, and executed tens of thousands of Afghans. The horrors inflicted by the late, unlamented Hafizullah Amin on "enemies of the state" were continued, and even improved upon, by the KHAD. Gravediggers could not keep up with their workload, and complained bitterly to the authorities that their quotas were impossible to meet.

The mujahedin confronted the Soviet war machine with the only weapons they had: raw courage, Islamic faith, and antique Lee-Enfield rifles. In one of those amazing trapdoors that sometimes open in history, a modern Soviet army, with armor, artillery, aircraft, and helicopter gunships, found itself pitted against a tribal force that, except for its rifles, could have ridden right out of the time of Haroun Al-Rashid and the *Arabian Nights*.

Though the public and media were indifferent, consolidation of the Soviet invasion of Afghanistan had caused panic among governments in Washington, the Mideast, and Western Europe. The badly unnerved and deeply confused Carter administration was advised by the Joint Chiefs of Staff and the CIA that the Soviets would quickly pacify Afghanistan. Then, it was widely feared, the Soviets would advance their armored units south through Pakistan, or southwest through the mountain passes of Iran, down to the oil-rich Gulf.

In August 1980, U.S. war planners advised Secretary of Defense Harold Brown and President Carter that there was "no other option" except the use of tactical nuclear weapons to prevent the Soviets from seizing the Gulf. The nearest U.S. ground forces were 7,000 miles (11,300 km) away. Even if the U.S. embarked on a massive effort to rush troops and aircraft to the Gulf, the soonest it could deploy the first heavy divisions to the region would be D+30, at which time the Soviets would enjoy a 14-to-1 tactical advantage.

American planners had good reason to fear a Soviet attack on the Gulf, which at the time supplied 32 percent of America's oil, 70 percent of Europe's, and 77 percent of Japan's. Interestingly, as a result of the August 1980 crisis, the U.S. steadily reduced its dependence on Mideast oil, which went from supplying nearly a third of its needs to only 4 percent today.

Soviet ground and air units in the backwater Caucasus and Turkestan military districts were normally maintained at "Category C," the lowest level of military readiness, and equipped with the oldest weapons systems. But in the seven months since the invasion of Afghanistan, the twenty-eight Soviet divisions based north of Iran had gone onto full war footing. Many units had left their garrisons and moved into the field. Soviet airborne divisions in Eastern Europe had been ordered on alert. Specialized communications, logistics, and Spetsnaz commando units were deployed in the region. Tactical air force units were reinforced and supplied with large stocks of munitions. Soviet units shifted to new radio frequencies, or maintained radio silence. The last time such activities were observed was just prior to the 1968 invasion of Czechoslovakia. By August 1989, the Soviets had massed 3,400 tanks, 8,000 armored personnel carriers, 370 combat aircraft, 350 helicopters, and 4,000 guns on Iran's border.

The distance from the Soviet border to the Gulf was 700 air miles (11,300 km), or 1,000 land miles(1,600 km). To reach the Strait of Hormuz, Soviet forces would have to cross the lofty Elbruz Mountains, then skirt the uplands of the Zagros Mountains through narrow defiles and over bad roads. Even so, the Pentagon estimated the Red Army's spearheads could reach the Gulf within ten or eleven days. Worse, Soviet armor based at Shindand in southwest Afghanistan was only 450 miles (724 km) from the Gulf.

Secretary of Defense Brown estimated that a minimum of three U.S. divisions and five air wings would be required, just to slow a major Soviet attack; none was available. A lightning Soviet thrust could be delayed by sending in special forces to blow up bridges and block mountain passes, but Pentagon war planners concluded a determined Soviet thrust could not be halted without recourse to tactical nuclear weapons.

This option, it was clear, would almost inevitably escalate to all-out nuclear war with the Soviet Union. Even in the unlikely chance that it did not, any American action in Iran would certainly have provoked the Soviets to launch a blitzkrieg in Europe. At the time, the massed tank armies of the immensely powerful Group of Soviet Forces in East Germany were believed to be capable of reaching the English Channel in only six or seven days of round-the-clock fighting. The indecisive Carter administration watched all this, paralyzed by shock and fear.

Most of the Muslim nations reacted similarly. Though always passionate oratorical champions of Islamic causes, in reality most Muslim nations followed a policy of every man for himself. The dictatorships and oligarchies of the Muslim world at this time were too preoccupied keeping themselves in power, or intriguing against their neighbors, to spare time or resources for less urgent matters. But when Soviet tanks rolled into Kabul, a shudder of fear coursed through the Arab world and Iran. Few in the Middle East believed Washington would risk nuclear war to prevent the Red Army from rolling into Tehran, Baghdad, or Kuwait.

But then, at this darkest of hours, two important events occurred that Moscow had not foreseen. First, Pakistan's leader, the tough former tank general Zia ul-Haq, concluded early in 1980 that the Soviet invasion of landlocked, resource-poor Afghanistan, a nation of no intrinsic economic value, could have only one objective: as the first stage of a massive Soviet push through Pakistan to the Arabian Sea.

Accordingly, Zia launched a secret plan to defend Pakistan by covertly organizing resistance by the Afghan tribes to the Soviet invaders. As his chosen instrument of policy, Zia ordered his crack military intelligence agency, Inter-Service Intelligence (ISI), to arm, supply, and organize the Afghan resistance. Zia put this vast, complex undertaking under command of his right-hand man, one of Pakistan's most

Islamic law at Kabul University; he had also written books on Persian poetry. His political party, the Jamiat Islami, had become a rallying point for non-Pathan anti-Communists.

The other significant presence was Sibgatullah Mojadidi, a short man with a long oval face, drooping eyes, and a downturned mouth that gave him a permanent look of deep melancholy, despite which his gaze was hard, intelligent, and sharp. Mojadidi was a respected Islamic theologian who had been educated at the Muslim world's leading religious institution, Cairo's Al-Azhar University; he was an authority on Sufism, a mystical branch of Islam. More important, Mojadidi was a Pathan, a member of the dominant ethnic group in Afghanistan, who live south of the Hindu Kush mountains. I quickly fell into conversation with Rabbani and Mojadidi.

Among the others present was an Uzbek chieftain from the northwest, close to the border with the Soviet Union. This man was a hereditary saint, known as a *pir*, who said little. There was also a rather pompous royalist wearing a heavy gold Rolex. Completing the ethnic mosaic of Afghanistan was a notable of the Shia Hazara, a people of Mongol origin.

One of Rabbani's lieutenants translated for us. The Afghans had been raising funds in the U.S. and Canada. They had just come up the lake from Buffalo. In each city, Muslims had flocked to meet the mujahedin leaders and press into their hands whatever small sums these people of modest means could afford. I asked Rabbani how he could expect to defeat the Soviets, or even hold them at bay. Rabbani looked at me and smiled gently, as a father would at a young son asking a naive question. "Our faith makes us strong. We are in the right. Allah will show us the way."

"Yes," I persisted, "but how can you fight the Soviet Army with World War I rifles?"

Rabbani shrugged. "Allah will provide. What is important is that our faith be strong."

Mojadidi cut in, with a more worldly explanation. "We do have a few friends. Some, *inshallah*, will come to our aid. But even if they do not, you know we Afghan have defeated every nation that tried to conquer us. We defeated Alexander the Great, and the British. We will defeat the Russians too, Allah willing."

This time, however, the redoubtable Afghans were fighting a modern army equipped with armored helicopter gunships, ground attack aircraft, poison gas, armored vehicles, and artillery. Courage was not enough. And how, I wondered, could these proud, fractious tribal chiefs from an age long past wage a national struggle against a superpower whose ruthlessness was without equal in modern history?

I also saw in the Afghan leaders that same deficit of human talent that afflicts so many backward societies. All too often the leaders of such nations have no grounding in the processes of politics, administration, economics, finance, or industry. Their training is as country doctors, mission teachers, postal clerks, common soldiers, or rural clerics. This poor man's "intelligentsia" passes for an educated class in their threadbare post-colonial societies.

When the British, French, Italians, and Belgians gave independence to their colonial empires, or simply abandoned them, in many cases these clerks and teachers were the only people who could read or write, and so they became, by default, the new ruling class. You could tell them easily: they had soft hands; they wore ill-fitting suits, often blue and shiny, that were always too short and threadbare; they almost always displayed the primary status symbol of the Third World intellectual or senior bureaucrat, a fountain pen in their breast pocket.

This is how Patrice Lumumba came to power in the Congo; and Ahmed Sukarno in Indonesia. Haiti's François Duvalier, that grandmaster of terror, began his bloody career as a humble country doctor combating yaws. Enver Hoxha of Albania, the Balkan Stalin, was a rural schoolteacher. Fidel Castro started out as a young lawyer with no clients, Idi Amin as a sergeant in the King's Uganda Rifles, and Anwar Sadat of Egypt as a passed-over major and an equally unsuccessful actor.

Most of these men burst from the profoundest obscurity onto the pages of history, propelled by cataclysmic historical events, the way the Himalayas were thrown skyward by the tectonic collision of a broken-off chunk of Africa with the land mass of Asia. The only thing they had in common was that lowest common denominator of political calculus: the instinct to cling to power at all costs.

Unfortunately, few of the men who would come to lead the Third World in the second half of the twentieth century had anything resembling what Russians term a "political culture." There was no tradition of compromise; no understanding of the need to accept dissenting views; no ability to accommodate different positions within one party;

no comprehension that there could actually be such a thing as a loyal opposition party or that government or media critics might not all be agents of the CIA, KGB or MI6. None of them had any sense of political direction or purpose, or awareness of the need to build enduring institutions—courts, a free press, independent universities, or opposition political parties—and certainly they gave no thought at all to providing the public with the kind of political education that would allow them, one day, to assume a larger share of the management of their societies.

Standing before me in Toronto were just such men. However splendid their faith, determination, and courage against daunting odds, however unmistakable their will to defeat savage injustice, these Afghans clearly lacked any knowledge of what to do with their country if they by some miracle actually won the war. All of them certainly failed to understand a basic fact of history: that big wars change everything. A nation, once having fought a full-scale, total war, will be irrevocably altered, and can never return to the way it was in the past. Yet these men were fighting precisely to restore a society that was dying, or already dead.

They truly believed that, once the hated Communists were all killed or driven out, Afghanistan would simply resume its antique ways. The ungodly twentieth century, with its dangers that could not be killed by bullets, would be repelled. The old ruling class—warlords, religious leaders, local nobles, perhaps even the weak king, Zahir Shah—could revert to the familiar, constrained chaos that was Afghanistan before 1979.

I asked Professor Rabbani and the other leaders what form of government they would create in a liberated Afghanistan. None could answer more than to say, "Allah will guide our hands...we will build a government according to the Sharia (Islamic Law)...we will be a nation of Muslims." Was there any Islamic nation that could serve as a role model? No. None. Egypt was corrupt; so was Pakistan. Turkey was not even a Muslim nation, having been "bought" by the Western infidels.

These answers left me uneasy, though at the time they did not seem particularly important. But in fact, they were a harbinger of the disaster to come to Afghanistan a decade later. A thousand tomorrows would be concerned with battle against the Soviets and their Communist satraps. Victory, if it were ever realized, was many years, or even decades, away. Ammunition was a far more pressing concern than political science. I told the Afghans I would do all in my power to make their cause known to the world.

As I was leaving, I said to Rabbani, *"Inshallah,* we will meet one day in Kabul." *"Inshallah,* my friend." He laughed with pleasure. "And perhaps in free Kashmir, as well," he added. The professor held my hand, and searched my face with his dark eyes for a long time. Muslims call this "reading the soul." In this manner, some Muslims have an uncanny ability to judge a person's motives and trustworthiness. I have had this done to me many times in my years among Muslim peoples, from Algeria to Indonesia, where studying a man's face, "reading his soul," is said to offer a surer bond than a battalion of lawyers or a library of contracts.

"You are now one of us," said Rabbani. "May Allah bless and protect you." I embraced each of the Afghan leaders. I walked outside, from one world into another. The time-lock snapped shut behind me: I was again back in the twentieth century. The wind off the lake had picked up, and it had grown much colder. Leaves flew up in spirals around the birches. Afghanistan again seemed two planets away.

Yet as I drove home, I kept hearing "Afghanistan" echoing in my mind. A great jihad had begun. I could not say precisely why, but I knew without a doubt that I had to go and join this war in the mountains at the very end of the Earth.

3

Dodge City Meets the *Arabian Nights*

PESHAWAR 1986

Peshawar, capital of the Northwest Frontier Province (NFP), the wildest city on Earth, the borderline between the Middle Ages and the twentieth century. I loved Peshawar the minute I laid eyes on its slim minarets, its bulbously domed palaces, its dark, mysterious souks, and still darker alleyways. Take away the cars and vans that clog the city's narrow streets, and Peshawar has changed not a whit since the days of

Kipling. Dust, incense, car fumes, sweet spices, and the reek of rotting garbage infuse its sultry air. A great din assaults the senses: honking horns, Pathan music, angry disputes, hawkers offering their wares, occasional bursts of gunfire, the *muezzin's* call to prayer. Women, veiled from head to toe in black, move like silent wraiths through the raucous crowds.

Walk down the Street of Leather, across the Street of Silver; wend your way through a barrel-vaulted gallery illuminated by shafts of dusty sunlight filtering down from the vaulted stone roof; and then go up the Street of Daggers. Cheap consumer goods from China trucked down from Kashgar along the Karakoram Highway, the world's highest and most treacherous road, are piled high. So are crates of Russian air conditioners, Japanese stereos, Korean rice cookers, French perfume, and un-Islamic brandy. Great woven baskets heaped with vermilion, jade-green, purple, saffron, and ocher spices. Rice of many hues, plump nuts, a cornucopia of dried fruits. Steaming, fly-covered goat carcasses putrefying in the rising heat of the day. Open sewers snaking down the long, winding streets, filled with black sludge and unspeakable refuse.

Tall noblemen—*sirdars* and *zamindars*—swaggering haughtily down the crowded alleys. Tough Pakistani soldiers. Chinese traders from beyond the great Taklimakan desert. Fair-skinned Kashmiris. Belligerent Sikhs with bristling black beards and orange turbans, always ready to take offense at the least slight. Tibetan lamas and Ladakhi herdsmen. Shifty-eyed Iranians and regal Baluchi tribesmen who might have stepped out of the Old Testament. And even a group of petrified Japanese tourists in pastel polyester leisure suits, cowering together in abject terror of all the germs and wild men surrounding them.

At the point where the Khyber Pass debouches onto flatter land rises the ancient city of Peshawar: guardian of the pass, one of Central Asia's most important trading centers, and, since the dawn of history, a renowned nexus of intrigue. To this day, Alexandrine coins are routinely unearthed around Peshawar. At almost every sharp turn of an alley, or in the maze of the covered souks, you encounter fair-skinned, blue-eyed men who might be Swedes or North Germans, yet they are Pathans.

Though Peshawar is within Pakistani territory, such political geography is only notional. The Pathans do as they please within the NFP—which Pakistan calls "Pakistani-administered tribal territory." The only reminders of the central government in Islamabad are a few nineteenth-century forts dotted along the border with Afghanistan, whose garrisons struggle to keep the Pakistani flag flying over a region that knows no political loyalty, and to maintain the often disturbed peace among the fractious Pathans.

In the first quarter of this century, two wonderfully colorful figures appeared out of the barren mountains of the Northwest Frontier. First, a fiery holy man, with a delightful name: the Fakir of Ipi. The old Fakir rallied the Pathans against the infidel *farangi* and came within a turban's length of taking Peshawar back from the British, who spent the better part of a decade chasing the elusive Fakir of Ipi through the mountains of Waziristan. Then there emerged an even more fearsome figure, the "Mad Mullah," who rode down from the Malakand Pass at the head of 20,000 savage horsemen, determined to put the impious city of Peshawar to the sword. Only British aircraft and heavy guns managed to save Peshawar from the "Mad Mullah" and his holy warriors. The British press railed against these "Islamic fanatics" with the same passion as that found in the *London Telegraph* today, still denouncing the modern versions of such troublesome Islamic malefactors, Muammar Gaddafi of Libya and Saddam Hussein of Iraq.

Peshawar was to serve for nearly a century as the British India's main army garrison on the permanently rebellious Northwest Frontier. From Peshawar, the British launched forty-seven major military expeditions into Afghanistan. All proved fruitless. In the end, not even the world's greatest power, Imperial Britain, could subdue the warlike, feuding Afghans.

I slipped into Peshawar after dark, to elude the many watchful eyes of the Soviet and Afghan Communist intelligence services. I spent the night at the inappropriately named Pearl Hotel; in the lobby, a large sign proclaimed: "Hotel Policy: Arms cannot be brought inside the hotel premisis [*sic*]. Personal Guards or Gunmen are requested to deposit their weapons with the Hotel Security. We need your cooperation. The Management." Who could not like Peshawar? It was a combination of Dodge City and the *Arabian Nights*.

I visited to the vast Afghan refugee camps that sprawled outside the city, where some of the 3.5 million civilians who had been driven from their homes by the war had sought shelter. This was a place of dislocation and squalor, but a more horrifying experience awaited. An Egyptian Islamic Red Crescent doctor took me on a tour of two hospitals for wounded mujahedin. "Up north"—that is, inside

Afghanistan—there were no field hospitals for the wounded fighters. The admirable French group Médecins sans Frontières had set up a few aid posts. These excepted, any of the tens of thousands of mujahedin or civilians who were wounded, and could not crawl or be carried to Pakistan, would simply be left to die.

The Peshawar hospitals, as I had feared, were gruesome beyond belief. They stank of putrefying flesh and gangrene. Bloody bandages and rusted bedpans were strewn across the floors. Beds, often shared by two men or three children, were soaked with brown dried, blood and green or yellow pus. Every third bed held an amputee. Many men and boys were missing both legs. They showed me their stumps and managed to smile or whisper a greeting. Others had shattered limbs wired up with clamps, or lay in traction. Many of the bodies of the patients had been peppered by scores of tiny steel darts from exploding antipersonnel bombs, shredded by shrapnel, or horribly burned.

What stunned me about this charnel house was that not one patient, no matter how horribly maimed, made so much as a whimper. Even the nightmare burn victims of napalm uttered not a cry. As I came to each bed, an injured Afghan holy warrior would struggle to sit up and grasp my hand in both of his, wishing me *"Salaam aleikum"* (Peace be unto thee). Those who could not speak would smile at me, and silently try to move their lips in greeting.

I remember one great bearded man who had lost both legs above the knee to a Soviet tank shell. What did he need? I asked. "Please, sir, get me a pair of artificial legs so I can go back and fight the Communists," he replied. Time and time again I heard this same answer. And I actually saw a one-legged mujahedin painfully . . . unbelievably . . . setting off from the hospital to make the long journey back to the war zone—on crutches. To another wounded Afghan with gangrene, I offered to go to a local pharmacy and buy antibiotics for him. "No, no," he insisted. "Get me my gun!"

These were the soldiers of Allah, the bravest men on earth. They had no material possessions save their ragged clothing and their rifles, but they had vast reserves of pride. They feared no man, and certainly not death. Each man believed that Allah stood at his right shoulder; Allah who was all-merciful, in spite of the cruel world that He had inexplicably created; Allah who would carry him to his final rest as a parent would wrap a sleepy child in his arms and take him off to bed.

Afterwards, I stood in front of the hospital and wept, not just for the horrors I had seen there, but also for the heart-wrenchingly courageous, burned, broken, shattered men who lay so silently within. It was the most noble and the most painful thing I have ever seen.

That night, a curtained jeep took me on a long ride through Peshawar's unlighted alleys, changing direction and doubling back to throw off pursuers, until we came to a low concrete villa in a quiet residential zone. Mujahedin guards prowled outside, their AK-47s at the ready.

In an anteroom, Prof. Burhanuddin Rabbani greeted me with arms spread wide, and a smile of welcome on his weathered face. We embraced. He had aged since I last saw him in that university apartment in Mississauga: his beard was now more white than black.

The "hopeless" war, Rabbani explained to me as we sat crosslegged on a fine Kerman carpet, sipping small glasses of sweet mint tea, was no longer hopeless. The Afghan people had risen *en masse* against the Soviets and their hated satrap, General Najibullah. His own forces, the moderate Islamist Jamiat Islami, had spread as far north as Mazar-I-Sharif, near the border with Soviet Uzbekistan, and west to Herat and Kandahar.

Professor Rabbani, a traditionalist who would later become president of Afghanistan, had become closely allied with the Americans, while his bitter rivalry with the mujahedin leader favored by Pakistan, engineer Gulbadin Hekmatyar, grew in intensity. Meanwhile, Rabbani's chief lieutenant, Ahmad Shah Massoud, a fellow Tajik, was fighting the Red Army to a standstill around the strategic Salang Tunnel north of Kabul. In the south, Hekmatyar's Pathan Hizbi Islami forces were beleaguering Communist garrisons between the Pakistani border and the approaches to Kabul.

Most important, the "friends" that Mojadidi had told me would come when we first met four years earlier had finally arrived, and were hard at work. You could see them in Islamabad, around the vast Ojhri arms depot run by the Pakistani Inter-Service Intelligence (ISI); and in Peshawar, particularly a few miles out of town, at the old American U2 airbase known as "Kanada," from which Gary Powers took off on his final, doomed spy mission over the USSR.

Tall, fit, gum-chewing North American men with sunglasses, crewcuts and nothing to say were all around Peshawar. There were some tough-looking British SAS types, and a motley collection of young Mideasterners: mainly Egyptians, Iraqis, Algerians, Saudis, and

Jordanians. A contingent of armed Chinese "merchants" discreetly patrolled a large warehouse on the outskirts of Peshawar. Every night, unmarked military transport aircraft flew in from the south; landed at remote, heavily guarded sections of the airports at Islamabad and Peshawar; and disgorged concealed cargoes under cover of darkness.

The secret war was under way. Britain's MI6, the CIA, Saudi intelligence, Chinese military intelligence, and Pakistan's ISI were in full swing with their covert campaign to train, organize, arm, coordinate, and supply the various mujahedin factions. The arms pipeline had opened, and through it flowed hundreds of millions of dollars of small arms, munitions, and war supplies.

"We can win this war, *inshallah*," Rabbani told me, as the hot light of a kerosene lantern played on the silver threads woven into the fabric of his gray silk turban. "But we must find some way to fight the Hinds. We can do nothing...nothing...against those terrible machines."

The much-feared Hinds were really flying tanks: even the big 12.7mm heavy AA guns supplied by China couldn't penetrate the Hinds' thick armor plate. The gunships could deliver devastating fire on fixed or moving targets, using advanced optical sighting systems to target their 23mm Gatling guns, and the pods of antipersonnel rockets, packed with thousands of needle-sharp flechettes, slung beneath their stubby wings.

In addition to the Hinds, the Soviet and Afghan air forces had large numbers of highly effective SU-25 Frogfoot armored ground attack aircraft, as well as squadrons of older MIGs and Sukhoi fighters. The open, treeless terrain of Afghanistan provided little cover for mujahedin bands. Once located, they were pursued relentlessly by a combination of Hinds and jets. If the mujahedin holed up in rocks or caves, special Soviet commando units would be air-assaulted in by helicopter, to first surround, and then kill them all, sometimes using poison gas.

By mid-1986, the Soviets had perfected their counter-insurgency tactics, sharply reducing the flow of Western arms to the mujahedin, and threatening the very survival of the jihad. Infantry backed by heavy artillery positioned in fortified fire bases would garrison all urban areas and larger villages. Armored units would keep the main roads open. Élite hunter-killer teams, using Hinds and aircraft, would then track down and liquidate the mujahedin in the field.

Rabbani looked profoundly sad and spoke with immense pain in his voice. More than a million of his people—one in fifteen—had been killed, and his country laid waste. Three and a half million were refugees. Victory was still only a dream. And a new danger had crept into the Afghan war: tribal rivalry and growing animosity between the mujahedin commanders.

Unbeknownst to the mujahedin, Soviet KGB teams that specialized in stirring ethnic or tribal conflict were committing provocations designed to turn the seven mujahedin groups against one another. The KGB staged carefully calibrated assassinations, ambushes, and raids, complete with faked evidence left behind, that convinced mujahedin leaders they were being attacked by other allied mujahedin groups.

Tragically, four years later, just as victory in Afghanistan appeared to be at hand, the various mujahedin factions, riven by ethnic, tribal, and personal rivalries, fell to fighting among themselves. This evil development would shape the course of Afghan affairs for the next decade, plunging the nearly destroyed nation into a bitter civil war that inflicted yet more suffering and misery on its people.

Equally important, the civil war would eventually draw Russia back into the fray, engage Afghanistan's Central Asian neighbors in the conflict, and lay the groundwork for the appearance of the Islamic fundamentalist Taliban movement. The seemingly unquenchable chaos and strife in Afghanistan would come to destabilize the entire region, nearly cause a major war with Iran in 1998, and spill over into Kashmir in the 1990s.

4
Fadil the Kurd

My friend," Fadil the Kurd said to me, grinning broadly, "you must come with us into Afghanistan. We will shoot the Stinger missile together. We will shoot down many Russian planes and helicopters!"

I had met Fadil in the early 1980s. We had kept up our friendship over the years, meeting in Peshawar and Islamabad. Now we were again in Peshawar, which hummed with the excitement of the war next door.

Fadil was a handsome man in his mid-thirties, broad-shouldered, erect, and of medium height, who wore his dark blond hair short and never appeared without a stubble on his square jaw. His eyes were a striking blue-gray. He spoke fluent Arabic, Turkish, good Farsi, better English, some Urdu, and of course his native Kurdish.

After the Pathans, the Kurds are the world's second-largest tribal people. And like the Pathans, they are fierce, quarrelsome, and untamed, a fair-skinned people among those of darker hues, a nation of warriors seemingly destined to battle for all eternity.

History has been exceptionally cruel to the Kurds. There are 25 million, possibly even 35 million of them. No one knows for sure. Nomads to the bone, they will not sit still long enough to be counted—or killed.

Kurds, like the Pathans, are an Indo-European plains people whose Aryan ancestors migrated to the mountains of what is now eastern Turkey, Iran, southern Russia, Iraq, and Syria during the Bronze Age. Converted to Islam in the sixteenth century, the Kurds are ardent Sunnis, but have guarded their tribal culture and generally avoided mixing with their lowland neighbors. Throughout the centuries, they have fought endless wars to defend their mountain pastures, as often feuding with their own tribes as with Arabs, Turks, Armenians, Iranians, or Mongols. Today, the Kurds are a people without a homeland, dispersed across the uplands fertile crescent, living a precarious existence in nations that will not recognize their identity, surrounded by enemies, and by great oil fields, as at Mosul and Kirkuk, that will never be theirs. As Kurds say, their only friend is the mountains.

Kurdish military prowess is legendary. Salah ed-Din, or Saladin, the great general who defeated the Crusaders, was a Kurd. Like the Pathans, all Kurdish males are warriors from youth and bear arms as a matter of course. Their enemies have justly learned to fear the ferocious Kurdish war bands, the *pesh mergas*.

Fadil had come from one of the pesh mergas that had battled both Iraq and Iran. In the 1970s, the CIA, Israel's Mossad, and Iran's Savak secret police secretly trained and armed Kurds in a effort to destabilize Iraq. Fadil learned his English and his mastery of weapons from CIA instructors in northern Iran.

Later, he drifted away from the endless war against Iraq, and went to Egypt to study engineering at Cairo University. There, he became involved with the Muslim Brotherhood, the powerful underground Islamic organization that was politically conservative and intensely anti-Communist. In the early 1980s, the Brotherhood began organizing aid for the Afghan mujahedin.

Soon after that, the CIA and the Brotherhood began discreetly cooperating to oppose the Soviets in Afghanistan. The CIA supplied money and East Bloc arms, covertly acquired through international arms merchants and China; the Brotherhood provided skilled fighters and also opened doors for the Americans in the Islamic underground from the Gulf to Peshawar. Saudi Arabia, eager to oppose the Soviets and to channel Islamic ferment away from its borders, joined the CIA in financing the Brotherhood.

Fadil was sent to Pakistan to train mujahedin to operate Chinese-supplied heavy infantry weapons. His sharp mind, natural authority, and strong personality quickly resulted in his being given command of a mujahedin combat unit. He would often slip with his men across the border to mount night assaults on Soviet or Afghan Communist targets, or join larger offensives against important enemy bases.

Later, Fadil joined a carefully selected group of volunteers from various Middle Eastern nations for training by the CIA and ISI to become instructors in the use of the Stinger missile. This long, slim, shoulder-launched anti-aircraft missile was to prove as decisive to the Afghan war as the English longbow was at Crécy and Agincourt.

Finding some means of countering Soviet air power—above all, the deadly Hind armored helicopter gunships—was absolutely essential; otherwise the war would be lost. Britain sent in teams of SAS men to train mujahedin in the use of their Blowpipe anti-aircraft missile. Like so many British-made mechanical products, it was heavy, cumbersome, too complex for the mujahedin, and virtually worthless in combat. So was the Chinese portable anti-aircraft missile that had been supplied to the mujahedin, a copy of the Soviet SAM-7.

The American-made Stinger, however, proved exactly the opposite. The shoulder-fired Stinger could track a maneuvering target up to about 11,000 feet (3,350 m). Most important, the Stinger's extremely sensitive infrared seeker could lock on and hold a target at different angles, unlike less sensitive missiles that needed to be fired directly at the enemy aircraft's engine exhaust. Tracking fast-moving targets with the Stinger was still difficult, and required considerable skill, but even so the missile was remarkably deadly and proved the first effective man-portable anti-aircraft weapon. It provided infantrymen in the open the same decisive defensive capability against the danger of close air attack that bayonets and pikes had given them against cavalry attacks in the past.

The first teams of Arabs sent into the field by the CIA and ISI shot down a number of Soviet fighters and transport aircraft. Most important, their Stingers hit and destroyed two heavily armored Hinds. The course of the war changed abruptly. The Red Air Force and the fearsome Hind flying tanks would no longer be able to dominate the battlefields of Afghanistan.

● ● ●

Fadil had invited me to join his CIA-trained hunter-killer team, equipped with the new Stinger missiles. We crossed the Pakistani border at dusk and marched north for four days into Logar Province to provide anti-aircraft cover for a band of mujahedin attacking a group of important Afghan army posts.

We stood on a vast, beautiful plain. It was as flat as a table and covered by a delicate fuzz of green produced by recent spring rains. At the extreme horizon, encircling the plain on three sides, rose a great wall of majestic, snow-capped mountains. The warming air shimmered. Insects hummed about the red and gold flowers that dotted the plain.

Fadil pointed. "There, there, at about two o'clock." Squinting against the sun, I could just make out dark shapes approaching us from the north, moving fast in the cobalt-blue sky.

There was no cover anywhere. The dark shapes drew closer. Fadil watched them calmly through his field glasses. "Sukhoi-25s. Three!" These were Soviet-built, heavily armored attack aircraft, probably flying out of the huge Bagram airbase near Kabul. The 25s were configured for ground attack, carrying cannon, rockets, and antipersonnel bombs.

The Sukhois were coming because another group of mujahedin had just shelled and were assaulting an isolated Soviet outpost a mile to the west of us. Fadil and his team were in an overwatch position, providing air defense cover for the attack.

Intent on the besieged outpost, the Soviet pilots failed to see our group. They deployed their dive brakes, slowed down, and prepared for a strafing run on the mujahedin attacking the outpost's heavily wired perimeter. Fadil directed two of his men who held Stingers on their shoulders. He carefully adjusted their aim points: "Five degrees left, Selim.... Lead more, more ... wait, wait, wait...."

"Fire," Fadil said, his voice flat and emotionless. The two Stingers launched with an intense backblast. They flew toward the three Sukhois, corkscrewing slowly. Their progress toward the Soviet warplanes seemed agonizingly slow. Surely the aircraft would be gone by the time the missiles reached their original aim point.

We heard an explosion in the distance, then a saw puff of black smoke where the Sukhois had been. The first Stinger had found its mark. The other one continued its flight, disappearing from our sight. Moments later, we saw a wing tear off one of the Sukhois. The plane nosed up, then began to cartwheel down, until it smashed into the earth. The two other Soviet aircraft immediately went to full military power, pulled maximum-g turns, and fled the scene at speed. Soviet pilots were quickly learning to fear the deadly Stingers.

"Allah Akbar! Allah Akbar!" Fadil and his men cried out, shaking their fists at the fleeing Soviet warplanes.

• • •

Fadil and I celebrated our small victory over the Sukhois at my hotel in Peshawar with a group of Muslim volunteers who had come to fight in the jihad. We laughed and joked, sharing the uniquely intense camaraderie and ease of soldiers. The petty squabbles and jealousies that divide the Muslim world into warring tribes were temporarily forgotten.

These were men of the Islamic International Brigade. Some ten thousand volunteers from every corner of the Middle East, and some from places as distant as Indonesia or Mali, had volunteered or had been recruited by the Muslim Brotherhood and various Saudi religious or welfare organizations to go and fight the jihad in Afghanistan.

They were not mercenaries. The great Arab oil rush was still on and educated workers of every sort were in great demand across the Mideast. Many members of the International Brigades had in fact given up good jobs and left their families to go on the jihad, just as young, idealistic Americans, Canadians, and Europeans had done for another International Brigade in Spain half a century earlier.

What moved men from deeply selfish Arab societies, where loyalty normally extends no further than family, clan, and tribe, to head off to war in the distant and dangerous mountains of Afghanistan against the world's largest and best-equipped land army? For some, the motive was no deeper than a youthful desire for adventure. But most of the volunteers were driven by two more potent forces: their faith in a militant, activist Islam, and their determination to avenge the humiliation and shame suffered for so long by the Muslim world at the hands of its two greatest modern foes, the Western powers and the Soviet Union. These Islamic volunteers aspired to undo on the battlefields of Afghanistan the defeats, disgraces, failures, and follies of a thousand years of Muslim history.

A decade later some of these same men, by now battle-hardened and scarred, would go to neighboring Kashmir to join the battle against Indian rule. Another "Afghani" (in reality a Saudi) named Osama bin Ladeen, would embark on a quixotic one-man crusade to drive the United States from its Mideast raj.

Before going off to war, the men of the International Brigade were trained by military instructors from the U.S., Britain, and Pakistan. Imams in the camps filled their ears with prayers and their hearts with the passion of Islam, teaching that being a true Muslim means actively advancing Allah's will on Earth.

Many—certainly thousands—died in battle, or later of their wounds. Others succumbed to hepatitis, malaria, pneumonia, and a legion of other diseases. After the fall of the Communists, some stayed on in Afghanistan, mainly around Peshawar, where they joined religious schools, called *madrassas*, devoting themselves to theological studies. Others, unwilling to leave their new fraternity of Islamic warriors and determined to advance the cause of militant Islam, went off to fight in Indian-ruled Kashmir.

The rest, seasoned warriors infused with the spirit of Islamic revolution, returned to their homes: to Algeria, Morocco, Iran, Lebanon, Egypt; to Jordan, Arabia, and the Gulf. Fadil, who as a Kurd had no homeland, returned to an adopted one, Egypt, where he vanished into the teeming slums of eastern Cairo to carry on his personal jihad. In all these places, whatever their origins, the veterans quickly became known as "Afghani": men of honor and courage whose faith had defeated the mightiest foe. They were spearheads of the Islamic renewal, the scourge of oppressors—soldiers of Allah.

• • •

The Americans, Soviets, and Indians all agreed that they desired a weak, divided Afghanistan rather than a united one that might become the launching pad for Islamic nationalism in Central Asia. The great powers determined that Afghanistan was to return to its former status as a neutral buffer state.

The Islamic revolution had served its purpose, at least for the United States. Once the Soviets had been driven from Afghanistan, and the threat to the oil-rich Gulf accordingly removed, Washington cut off all arms and money to the mujahedin. The Islamic warriors who had been America's ally, and surrogate army, were now denounced as "Islamic terrorists." The United States and the Soviet Union/Russia quietly joined forces to combat the spread of political Islam. The evil Muslim genie was to be put back in its bottle.

5

The Secret War

RAWALPINDI, PAKISTAN

'm an optimist," said President Zia ul-Haq, "but the situation could not be worse." Sitting in the den of his unassuming house in the Rawalpindi military cantonment, Pakistan's embattled leader looked remarkably calm and relaxed. The room was cluttered with books, newspapers, and toys that had been left scattered about by his grandchildren.

Dressed in a white palwar and khamiz, Zia looked like a mid-level Pakistani civil servant on his day off. The former tank general was of medium height, rather stocky, but muscular and fit from the tennis and golf he so dearly loved. His pomaded hair, just beginning to gray, was combed straight back. Zia's smile, which revealed flawless, gleaming white teeth, was intense, and notoriously infectious. He laughed often, deeply.

When recalling Zia, I always picture his powerful smile. But what struck me even more forcibly were his eyes and his hands. Zia's eyes were surrounded by dark-pigmented circles, almost like a harlequin's domino mask. They would quickly shift from warm to steely cold; from friendly and sparkling to hard and ruthless. His hands were like two chunks of rough-hewn marble, thick and strong; they attested to the tough, even brutal side of the general-turned-president. But then, no one with soft hands or a soft heart could possibly rule Pakistan, one of the world's most turbulent, maddeningly fractious, and unstable nations. Zia would make a marvelous friend, I concluded, and an exceptionally dangerous enemy.

Zia was also an extremely modest man, and a genuinely religious one. Among pious Muslims, modesty in appearance and behavior is considered a cardinal virtue. Zia had none of the hand-me-down pomp of the British Raj adopted by India's Gandhi dynasty and its successors; none of the ludicrous, nouveau-riche ostentation of Iran's vainglorious Shah; and none of the demagoguery, hard drinking, and wenching of his predecessor, Zulfikar Ali Bhutto.

Zia was widely respected, even by many of his bitterest critics, as an honest man. This was a rare attribute for a politician in Pakistan, a nation steeped in the most pervasive and corrosive corruption, where political office was the golden staircase to self-enrichment. Almost unique among Pakistan's leaders, Zia died without leaving his family a fortune.

His mood that day in Rawalpindi was exceedingly grim. It was 1986, and bitter hostilities had erupted between Pakistan and India. Four hundred thousand Indian troops had massed on the border with Pakistan. Under the late Indira Gandhi (who had been assassinated in 1984, two years before), India had become the USSR's closest ally and the largest recipient of Soviet arms. The two enjoyed a "special relationship" akin to the old U.S.–British entente, and their alliance meant that all the best units of the Pakistani army were tied down defending the long, vulnerable border with India. Only two weak infantry divisions were left to guard against Soviet incursions across the long Afghan frontier.

By the mid-1980s, Soviet troop strength in Afghanistan had risen to 140,000 men. Resistance to the occupation, though fierce, was fragmented and had largely been contained to rural areas. The Soviets were busy building major bases in remote southwestern Afghanistan at Farah and Shindand: their purpose could only be to support a major military thrust into western Pakistan and the Gulf. At Shindand, the Soviets had also set up highly sophisticated electronic warfare systems and medium-range missiles.

"Shindand," Zia explained to me, "is only 500 Ks [300 miles] from our port at Gwadar—maybe four days, at most, by tank." Gwadar lay on the Arabian Sea, next to Iranian Baluchistan, west of Pakistan's main port, Karachi. The warm waters of the Arabian Sea gave onto the Indian Ocean, and thence to all the world's seas.

"Russia's—and now the Soviet Union's—historic grand strategy is to expand to all of its potential maritime borders," Zia continued. Five hundred years earlier, the USSR had begun as Rus, a collection of land-locked principalities around Kiev and Novgorod. Ever since Tsar Ivan IV (the Terrible) united the Russian state in the sixteenth century, it had pressed relentlessly outward: down the Volga to conquer the lands of the Muslim Mongol Golden Horde around Astrakhan and the Caspian; south to Rostov, to Kerch on the Black Sea, and to the Muslim Khanate of the Crimea; then northwest, to the shores of the Baltic, and east across Siberia to the distant Pacific Ocean. In the 1840s, the Russian Empire again began to expand southeast, into Muslim Turkestan, a vast area of steppe and mountain stretching from the Caspian to China. And on into the wild Caucasus, where warlike Muslim mountaineers— Daghestanis, Chechen, Ingush, Cherkass—rose in a holy war against the Russian invaders. Their heroic resistance continues to our own day.

Zia took a piece of triangular red plastic from his bookcase and held it flat against the wall map, point upward. "This is the course of Russian expansion into our part of the world over the past two hundred years. Moscow's expansion into Muslim Central Asia has been relentless. Look at the dates of the fall of the Muslim Khanates: Bukhara 1848, Tashkent 1851, Samarkand 1853, Balkh 1865, Khiva 1868." Each year, the Czar's armies moved closer to the Himalayas, to India, and to the Arabian Sea. It took the Afghan tribes and the power of the British Indian Raj to finally halt—or delay—the Russian drive south, the long, hard-fought struggle for Central Asia that Kipling called the "Great Game."

Russia could wait years, even a century, to attain its strategic goal, said Zia. "One day, Russia will reach the southern shore." The general went to a bookcase and extracted a slim volume. "This book—it's a statement of Soviet foreign policy—was given to me by the Soviet Ambassador. He said to me, 'Your Excellency, this is our foreign policy. You can take this book and read it one hundred years from now, and nothing will have changed. Your American friends change policy every year. Russia's policy never alters. You should remember this.'"

As a writer on naval strategy, I immediately understood Zia's argument. By the early nineteenth century, the fleets of the Russian Empire had managed to secure access to all the world's great oceans and seas save two: the Mediterranean and the Indian Ocean. And for these two great bodies of water, Russia's czars ached with desire, knowing that when Russia finally reached its historic goal of the "warm waters," the Third Rome would truly rule the world. The collapse of the Soviet Union in 1991 delayed this grand strategy, but it has no way changed Russia's historic quest to reach all its ultimate maritime borders.

Russia's four great fleets—Northern, Baltic, Black Sea, and Pacific—suffered from a fatal disadvantage: they could not concentrate. Their bases and operational areas were all widely separated. In time of war, none could support the others. As the 1904 Russo-Japanese war disastrously showed, enemy fleets could, by concentration, gain tactical superiority over each separate Russian fleet, and defeat them in detail, before they could join forces. To make matters worse, the Pacific fleet guarding the distant, thinly populated Far East was dependent on two vulnerable rail lines of the Trans-Siberian and Baikal-Amur Railways for its supplies and communications.

Here was the classic military predicament of operating on exterior lines. The grand geopolitical solution to this problem was clearly understood by past Russian strategists:

First, seize Istanbul and the Dardanelles; then join with Serbia, a loyal ally, to gain the Adriatic coast, seizing the strategic Albanian deep-water ports of Vlore and Dures. Successful execution of this plan would turn the Eastern Mediterranean into a Russian lake.

Second, complete the drive to the south through Central Asia by reaching the shores of the Arabian Sea. The next step: establish a Soviet Gibraltar at Gwadar, in Baluchistan, or outside Karachi, and link this new naval, base complex to the Soviet rail system at Tashkent. Such a coup would allow the USSR to create the logistical base for a powerful Indian Ocean fleet, which would be the strategic nexus between the Pacific and Northern fleets and could dominate the Western world's oil artery from the Gulf.

Reaching the coast of the Arabian Sea would open all East Africa and Arabia to Soviet influence; then, once the strategic alliance with India was cemented, Singapore and the Straits of Malacca would be brought under Soviet naval guns. This final act in the historic Russian expansion would alter the entire geopolitical balance of the world, transforming Russia from a primarily land power into a genuine naval superpower, breaking the stranglehold on maritime commerce and naval power held by the Anglo-American alliance.

The occupation of Afghanistan was a breathtaking geopolitical gamble, first step of a master plan that would ultimately mean the attainment of Russia's profoundest historic ambition. It was a move that could shake the world and make the Soviet Union master of both the land and the seas. The timing was ideal: the West quailed before Soviet power. President Carter might be ready to cede the Middle East without a fight. From southern Afghanistan, the Russians could almost smell the warm, salty waters of the Arabian Sea. Only some poorly armed Afghan tribesmen, a thousand kilometers of Pakistani territory, and General Zia ul-Haq stood in their way.

"We decided," Zia said in his usual unassuming way, "that the Soviets would destroy Pakistan if we did not act." ISI, Pakistani military intelligence, was convinced Moscow and its ally India would invade Pakistan as soon as the Afghan resistance had been crushed. "The only reason the Soviets didn't invade sooner was that they had to secure their supply lines through Afghanistan from attack by the mujahedin." An invasion of Pakistan would not be possible until Soviet communications from Tashkent to the Khyber Pass were secured.

Abandoned by the United States, assailed by supporters of the executed Zulfikar Ali Bhutto, and threatened by a joint Indian-Soviet invasion, Zia and his right-hand man, General Akhdar Abdul Rahman Khan, decided the only way to save Pakistan was to confront the Soviets head-on in Afghanistan. Pakistan, an impoverished, backward nation of 130 million, would launch a covert war against the world's greatest land power.

General Akhdar Abdul Rahman Khan was one of the most intimidating men I had ever met. The director general of Pakistan's Inter-Service Intelligence agency briefed me on the course of the war and Pakistan's growing involvement. Pakistani army officers, seconded to the jihad, provided most of the technical services for the mujahedin: radio, logistics, medical support, ordinance, combat planning, and intelligence. I was shown films of ISI men in Afghan garb blowing up Soviet oil pipelines and microwave relay towers, firing heavy weapons, servicing arms and equipment, or directing tactical and staff operations.

Logistics were the single most important element in the war. Every bullet, every mortar shell or rocket, that was fired in Afghanistan had to be transported by trucks, then on horses, mules, and, finally, men's backs from secret ISI arms depots in northern Pakistan. Without the efficient ISI logistics network, the jihad would have been crushed by 1985.

Pakistani covert assistance turned the war from an inevitable defeat for the mujahedin into a bloody stalemate that halted the Soviet *Drang nach Süden*. Mideastern and American money continued pouring into ISI coffers to support the war. The CIA and MI6 quickly became allies of the ISI in the secret war. At its peak, in 1988, more than $600 million annually was flowing through the ISI to the mujahedin. And it was through the ISI and the Muslim International Brigade that the deadly Stingers were deployed, altering the course of the war and so greatly contributing to the ultimate Soviet defeat.

I asked Zia where he found the courage to face the incessant, furious Soviet threats to invade and "punish" Pakistan. "I stay calm. I am a Muslim. I believe that Allah defends the just, and our cause is just." Coming from a Western political leader, such words would cloy and reek of hypocrisy. But Zia was a passionate Muslim who ardently believed in what he said and truly thought of himself as a Muslim soldier whose duty, as the Koran says, is to defend the Muslim community when it is attacked. "My faith and my people's faith gives me strength to fight against odds that are"—Zia smiled his big smile—"impossible."

Zia and Akhdar made the impossible happen. Thanks to them, and to the heroism of the mujahedin and the Afghan people (of whom 1.5 million became *shaheed*, or martyred, in the Great Jihad), and thanks also to the Stingers, the Islamic Brigades, and Western and Muslim money, the Red Army—the most powerful military force on Earth— had been stopped in its tracks.

When the USSR's new leader, Mikhail Gorbachev, came to power, he ordered a complete review of the Afghan war and its mounting economic cost to the foundering Soviet economy. Appalled by the stalemated war's expense, and bowing to widespread public anger over losses in Afghanistan, Gorbachev called an end to the conflict. By mid-1989 the last units of the Soviet army crossed out of Afghanistan over the bridge at Termez.

Defeat in Afghanistan shattered the myth of Soviet military invincibility in the most humiliating possible manner: the ever-victorious Red Army had not been beaten by the redoubtable Germans, or even by high-tech Americans, but by primitive tribesmen, and even worse than that, by Muslims, who are to Russians the most hated and despised of people. It would be as if a ragtag army of Puerto Ricans and Mexicans had defeated America in a war.

The demoralized Soviet soldiers who returned from Afghanistan also brought back with them a political virus that would soon infect and then destroy the entire Soviet Union. The Communist empire was bankrupt, corrupt, frozen rigid by incompetence, laziness, cynicism, and despair. On the outside it seemed virile and aggressive. But like the Wizard of Oz, it was all sound and colored smoke. As the Russians retreated from Kabul, a great wind arose and raced across the Russian heartland, sweeping all before its fury.

The storm from Afghanistan blew down the Potemkin village that was the Soviet Union. It blew away the ingrained, pervasive fear that had held the rickety Soviet system together. When the fear was dispelled, the many peoples of the USSR opened their eyes and saw that they lived not in a bountiful, heroic state, but in a vast, dilapidated ruin, a modern version of the moribund Ottoman Empire. The USSR's subject races and nations saw Moscow humbled by primitive Afghans and promptly decamped from the union, no longer terrified of a punitive invasion by the Red Army, or midnight arrests by the KGB. Local chiefs and party bosses in the republics—collectively known as "mafias"—concluded they were better off without Moscow, and could keep their wealth at home instead of paying it into the Kremlin's coffers. The generational revolution that was sweeping Eastern Europe hit the Soviet Union full force, bringing down its elderly, discredited power structure.

Three years after the last Soviet troops left Afghanistan, the Soviet Union and the once mighty Communist party, having run out of lies, and no longer able to inspire fear, simply collapsed from internal rot and oozed away into the gutter of history.

The Soviet Union and communism probably would not have fallen so soon without the blows struck by Zia ul-Haq, who decided to draw his sword and stand almost single-handedly to face the world's greatest and most ruthless land power. The heroic Polish uprising, secretly organized and financed by the Vatican, and President Ronald Reagan's decision to engage the USSR in a massive and ultimately ruinous arms race, had undermined Soviet power. Zia and the mujahedin delivered the death blow to the Soviet Empire.

Without Zia, there would have been no victory in Afghanistan. Had the secret war not been waged, the Soviets might have reached the warm waters of the Arabian Sea by 1988. In many ways, the victory of Zia and the mujahedin in Afghanistan was as great a historic triumph as the defeat of 110,000 Byzantine troops on the banks of the Yarmuk in November 632 by 50,000 Arab holy warriors of the great general, and first *Saif-ul-Islam* (sword of Islam), Khalid ibn al-Walid. In our day, another Saif-ul-Islam, Zia ul-Haq, helped bring down an evil empire that was the worst oppressor on Earth of Muslims and non-Muslims alike.

Modest to the end, Zia kept the details of Pakistan's epic resistance a secret. In spite of having been fully briefed in 1986, I never revealed this remarkable story until the war was over, for fear of endangering the jihad and Pakistan's secret role in this epic victory.

The last time I saw Zia, I asked him if he planned to retire. "By 1990 I will have contributed enough." He paused, and then produced his trademark dazzling smile: "I will then concentrate on improving my golf and tennis."

But he would not have the opportunity. In June 1988, the Soviet proconsul in Kabul, Yuli Vorontsov, openly threatened that Zia and Akhdar would "pay personally" for the looming Soviet defeat in Afghanistan.

On August 17, 1988, a c-130 military transport carrying Zia ul-Haq, Akhdar Abdul Rahman, thirty of Pakistan's most senior military officers, and U.S. Ambassador Arnold Raphael took off from Bahawalpur, in central Pakistan. Minutes later, the C-130 went out of control and crashed into the desert, where it exploded and burned. All aboard were killed.

Pakistan's government investigated the crash, aided by U.S. Air Force accident investigators. The inquiry concluded that Zia's C-130 had been sabotaged by the introduction of a poisonous, incapacitating gas into the cockpit. Just as the FBI was about to open its own detailed investigation, the State Department intervened and blocked the FBI investigation, leaking claims to the media that the crash was caused by mechanical malfunction. This was to become the official American version of events, even though U.S. Air Force investigators flatly contradicted the claim.

The new Pakistani government of Benazir Bhutto moved swiftly to cover up or destroy evidence from the crash. The flight crew's bodies were never autopsied, but quickly buried. Key components from the aircraft vanished. Records were "lost." Senior officials appointed by Zia were purged *en masse*. It was as if a giant eraser had wiped away the memory of the general who had faced down the Soviets in Afghanistan.

Pakistani Air Chief Marshal Hakimullah, who chaired the inquiry, told me it was also his own personal view that the aircraft had been sabotaged, and the ensuing investigation short-circuited by both Washington and Benazir Bhutto's government. "I am afraid we will never find out the true story," he told me, eight years after the crash.

Zia had many enemies. Which of them murdered him?

In 1988, when I was one of the first Western journalists to gain access to KGB headquarters in Moscow, I asked two senior KGB generals if their agency had been involved in the Zia assassination. They denied any involvement, but suggested the Afghan KHAD had "played a role." This is unlikely. KHAD was a faithful satrap of the KGB and would not have mounted a major assassination without full approval from Moscow Center. In any case, it lacked the expertise and technical capability to sabotage Zia's aircraft by the sophisticated method that was used. India's intelligence agency, the Research and Analysis Wing (RAW), was also an unlikely candidate, being in a similar position.

This process of elimination leaves three possibilities. The first is Gen. Mirza Aslam Beg, who was the sole senior officer to escape the crash, and other senior officials, acting in collusion with either Benazir Bhutto or a foreign power.

The second possibility is the KGB. Over the past decade, I have heard from ex-KGB officers that the assassination may have been mounted by technical experts from Department 8 and "wet affairs" teams from Directorate S, using special unidentifiable gases perfected by KGB laboratories, like the cyanide compounds used to assassinate Ukrainian nationalists in West Germany.

According to the reports I heard, three KGB assassination teams had been assigned to kill Zia. They were ordered to stay in a constant state of readiness, waiting for an opportunity to strike. Shortly after Vorontsov's threat against Zia, Soviet Foreign Minister Eduard Shevardnadze warned Pakistan that its continued support for the mujahedin would "not go unpunished." Shevardnadze denied in a 1994 interview with me that he had had any part in Zia's assassination.

Six weeks after Zia was killed, Vladimir Kryuchkov was promoted to chairman of the KGB by Mikhail Gorbachev. Kryuchkov was head of the KGB's First Chief Directorate, to which Department 8 and Directorate S belonged.

The third and last possibility: a majority of Pakistanis believe to this day that Zia was murdered by the United States. Zia had ambitions for Pakistan to dominate Afghanistan, and then to go on to assume the leadership of the Muslim peoples of Central Asia. Neither Moscow nor Washington wanted to see a Pakistani-led Islamic *risorgimento* in Asia. The victorious Zia clearly threatened the tacit agreement between the U.S. and the USSR to demilitarize and isolate Afghanistan, as well as to leave the ex-Soviet republics of Central Asia within Moscow's sphere of influence.

In short, Zia had become a dangerous inconvenience. Pakistan and the mujahedin had served their purpose and were no longer needed. If FBI investigators discovered that Zia had, in fact, been murdered by the KGB, the trail of guilt would lead right to the man who would have had to authorize the murder: Mikhail Gorbachev. But Gorbachev was now ending the Cold War and dismantling the once menacing Soviet Empire. Accusing the Soviets of involvement in Zia's assassination might very likely derail START arms reductions negotiations.

No one in Washington wanted to embarrass or undermine the new Soviet leader, or endanger the fragile détente between the superpowers. After the attempt on Pope John Paul II's life, U.S. and European investigators had similarly shied away from following the evidence trail that led, via Bulgaria, to Moscow Center.

After years of investigation, my own view is that the most probable cause of Zia's assassination was a secret compact between Washington and Moscow to eliminate the Pakistani leader, made during U.S.-Soviet negotiations at Geneva, Switzerland, in the spring of 1988, to end the war in Afghanistan.

Zia was immediately replaced by the U.S.-educated Benazir Bhutto, darling of the Western media, enemy of Islamic forces, and a compliant ally of Washington. She could be counted on to keep the Pax Americana in South Asia. Rarely has there been a neater or more complete transfer of power than that between the Zia regime and Bhutto.

Another ISI director, General Hamid Gul, who had directed secret operations in Afghanistan, told me a decade later he was convinced the United States had assassinated Zia ul-Haq, probably with help from the Bhutto family and other senior officials. Zia, claims General Gul, had to die because he refused to obey directives from Washington, and kept insisting the Soviet Union still remained determined to dominate Afghanistan and, eventually, Pakistan.

So, having served his role and become an inconvenience, Zia ul-Haq was "surgically" removed. Some day, the sordid details of his murder will emerge. As Henry Kissinger noted in another context, it is far safer being an enemy of the United States than an ally.

• • •

The Soviet Union had suffered its first military defeat. While the West rejoiced in this historic victory, Afghanistan was left in ruins. Large parts of the country were devastated: villages had been reduced to rubble; bridges and irrigation systems destroyed; wells poisoned; farm animals slaughtered. Many of the ten million antipersonnel mines scattered by the Soviets remained active, rendering much of the nation's agricultural land lethal and unusable.

At least 25,000 Islamic mujahedin and 20,000 Afghan Communist troops died in the struggle. An estimated 1.5 million civilians, about 10 percent of the total population, were dead. Five million Afghans were refugees in Iran and Pakistan.

The psychological damage inflicted on Afghanistan equaled the enormous physical destruction. Before the war the multiethnic Afghans had coexisted reasonably successfully, but now the fragile regional religious, ethnic, and linguistic mosaic of prewar Afghan society was shattered. None of the Afghan leaders or warlords knew how to reassemble the jagged, jumbled pieces of what had once been a country.

Unseen by the West, the Soviet KGB's campaign to promote tribal turmoil had been a deadly success. The result was violent civil war in which all Afghanistan's neighbors, including Russia, intervened.

In 1995 a new force burst upon the scene. An army of supposed seminarians, or "Talibs"—from Islamic *madrassas*—suddenly took the field armed with tanks, artillery, and even a small air force. With AK-47s in one hand, and the Holy Koran in the other, Taliban quickly captured the important western cities of Herat and Kandahar. Then they advanced on Jalalabad, and finally took Kabul. Their enemies seemed to melt away before the Islamic host.

Taliban was yet another product of the inventive military minds at Pakistan's Inter-Service Intelligence. The ISI boys had somehow cooked up the idea of Taliban as a sort of crusading army that would rid Afghanistan of anarchy, rapine, and banditry, all very real plagues at the time. Talibs from the many madrassas in Pakistan, some of them members of the old Islamic International Brigade, were trained and armed by the ISI, then sent into battle.

Led by the one-eyed Sheik Omar, the new faction preached a medieval faith that often employed Islamic terminology to foster the most archaic customs of tribal Afghanistan. The heavily armed Talibs did not give a hoot for foreign opinion or diplomatic niceties. These wild mountaineers did as the pleased, and told the rest of the world, in particular horrified Western aid agencies and their idealistic workers, to go straight to the devil. Women were to work only in the home, and be veiled from head to toe when they went out, lest they cause good men to sin by rousing their lusts. Men had to wear beards to show they belonged to the faithful, and were not sissified, Westernized Afghans or, worse, Communists.

Taliban's medievalism was a direct reaction to the Communist era. The Afghan Communists had championed social modernization, education, and women's equality. Communist Afghan men shaved their beards; Communist Afghan women went unveiled, and worked in offices, stores, schools, and hospitals. They were thoroughly modern Marxists. In Kabul, leftist intellectuals drank whiskey and vodka, which traditional Muslims view with as much disapproval, or even horror, as Westerners do the public consumption of addictive drugs.

When Taliban seized Kabul, its first act was to string up Najibullah; then it went on to smash bars, order men to grow beards, and forbid women to work or appear unveiled in public, so expunging the lingering vestiges of communism. De-communization meant returning to traditional tribal ways—at gunpoint if necessary.

After the Pakistani-supported Taliban movement seized much of Afghanistan, its neighbors Russia, Uzbekistan, and Khazakstan also delivered arms, munitions, and military supplies to the Uzbek forces of former Communist warlord Gen. Rashid Dostam, in Mazar-I-Sharif. Russian military advisors served with Dostam's forces and piloted his small air force. It was noteworthy that, while Russia was begging loans from the West, it managed to find $2.4 billion to spend on the war in Chechnya, and at least $1 billion to battle Taliban in Afghanistan.

Russia viewed Taliban as a grave threat to the neo-Communist rulers of Central Asia. These newly independent states were still reliant on Moscow for military protection; their feeble economies remained linked to Russia's, and dependent on trade with the Russian federation. As far as the leadership in Moscow was concerned, the Central Asian states had merely decamped temporarily from the union in 1991. Once Russia was restored to political and economic stability, Central Asia would fall back into Moscow's orbit.

In a highly significant statement of policy that was totally ignored by the West, Moscow made clear that its "strategic borders" were identical to the old borders of the USSR. Any threat to Central Asia or the Caucasus would be acted upon as a threat to Russia. In military terms, Russia's "near abroad" was still part of the motherland. Substantial numbers of Russian troops remained at bases in Central Asia and the Caucasus, where they were frequently employed to combat Islamic rebels. Russian foreign intelligence doubled the number of its agents and covert operations in Central Asia and Afghanistan.

Iran eagerly cooperated with Russia to combat the advance of Taliban. Iran had another important objective in Central Asia. Tehran was determined to thwart Pakistan's plans to build a pipeline from Central Asia to Karachi, a project that would directly challenge its plans to export the Central Asian region's resources by rail and pipeline through Iranian ports on the Gulf. Tehran determined the most effective method of blocking the proposed north-south pipeline project to Pakistan was to keep the civil war raging in Afghanistan.

Further complicating this already murky situation, the militantly anti-American agitator Osama bin Ladeen sought refuge in southern Afghanistan, where he had served during the 1980s as a volunteer in the Islamic International Brigade. I had not met bin Ladeen, but knew some of his men, and the camps in which they were based. Whether bin Ladeen was the arch-terrorist that America claimed is uncertain. One must be cautious about Washington's demonizations. Each decade, the U.S. government and media select a Muslim malefactor of choice. In the sixties, it was Nasser; in the seventies, Arafat; in the eighties, Gaddafi; and in the nineties, Saddam Hussein.

The shadowy bin Ladeen's stated goal was to "liberate" the Muslim holy land of Saudi Arabia from its "puppet regime" and American military occupation. Just as Soviet troops in Afghanistan kept the quisling Najibullah in power, so, asserted bin Ladeen, it was the American military garrison in Saudi Arabia that kept its royal family on the throne. Islamic forces had liberated Afghanistan from foreign domination; now they would do the same in Saudi Arabia. What was the difference between Russian and American occupation of Muslim lands? bin Ladeen asked. It was time to overthrow the Saudi puppets of the West who were stealing the nation's wealth and squandering it on unusable arms, blonde prostitutes, gambling, and palaces.

Bin Ladeen was widely seen as a hero across the Islamic world, a Muslim David standing up to the American-Israeli Goliath. To the U.S., of course, bin Ladeen was a terrorist and grave national threat. The U.S. brought intense pressure on Taliban to expel bin Ladeen; when Taliban refused, and American embassies in East Africa were bombed by parties unknown, the U.S. fired more than one hundred cruise missiles at bin Ladeen's camp, killing a score of Afghans and Pakistanis, but missing the shadowy Saudi militant.

The Clinton administration described Afghanistan as "a hotbed of Islamic terrorists." Ironically, this terminology was almost identical to that used by the Kremlin. The U.S. and Russia were now united in their common objective of defeating the forces of political Islam.

The Afghans won the war, but lost the peace. Jealousy, tribalism, and the lust for power had replaced the holy war. It was a demoralizing spectacle, humankind at its lowest ebb: politics as usual. Victory had been thrown away; the Russians and their Communist Central Asian allies were worming their way back into Afghanistan. The world regarded the once heroic mujahedin as dangerous wild men and fanatics. Many Americans would even foolishly claim they should never have aided the anti-Soviet resistance.

The fragile mosaic of Afghanistan had been shattered by twenty years of war; it could not be put together again. The great powers used Afghanistan as a battlefield for their proxy wars, then left this once beautiful nation a smoking ruin, covered with millions of active mines, ruined villages, and warring factions.

Disgusted by the bloody mess in Afghanistan, many mujahedin, both Afghan and foreign, turned their attention to neighboring Pakistan and Kashmir. A year after the Soviets withdrew from Afghanistan, rebellion erupted in Indian-held Kashmir. The explosion in Kashmir was spontaneous, but there is no doubt the Islamic victory in Afghanistan ignited the new *intifada*. Muslims across the world were elated, emboldened, and made proud by the victory over communism in Afghanistan.

If the world's leading conventional military power could be beaten in Afghanistan by Islamic faith and ardor, many Muslims reasoned, they could just as well liberate themselves from oppressive regimes everywhere else, be it from Egypt's pro-Western military regime, the Israeli occupation of southern Lebanon, Saudi oil oligarchs, Indian misrule in Kashmir, Catholic oppression in the Philippines, or Russia's brutal repression of the Caucasus.

Accordingly, small numbers of battle-hardened mujahedin left their bases around Peshawar, and made the short voyage from Afghanistan to the Pakistani portion of Kashmir. Next door, in Indian-held Kashmir, Muslims were being ferociously repressed and abused by the infidel Hindus. It was the duty of all good Muslims to succor them in their hour of need.

A new jihad had begun.

PART TWO

Kashmir—War in Paradise

Prologue

*Fight in the way of God against those who fight against you,
but do not yourselves be aggressors; for verily, God does not love
aggressors. . . . Fight against them until there is no longer
oppression and all men are free to worship God.*

HOLY KORAN

KASHMIR. LINE OF CONTROL. 0243hrs.

Two star shells drifted slowly down from the moonless sky, blazing an intense, sharp-edged magnesium light over the pine forests below. Off to our left, beyond the next hill, Indian border guards began firing shimmering volleys of tracer bullets. From somewhere farther behind the fortified Line of Control (LOC) that divides Kashmir, a battery of Indian 81mm mortars opened fire.

Rashid laughed. "They are frightened. The Indians are firing at ghosts again." Indeed, Indian troops guarding the ceasefire line in Kashmir were jumpy and trigger-happy. Small bands of *mujahedin* (holy warriors), were slipping across the hilly, wooded border each night to join the national uprising in the Indian-held portion of Kashmir. The nervous Indians fired at every sound, at anything that moved in the night.

We were huddled down behind a small knoll, shivering slightly as the damp cold of the Kashmir mountains penetrated our olive-drab field jackets. After a few minutes, the firing abated, then ceased completely. The rising wind stirred the tall pines around us. Rashid rose to his feet and began surveying the Indian positions below us through a pair of powerful German field glasses. He had come up to the front line that night to study Indian defenses. I had joined him on the reconnaissance mission, eager to have a close look at the barrier defenses on the Indian side of the Line of Control, a series of strongpoints behind a lethal barrier of thick razor wire, minefields, and delicate sensors that detected movement and sound.

Rashid had made, as I had, a very long, arduous journey to join the *intifada* in Kashmir. At some time in the distant past, Rashid had been an engineering student in Iraq. He showed me an old, dog-eared photo of himself: youthful, beardless, and slim. Now, many years and more pounds later, the burly Rashid looked the picture of a modern Islamic holy warrior, with his thick black beard, regulation Chitral knitted hat from Afghanistan, green field outfit and combat boots, AK-47 Kalashnikov, and a brace of Chinese-made grenades.

Soon after graduating from university in Baghdad, Rashid went off to Pakistan to join the great *jihad* (holy war), that was being waged against the Soviet army in Afghanistan. For Rashid, and thousands of other idealistic young Muslim men and women, the struggle against the Communists in Afghanistan was not merely a crusade against evil and oppression; it seemed, at the time, a path that would lead the downtrodden Islamic world to renewal and dignity.

Rashid had joined the Islamic International Brigade and fought the Communists for four years in the 1980s in Afghanistan, where he was trained by the CIA as a heavy weapons specialist.

We heard a series of rapid explosions about a mile off to our left. Rashid told me Indian howitzers were firing at a *nullah*, a narrow, dry gully that intersected the border at a right angle, and that provided a sheltered corridor along which mujahedin units slipped across the border between the Indian and Pakistani parts of Kashmir. Indian patrols were either using newly acquired night-vision devices to spot and then bring fire down on a group of holy warriors who were trying to penetrate the minefields and wire along the LOC, or were merely interdicting a known crossing point with random shelling.

The Muslim uprising in the two-thirds of Kashmir occupied by India had been under way for more than four years. After nearly half a century of Indian rule that was as inefficient and capricious as it was corrupt and brutal, Kashmiri Muslims had unexpectedly exploded in rebellion. The uprising surprised everyone, not least the Kashmiris themselves, who had long had a reputation for passivity, and wholly lacked the martial reputation of their other northern neighbors.

But the victory in 1989 by Islamic forces over the mighty Soviet Union and its Afghan Communist satraps had galvanized the entire Muslim world, including the Muslim majority in neighboring Kashmir. For the first time in memory, Muslims had defeated a mighty colonial power, the USSR, which was also the world's leading oppressor of Islam.

The struggle to free Muslim lands from European and Russian colonial rule had been going on for sixty years. In the 1930s, bands of Libyan mujahedin had breached barbed wire and minefields laid by the

Italians along the border with Egypt. Twenty years later, Algerian muja-hedin had fought their way across the minefields and electrified wire of the lethal Morice Line, built by the French to halt infiltration and the resupply of the rebel forces. In the 1950s and '60s, Palestinian *fedayeen* had been cut down trying to breach the wire and minefields defending Israel's border. Now it was Rashid's turn to lead his holy warriors across a new line of death on a new jihad.

6

The Kingdom of Sikander

The fabled state of Kashmir lies in majestic isolation amid the tower-ing mountain ranges separating the overpopulated plains of India from the endless steppes and deserts of Central Asia. Kashmir has long been called the jewel of India, the Switzerland of Asia, and the abode of the gods.

The noted nineteenth-century geopoliticians Sir Halford Mackinder and Baron Karl Haushofer described this region as one the world's primary strategic pivots—the nexus of continents, empires, and civilizations.

Kashmir is surrounded by a great bowl of crags: the Himalayas and Karakorams. Its borders are disputed but Kashmir's total area is approximately 92,200 square miles (239,000 sq. km), roughly the size of Great Britain. With a population of 11 million, Kashmir is larger than half the world's nations. Eight and a half million Kashmiris live in the Indian-held sector, 2.5 million in the Pakistani portion, or Azad Kashmir. Another million people of Kashmiri origin live in the Pakistani-administered Gilgit-Baltistan region, or Northern Territories, an area claimed by Kashmiri nationalists as part of their nation. A further million live in Pakistan, or are scattered in a dias-pora around the globe.

The majority of Kashmiris are tall, slender, fair-skinned people of

Aryan, Indo-European origin. A minority, concentrated in Ladakh, the Gilgit Valley, and Baltistan, are Mongol-Tibetans, short, dark-skinned people little different in physical appearance from the tribes of Tibet. Kashmir also has two small groups of nomadic mountaineers, the Gujars and Dards. Culturally, Kashmir's peoples have traditionally looked northward to Central Asia and Tibet, rather than south to India.

Unless you are a yak, or a bird, there are only two ways of getting into the Indian-ruled portion of Kashmir. The first is an interminably long, physically excruciating, and often perilous 435-mile (700-km) road voyage from New Delhi, India, over rising hills and steep mountain passes, which are often blocked by snow or landslides, to Srinagar, Kashmir's lake-girded capital.

A flight into the Kashmir Valley from New Delhi on one of India's internal airlines is also rather risky: their pilots are notorious for drink and incompetence; maintenance is shoddy; and aircraft are old, tired, and often suffering from advanced metal fatigue. Indian air carriers are almost always late; flights are frequently canceled because of mechanical problems or for other, more mysterious reasons.

Weaving and bobbing in a small Indian airliner between snow-capped mountains and around huge banks of cumulus clouds is a grandly hair-raising experience, even for the most phlegmatic or jaded traveler. But however dangerous flying inside India may be, it is quicker and considerably safer to take a plane than to brave the sustained terror and intense discomforts of road travel.

The Pakistani portion of divided Kashmir, called Azad ("Free") Kashmir, can be reached only by a long, tortuous journey over evil mountain roads, a trek that begins at Pakistan's capital, Islamabad, in northern Punjab, where the foothills of the mighty Karakoram range start to rise. Islamabad itself is no easy destination to attain. I had decided to go to Azad Kashmir to follow the new jihad in the Indian-ruled part of the divided state, and to renew my contacts with some of the mujahedin I had met during the Afghan conflict.

• • •

Custom-made capitals are disturbing, sterile places, unnatural creations that are half ghost town, half Potemkin village. Their awkward locations are determined not by the natural evolutionary logic of urbanism, geography, and trade, but by fear of foreign invasion, desire to escape the evils of commercial contamination, the need to be in friendly tribal territory, or, worst of all, rampant megalomania.

Think of Brasilia, a sort of bureaucratic Devil's Island, preposterously sited in the middle of a vast nothingness, a good 1,000 miles (1,600 km) from the inhabited coastal regions of Brazil. Of Romanian tyrant Nicolae Ceaușescu's monstrous Megalomaniapolis of neo-Stalinist palaces, built on the bulldozed ruins of elegant old Bucharest. Abuja, the new Nigerian capital, fallen into semi-ruin and slipping back into the jungle even before its construction was completed. Or the latest folly of would-be grandeur, the new Kazakh capital at Astana, a windblown former caravan stop on the empty Central Asian steppe.

Islamabad, Pakistan's capital, was created in 1954 for all these bad reasons by its then president, Field Marshal Ayoub Khan, a tough Pathan soldier from the Northwest Frontier. Ayoub sought to remove government from the nefarious clutches of corrupt, wicked Karachi; to move away from unfriendly Sind Province to his political, military, and tribal power base in the north; and, of course, to leave a grandiose monument of his enlightened rule.

Five decades later, Islamabad remains a monument of sorts to Ayoub, with its squat, uniform blocks of banal, white marble government buildings set among leafy trees and lush gardens. Streets are laid out in an eminently logical grid pattern, and numbered, appropriately, like so many office files. The city is whistle-clean, orderly, tranquil, and odor-free, a leafy bureaucratic oasis carefully set apart from the otherwise ubiquitous squalor, tumult, and disorder of South Asia. Islamabad looks and smells nothing like the rest of Pakistan. The capital is a brain detached from the nation's body, floating, as in a B-grade science-fiction film, in a sterile, liquid-filled container called Islamabad.

After two steamy nights in Islamabad, I set off for Azad Kashmir, wedged in the back of a Japanese car whose features included exceptionally bad springs, a struggling motor, and an impaired braking system. My ultimate destination was Chokoti, a village that lies at the apex of a sharp salient along the mountainous ceasefire line between Indian and Pakistani forces in Kashmir. The road to the north is deceptive. You first leave Islamabad along a smooth-surfaced highway with four luxurious lanes, bordered by impressive white curbstones. Once out of sight of Islamabad, however, this Pakistani autobahn soon dete-

riorates into a two-lane pot-holed road that winds laboriously upward
to the hill station of Muree, a famous refuge of colonial British from
the murderous summer heat of the Indian plains.

Muree, a cluster of low wooden buildings atop a steep hill, has little to recommend it save its 7,500-foot (2,286-m) altitude and
panoramic views of the Karakoram Mountains to the north. Any pretense at modern arterial communications ceases at Muree. Beyond, the
road hugs the side of Jhelum River, one of the five main tributaries of
the great Indus River. The road, by now a narrow strip of intermittent
asphalt punctuated by deep potholes, interrupted by water courses,
and liberally peppered with fallen rocks and branches, wound down
through narrow gorges.

Overladen trucks, threatening to capsize at any moment, careened
perilously around blind corners. Animals and pedestrians ambled along
the road, as heedless of danger as if it were a country lane. Gaily
painted buses, known as "flying coaches," navigated with an equal dis-
regard for safety, as if eager to deliver their tightly packed human cargoes into the hands of Allah the Merciful. In fact, each year numerous
flying coaches miss turns and fall into the Jhelum or the even might-
ier Indus, vast torrents of roiling, vicious, gray water filled with an
aqueous avalanche of rocks, boulders, and logs. The unfortunate chara-
bancs and their passengers are ground to unidentifiable bits in this
lethal Himalayan slurry.

As the road again rose, the air grew steadily cooler. The torrid heat
of the plains below was forgotten as we climbed through thick forests
of spruce, beech, and pine. Clouds and mist hung low, gray and moist.
Freshets of icy water poured down the mossy sides of the ever-steeper
cliffs banking the road and river.

Wet, muddy, and unstable, the road grew more perilous as we progressed. Each hairpin turn threatened either a watery grave in the
Jhelum River or instant pulverization by a hurtling truck or bus. Road
travel seems to be Pakistan's natural form of population control.

One quickly gets what I call "Pakistani road terror," a condition
that combines utter helplessness with panic, flashes of fatalism, and
nervous frenzy. It's impossible to close your eyes for a second, even during a twenty-hour ride, lest you fail to see your last moments on Earth.
Screaming at the drivers, who keep their pedals to the floor and horns
blaring, is pointless. They shrug, laugh at the foolish *farangi*, mutter

curses in Baluchi or some obscure dialect, and go even faster. You cling desperately to the seat back, or straps, brace your battered body and pray to Allah, Vishnu, Buddha, and the Holy Virgin of Santiago that you will survive the next mile.

After six hours of this unrelenting torture, we arrive at Muzzafarabad, the grandly named capital of the third of the mountain state controlled by Pakistan, Azad Kashmir. The city is very far from impressive. It is a dismal collection of moldering concrete buildings and wooden shacks set in a dreary valley, with the usual Indo-Pakistani urban backdrop of broken-down vehicles, stray animals, street urchins, refuse heaps, ugly overhead power lines, and squalid shops lit by a single, dim fluorescent bulb giving off a funereal blue glow. I was not impressed. Could this truly be the gateway to fabled Kashmir?

I was escorted, with much solemnity, to meet the prime minister of Azad Kashmir, a soft-spoken, venerable gentleman with a very white beard, neatly attired in a gray Nehru jacket and a high Karakul fur hat. Very politely, in his gentle voice, he denounced the impious, godless Indians who were raping and pillaging his beloved Kashmir. "You must study the Holy Koran," he admonished me gently, wagging a finger and showing grandfatherly concern for the visiting nonbeliever. "Allah will guide us to the true path in Kashmir, and smite the ungodly." Brave words, but there were some 840 million ungodly Hindus across the border.

The prime minister seemed to have little else of note to say. We exchanged platitudes, and drank milky tea. Known as *chai*, this form of tea is unique to the Asian subcontinent. To make it properly, you must take a battered, blackened, greasy aluminum pan; add contaminated water, two or three tablespoonfuls of insect-infested sugar, raw, unpasteurized milk, and black, perfumed tea; then boil it all up into a sweet white drink that will either cure whatever ails travelers to these parts or, more likely, leave you with Q fever, cholera, and assorted parasites. In these parts, tea cannot be refused when offered, which it always is. I discreetly gulped down an antibiotic capsule I had learned to always keep secreted in my pocket for just such social occasions.

I was relieved to bid the venerable prime minister farewell and continue our journey to see the refugee camps in Azad Kashmir and continue on to the front at Chokoti. We left town, and crossed the rushing river over an old, groaning Bailey bridge left over from World War II.

There was a large flag-decked stone arch surmounting its far end, bearing a sign proclaiming "Welcome to Azad Kashmir." We drove through, leaving melancholy Muzzafarabad well behind.

As before, the narrow, wet, crumbling road followed the sinuous gorge hewn by the raging Jhelum River into the heart of the granite mountains, ever deeper into Kashmir. Sprays of water from the raging river washed over the road and our car. Occasional clusters of hovels and orchards clung to the side of the road. Otherwise, we were alone in the great fastness of soaring mountains, rushing water, and winding defiles.

By now, the mountains had become taller and more jagged, so that their serrated peaks seemed to shred the thin white clouds scudding over them. We were awash in green: thick stands of trees and bush; lichen-covered rocks; and broad slopes blanketed with tall, damp, glistening grass. A sea of welcome luscious green after the endless aridity of the dun-colored plains. And everywhere precious water, worth more than human life in the dry south, gushing forth from rocks, running like quicksilver down granite slopes, collecting in sparkling pools, cascading with abandon into the Jhelum River. This seemed an outrageous, criminally extravagant waste of precious water, like gold coins thrown into the sea for the entertainment of children. I recalled an old love poem of the Gujar nomads: "I am thirsty; you are my water..."

At that precise moment, I suddenly understood why Indians and Pakistanis were willing to kill for Kashmir, why they had warred fifty years over this kingdom in the clouds. Kashmir aroused the most ferocious and unique passions in everyone, passions that brooked neither compromise nor concession. The place quite simply was heaven. And no one was about to hand over heaven, of all places, to a hated enemy. To dwellers on the flat, sere, furnace-like plains of north India and Punjab, Kashmir was a dream: inexhaustible sweet water; cool air; lush, dark soil; trees, flowers, fruits; and beautiful, fair-skinned women. No matter that few Indians had actually seen Kashmir. It was truly the jewel of India, the guardian of the holy rivers, the abode of the gods.

To comprehend the importance of Kashmir to the Indian psyche, one must first understand the role played by race in India's ancient culture. Few outsiders understand how important caste and skin color are in Hindu society.

The linguistic origin of the word *caste* comes from the Portuguese and

Spanish term for race, *casta*. Rightly so, because the caste system discriminates by race and enforces social stratification; one of its prime goals in India is to keep the darker-skinned lower orders, in particular, Dravidians, from mixing socially or sexually with the lighter-skinned high castes. The caste system has become so fragmented into subcastes, and so much a part of India's social fabric, that its racist origins have come to be widely ignored or forgotten. India, for example, became a leading foe and constant critic of South Africa's apartheid system, unconscious of the irony that its own caste system was just as racially driven and pervasive as that imposed by the regime it so ardently denounced.

High-caste India, however, was not alone in seeking to maintain the Aryan whiteness of its skin. In neighboring Burma, Thailand, and China, aristocracy and high class were always denoted by fair skin, and remain so today. This is also the case in many parts of Africa, where non-Negroid Hamitic blood, as in the case of Somalia and Ethiopia, or among Tutsis, is deemed a sign of great beauty. Even African-Americans have been accused of this practice, with successful black men picking light-skinned women for girlfriends or wives. Seeing fair skin as more attractive and desirable than dark appears to be a custom practiced around the world.

At the apex of India's caste pyramid are Brahmins, who believe themselves defiled if any of the food they consume has been touched by a lower-caste person, or if even the shadow of such a person falls upon them. Economics reinforces caste for the large numbers of Indian peasants who are condemned to permanent indentured servitude, unable ever to escape the crushing debts and accumulating interest they owe to rapacious moneylenders. Indebtedness passes from one generation to the next, ensuring the permanence of their near-slavery. At the bottom of the caste system are 160 million untouchables, today known as *dalits*, a group whose original function was menial chores and the sweeping up of feces deposited in the street by higher-caste defecators. Some years ago when I was in India, sociologists were amazed to discover an unknown subcaste of untouchables who had never previously been identified because they were not allowed to appear in daylight. These wretches lived exclusively in garbage dumps, where they fed on refuse, emerging only at night to do washing for slightly higher-caste untouchables.

The Brahmin caste has long provided Hindu India's ruling élite. Brahmins and other high castes are generally of Indo-European, or

Aryan, blood. Groups of nomadic Aryan tribes from Western Asia—the progenitors of Europe's Indo-European settlers—came down into north India through the Khyber Pass around 1500 BC, spreading rapidly across the subcontinent as far east as Bengal. The religion of these Aryan tribes, based on the holy books of the Veda with their pantheon of warrior sky deities, spread in the wake of the invaders; by 1000 BC it had developed into Brahmanism, a more complex, nuanced faith, the precursor of today's Hindu faith.

Hinduism divides society into four basic castes: Brahmins (priests), Ksatriya (nobles, warriors); Vaisya (merchants or farmers); and Sudra (workers). Over the centuries innumerable subcastes have developed. The only way for a Hindu to rise from a lower to a higher caste is through the process of reincarnation.

The Aryan Hindus were racially and linguistically akin to the early Germanic tribes that migrated into Europe. This link can easily be distinguished by the word for "king." In Europe's languages, *roi, rex,* and *rey* all share the same ancient Aryan linguistic root as the Indian term, *raja.* The Aryans displaced India's indigenous Dravidians, a smaller, dark-skinned people, pushing them down into southern India. Today, skin color and language are the great divide of India: in the north, Hindi-speaking Aryans; in the south, dark-skinned speakers of Dravidian languages such as Tamil, Kannada, Malayalam, Telugu. A northern Indian from Punjab or Uttar Pradesh is as distinct racially and linguistically as a Norwegian is from a Sicilian.

Brahmins from Kashmir, who held the highest rank on this racial-religious-social scale, are held in great esteem for their fair skin, fine features, and aristocratic ways. To Hindus, Kashmir is a repository of the pure essence of Aryan Hindu culture. Jawaharlal Nehru, India's first prime minister and founding father, was a Kashmiri Brahmin. Brilliant, haughty, and imperious, Nehru was the embodiment of Hindu hereditary royalty.

Legend has it that the light-skinned peoples of Kashmir, Gilgit, the Hunza Valley, and Baltistan are descendants of the soldiers of Alexander the Great. Those who know Rudyard Kipling's *The Man Who Would Be King,* or the superb film that was made of it, will recall how the local tribes awaited the return of Sikander, Alexander's son. There may, in fact, be substance to this charming legend. Alexander fought his way through the Khyber Pass and entered northern India via the

Indus valley in 327 BC. The following year, Alexander won a major battle against the local king at Hydapses, but his army refused to march any deeper into India.

Alexander returned to Persia, but he left behind many thousands of his élite Macedonian troops, with orders to marry local women and found Greek satrapies. In classical times, Macedonians and most Greeks were a fair-skinned, blue-eyed people who showed their Germanic roots—a far cry from today's Hellenes, who are the product of centuries of racial mixing with multiethnic Ottoman Turks, Slavs, and other Balkan peoples.

Cut off in Kashmir from India and Afghanistan by the ramparts of the Karakorams and Himalayas, the Greco-Kashmiri gene pool remained relatively isolated until modern times. The result is a people who appear strikingly different from their neighbors, rather like marooned survivors from a lost ship—wrecked, beached, and forgotten long ago on a strange, uncharted island.

On my way from Gilgit I passed through the fabled Hunza Valley, the ancestral home of the Aga Khans, the powerful hereditary *imam* of one branch of Shiism. Stopping for chai at a tea shop at the crest of a long, winding pass, I saw a blond man in a parka, about 6 feet (1.8 m) tall with very fair skin and blue eyes, and taking him to be British or north German, I addressed him in English. He could not understand me. The shop owner said, "Sahib-sir, he only speaks our local language." I was stunned and abashed. Later, I was to see many natives of Hunza, Kashmir, the Swat Valley, and Chitral who looked as Aryan as the man in the blue parka. The Kafir Kalash, a little-known non-Muslim tribe with the interesting custom of picking the strongest man in the village to mate with all its virgins, look as if they had just flown in from Hamburg. Where did these fair-skinned people come from, if not Alexander's hoplites?

For Muslims, passions over Kashmir run even deeper. Kashmir is the only Indian state that has a Muslim majority; it had been a stronghold of high Islamic culture for centuries. More important, Kashmir's famous gardens, shimmering lakes, snow-clad mountains, waterfalls, beautiful women, and Alpine climate seem to embody the Holy Koran's description of Muslim paradise. For 200 million illiterate but deeply pious Muslims in Pakistan and India, Kashmir is literally heaven on earth.

To politicians and generals on both sides, Kashmir has always been of such enormous strategic importance that its loss simply cannot be contemplated. To bitter enemies India and Pakistan, Kashmir plays the same inflammatory role as Alsace-Lorraine did between France and Germany from 1870 to 1945, a jealously disputed territory that arouses fierce irredentist hatreds and exaggerated fears in both nations.

• • •

The region today known as Kashmir was a Buddhist kingdom that paid fealty to Tibet until the seventh century AD, when it fell under Hindu rule. Muslim rulers ousted the Hindus in the fourteenth century. The great Muslim Mogul emperor Akbar conquered the valley in 1586 and made it his summer residence. In 1757, wild Afghans overran Kashmir. Then in 1819 came the warlike Sikhs, until they in turn were defeated in the Sikh Wars by the army of the British East India Company, which annexed Punjab and Kashmir.

In 1846, the British East India Company sold Kashmir to Ghulab Singh, the Hindu maharaja of Jammu, giving him the status of an independent princely ruler under the Raj, to which the maharaja paid annual tribute. Supported by the British, Ghulab Singh annexed the neighboring regions of Gilgit, Hunza, Nagar, and Chitral to his kingdom of Kashmir and Jammu, creating the region today termed Kashmir. Muslim Kashmiris rebelled repeatedly against their new Hindu ruler, but the revolts were put down by the maharaja's forces, aided by troops of the British Indian Army.

At the time of India's partition by Britain in 1947, today's Indian-ruled part of Jammu and Kashmir was about 77 percent Muslim, 20 percent Hindus, and 3 percent Sikhs and Buddhists. What was to become the Pakistani portion, or Azad Kashmir, was 100 percent Muslim. The Indian-controlled state was ruled by Ghulab Singh's descendant, Hari Singh. Economically, Kashmir was closely linked to the eastern Punjab, the region that was to become Pakistan after partition. Poor roads, high passes, and landslides made communication with India difficult, even in clement summer weather. The roads leading northwest from Pathankot to Jammu and Poonch in southern Kashmir were often closed by rockfalls, or snow. Srinagar, Kashmir's capital, was four times closer to Islamabad than to Delhi.

Though an independent united India extending from Iran to Burma was the most cherished dream of the Congress Party, led by Mohandas K. Gandhi and Jawaharlal Nehru, by the end of World War II it became clear the subcontinent was headed for partition. The leader of the powerful Muslim League, Mohammed Ali Jinnah, pressed relentlessly for creation of a state for India's minority Muslims that would offer them a haven from frequent persecution by Hindus, and the opportunity to create the world's first nation guided by Islamic thinking.

By the eve of India's independence in 1947, Britain's new socialist government was eager to wash its hands of colonialism and India, and Lord Louis Mountbatten, the British viceroy, hastily agreed to Jinnah's plan to create a separate Muslim state out of predominantly Muslim regions in Bengal, the western Punjab, and Sind, though the latter two areas were separated from the former by an entire continent. Nehru and Gandhi protested bitterly, prophetically warning that the decision to split the British Raj in two (or three) would destabilize the subcontinent and lead to future strife. Mountbatten and his advisors rebuffed these warnings and made few plans to deal with any breakdown of law and order.

India was partitioned on August 15, 1947. Communal violence between Hindus, Muslims, and Sikhs immediately erupted. In one of modern history's largest population transfers, seventeen million Hindus and Muslims fled their homes. An orgy of mass killing, rape, arson, and looting ensued that the confused British authorities proved powerless to prevent or suppress. Estimates of the number of people who died in the bloodbath range between 500,000 and 1 million.

India's 500-odd princely states, which had formerly been vassals of the British Raj, were left to decide on accession to India or Pakistan. The largest such state, Hyderabad, with a large Muslim population, elected to join India, which surrounded it. But Kashmir, which lay between India and Pakistan, presented a unique problem.

The terrible trauma of partition hit Kashmir with full force: it quickly became the focus of ferocious Indo-Pakistani rivalry. Lord Mountbatten went to Kashmir shortly before partition and advised the maharaja, a reactionary and dissolute potentate, to determine whether his people wished to join India or Pakistan—or whether they preferred a third option, to remain an independent princely state. Gandhi hurried north to Kashmir and convinced the maharaja to accede to India and dismiss his prime minister, who favored independence. Muslim

Kashmiri leaders, notably Sheik Abdullah and Ghulam Abbas, were thrown into prison by the maharaja.

Mountbatten advised that the Kashmiri majority be allowed to choose their own allegiance, and Nehru publicly promised to respect their wishes, but in the end both advice and promises were ignored. Mountbatten's strong-willed wife, Edwina, who was openly carrying on an affair with Nehru, may well have influenced her wavering husband to tacitly favor Indian rule over Kashmir—or, at least, not to impede it.

Britain's socialist government failed to ensure that its pre-Partition assurances were observed. Kashmiri Muslims, who overwhelmingly desired to join Pakistan, were ordered to surrender their arms, and promptly revolted. In September 1947, in the southern Kashmir regions of Poonch and Jammu, which had and still have sizeable Hindu majorities, mobs of Hindus and Sikhs, aided by the maharaja's Sikh soldiers, began slaughtering Muslims. Muslim sources claim 200,000 of the region's total Muslim population of 500,000 were killed, and the rest driven as refugees to Pakistan. Muslim mobs turned against Hindus and Sikhs, slaughtering thousands.

As communal fighting spread across Kashmir, Pakistani leaders organized a "spontaneous" counterattack in October 1947, by Pathan tribesmen from the Northwest Frontier. The war-loving Pathans proclaimed a holy war, and promptly attacked the maharaja's small ragtag personal army of Hindus and Sikhs. The fierce Pathans routed the maharaja's troops, and advanced swiftly to within 19 miles (30 km) of Srinagar, the Kashmiri capital, and were poised to seize its vital airfield, the only one in Kashmir. The panicky maharaja appealed to Delhi for immediate military aid. Nehru agreed to succor the beleaguered Hindu ruler, but only if he would immediately join India. Hari Singh quickly agreed to Nehru's demand, and signed the Instrument of Accession to India on October 26, 1947, but with an important proviso: Kashmiris could decide on the future of their state once the military emergency was over. Lord Mountbatten confirmed this in a letter to the maharaja on the following day.

Meanwhile, in typical tribal fashion, the Pathans delayed their attack on Srinagar and its airfield in order to devote themselves to looting and pillage. This delay allowed India time to mount an air bridge to Srinagar. The Indians used their entire inventory of thirty Dakota military transports to airlift a battalion of Sikhs, blood enemies of the

Pathans, to Srinagar's airfield. A three-thousand-man army brigade was rushed up the terrible roads from the plains to Kashmir. After a month of chaotic fighting, the Pathans and Muslim irregular forces were pushed westward by arriving Indian Army troops. Further inconclusive fighting, which was joined in 1948 by regular Pakistani army units, sputtered on until the United Nations imposed a ceasefire in January 1949 between India and Pakistan.

When the fighting ended, two-thirds of Kashmir was in Indian hands, and a third in Pakistan's. The ceasefire line between the warring forces, known as the Line of Control (LOC), became the *de facto* border, along which both sides constructed field fortifications and deployed large numbers of troops and artillery—and there they remain today, half a century later, in a state of constant skirmishing and occasional major clashes. The lush Kashmir Valley, Srinagar, and mountainous Ladakh remained in Indian hands. In addition to the western third of the Kashmir Valley, Pakistan ended up in possession of the more northern Kashmiri regions of Gilgit and Baltistan, which it terms "the Northern Territories."

The border up to the top of Kashmir, which abuts China and Tibet, a rampart of soaring, snow-capped mountains and the great Baltoro and Siachen Glaciers, was left undemarcated—it was judged that no one could have any possible interest in such an uninhabitable, lethally high range of frozen crags. Such common sense would later fall victim to the poisonous hatred between Indians and Pakistanis, driving them to fight ferociously over utterly remote, absolutely worthless peaks that even mountain goats would not inhabit.

Beginning in 1948, the UN Security Council passed a series of resolutions calling for the status of Kashmir to be decided by a free, impartial plebiscite under supervision of the UN. Pakistan readily agreed, knowing the outcome would favor it. But Delhi refused to accept the UN's will, and set about integrating Kashmir into India. Subsequent UN resolutions reaffirming the original call for a plebiscite were also ignored or dismissed by India as non-binding, irrelevant, and an unacceptable intrusion into India's internal affairs. Pakistan refused to withdraw its forces from Azad Kashmir.

Kashmir has become the oldest, longest-running world dispute before the UN, predating even the Arab-Israeli conflict and the intractable dispute over Cyprus.

After 1949, riots by Kashmiri Muslims were put down ruthlessly, and Kashmiri Muslim leaders were repeatedly jailed, bribed, or intimidated into silence. In 1957, after years of creeping legal and administrative expropriation, India officially annexed Kashmir. Delhi was also subsequently to annex the former Portuguese territory of Goa, and turn the remote, but strategic, Himalayan states of Bhutan and Sikkim into Indian protectorates. Aside from protests by Pakistan, Portugal, and, ominously, China, all three annexations were greeted by the outside world with deep indifference. Few observers at the time noted that India, a vociferous champion of non-alignment and self-proclaimed scourge of Western colonialism, had itself become something of a regional colonial power.

· · ·

Another important element in the interlocking conflicts at the top of the world lies in a region deep in the fastness of the Karakorams. Remote Ladakh, known for centuries as "little Tibet," occupies an area on the northern shoulder of Kashmir. It is India's only region with a Buddhist majority. Ladakh's people are of the same ethnic and linguistic group as Tibetans, and in fact form part of historic ethnic Tibet.

Ladakh is one of the Earth's least-known places, a long, lonely series of desolate, arid valleys, girded on the southwest by the Zanskar Mountains, to the northeast by the Ladakh Range and the Karakorams, and the southwest by Kashmir. Geographically, it forms the extreme western end of the Tibetan Plateau.

A single narrow military road, open only six months of the year, leads up from Srinagar, across the Zoji La (*la* means "pass"), at 11,578 feet (3,529 m) to Kargil. Then the road struggles over a series of even more vertiginous passes to the capital, Leh, which lies near the upper reaches of the mighty Indus River, Pakistan's principal source of groundwater. Leh, which has 20,000 inhabitants, resembles a miniature version of pre-1950 Lhasa in culture and language. In fact, today Ladakh looks much more like traditional Tibet than the neighboring Chinese-occupied state. Harsh Chinese rule and immigration by some two million Han Chinese settlers have permanently altered the ethnography and character of Tibet; Ladakh, by contrast, still retains some of its original Tibetan culture, Buddhist-Lamist religion. The

Indians have fortunately taken little action to alter Ladakh's way of life.

Like the rest of Kashmir, Ladakh has been the frequent victim of invasions by neighbors, including Tibet. The Dogra maharajas of Jammu and Kashmir established their rule over Ladakh in the mid-1800s. At Partition, in 1947, India forces occupied Ladakh, keeping on its king as a figurehead. The Chinese occupation of Aksai-Chin, and the 1962 border war between China and India, spurred Delhi to build the military road linking Srinagar to Kargil and Leh, and to deploy large numbers of troops in Ladakh, parts of which are permanently restricted as sensitive military zones. When the Dalai Lama fled to India from Tibet after the Chinese invasion, he sought permission to settle in Ladakh. Fearing his presence would kindle Ladakhi nationalism and pro-Tibetan sentiments, India denied the request.

The failure by the nineteenth-century British Raj to clearly demarcate borders in the Himalayas, the Karakorams, and Kashmir would come back to haunt twentieth-century India, China, and Pakistan. As an Arab diplomat told me, "Most of the problems today in Asia and Africa are the fault of British imperialism." An exaggeration, to be sure, but one that contains an important kernel of truth.

China holds Ladakh to be an extension of Tibet, and thus part of China. Tibetans insist Ladakh is part of their ancient kingdom. Pakistan contends Ladakh is part of Kashmir, which is claimed by Pakistan. India insists Ladakh is part of the Indian union; Delhi has possession, of course, and troops on the ground, to support its claim.

The little mountain state of 130,000 people is of great strategic significance to India: its northwest border runs along the notional cease-fire line with Pakistani-held Baltistan, from the region around Kargil to the enormous Siachen Glacier on the border of Tibet. Its northeast frontier abuts the strategic Aksai Chin plateau, annexed by China in the 1950s. Leh is filled with Indian military personnel, producing an uncomfortable comparison with Chinese-occupied Lhasa.

India has long restricted visits by foreigners and journalists to Ladakh, citing military security. Another reason may be reported unrest by Ladakhis against heavy-handed Indian rule. India is extremely sensitive to potential accusations that it may be suppressing or illegally occupying Little Tibet, just as China suffers international rebuke and protest over its seizure of "Big" Tibet.

Like two other, similar mountain kingdoms, Bhutan and Sikkim,

Ladakh is a historical orphan, caught between two of the world's largest nations, and destined, inevitably, to be absorbed by them.

• • •

While India and Pakistan were fighting over the Kashmir Valley, China quietly took advantage of the confusion to advance its own territorial claims on the remote eastern end of Kashmir. Northeast of Ladakh, abutting Tibet, lies Aksai Chin, another chunk of disputed Kashmir that was of enormous strategic interest to China. Aksai Chin is a vast, arid, almost uninhabited plateau of icy lakes and frozen peaks, averaging 15,000 feet (4,572 m) of elevation, on the western extension of the Tibetan plateau. China seized Aksai Chin in the 1950s because the region offered the only possible route for a planned military road that would provide a vital southern link between Tibet and strategic Sinkiang, China's westernmost province.

Aksai Chin was so remote, Indian intelligence didn't even find out China had driven a strategic road across it until early in the 1960s. Pakistan gave tacit approval to this annexation because it badly needed Chinese political and military aid in its long struggle with India. Delhi insists to this day that Aksai Chin is Chinese-occupied Indian territory. Tibetans say Aksai Chin is part of historical Tibet, which it most likely is. No one has ever bothered to ask the opinion of the few yak herders of Aksai Chin who scratch a precarious living from this vast, forbidding wilderness of clouds, snow, and ice.

7

Revolt in the Mountains

In 1963, growing anger at India's often brutal, corrupt rule over Kashmir, and the theft of a sacred hair of the Prophet from the famous Hazratbal Mosque in Srinagar, ignited widespread protests and riots by Muslims. The protests raged on for two years, and were brutally suppressed, with heavy bloodshed, by Indian security forces.

The surging violence in Kashmir finally sparked a second full-scale war between India and Pakistan in 1965. The two nations battled for seventeen days before the UN imposed a ceasefire. Each tried to cut off the other's access roads to Kashmir through northern Punjab. Both the Indian and Pakistani armies soon bogged down along the long front from Kashmir to the Arabian Sea, quickly exhausting their inadequate stores of munitions and supplies. Like nearly all Third World armies, neither side could mobilize rapidly enough to sustain or provide logistical support for a fast-moving armored offensive. As so often in Indo-Pakistani wars, blitzkrieg soon turned to sitzkrieg.

Pakistan, which had believed its superior armor, its pilots, and the fighting spirit of its renowned "martial races"—Punjabis and Pathans—would overcome Indian numerical and material superiority, was forced to realize it lacked the military or economic power to decisively defeat seven-times-larger India. In addition, it was clear that, in any conflict, India held the important advantage of strategic depth, which allowed it to trade territory for time to mobilize and concentrate its superior forces. Narrow, wasp-waisted Pakistan had no such luxury.

During 1970–71, India's aggressive leader, Indira Gandhi, emboldened by her new strategic alliance with the Soviet Union, took advantage of an uprising in East Pakistan (today Bangladesh) against harsh rule by West Pakistan. Indira Gandhi had special Tibetan troops of the Indian armies, disguised as Bangladeshi rebels, infiltrate into East Pakistan to begin guerrilla warfare. As the revolt spread, Gandhi sent her rearmed, expanded army to conquer indefensible East Pakistan, which was easily overrun in three weeks by the very able Indian commander-in-chief, General Sam Maneckshaw.

Once again, Pakistani forces in the West, supported by heavy air attacks, hurled themselves against Indian deployments in Kashmir, northern Punjab, and the Thar Desert of Rajastan. After initial dramatic successes, Pakistani attacks petered out. A major Pakistani armored thrust against Pathankot and Jammu threatened to isolate Kashmir from India. But it was halted before its objective. So was a second major thrust toward Poonch, in southern Kashmir. Pakistan lacked adequate air cover, strategic reserves, or supplies to sustain its offensives.

Superior Indian forces, concentrated in two corps commands, counterattacked in the north, driving toward Sialkot, attempting to isolate Azad Kashmir from the rest of Pakistan. In the south, an Indian strike corps thrust into the Thar Desert, with the objective of cutting the narrow, vulnerable 1,000-mile (1,600-km) rail and road lines between northern Punjab and Sind. Intense air and land battles raged as India gradually gained the upper hand. Both sides fought with gallantry and élan, but the tide of war turned relentlessly against Pakistan, which was forced onto the strategic defensive. For a while, it seemed Indira Gandhi would heed calls by nationalists to crush Pakistan once and for all. But heavy American pressure, including threats that the Seventh Fleet, which rushed a carrier battle group into the Arabian Sea off Pakistan, might intervene in the war, the exhaustion of Indian war stocks, and stiffening Pakistani resistance forced negotiations that ended hostilities.

Pakistan had suffered catastrophic dismemberment, losing its eastern half, which became the independent state of Bangladesh, but the impasse in Kashmir remained unchanged. Pakistanis emerged from the war badly shaken, militarily, morally, and politically.

In July 1972, India and Pakistan conducted lengthy negotiations at the old British hill station at Simla, under the aegis of their respective patrons, the USSR and the U.S. Moscow and Washington, concerned they might be dragged into the Indo-Pakistani war, and thus face the risk of a direct clash, pressed Islamabad and Delhi to reach a negotiated settlement.

After much bazaar haggling, India and Pakistan agreed, first, that they would settle all their differences by peaceful means through bilateral negotiations; second, that neither would take any action to upset the status quo, or aid any forces seeking to do so; and, third, that the Line of Control in Kashmir would form the temporary border between India and Pakistan until Kashmir's final status was resolved.

India, basking in its successful war, regarded the Simla Agreement as a final end to the long dispute. Pakistan, in India's view, had accepted the permanent division of Kashmir and recognized Delhi's rule over two-thirds of the state. Equally important, according to Delhi's interpretation, Pakistan had agreed that Kashmir was to remain a wholly bilateral issue, not subject to any outside intervention or mediation, particularly that of the UN. Kashmir was now an entirely internal Indian matter; no UN interference, notably a plebiscite, would be legal under the Simla Agreement. Delhi adamantly maintains this position, to this day.

Pakistan, negotiating from a position of weakness at Simla, portrayed the accords in a different light. Though on rather shaky legal ground, Islamabad held that the pact left the door open for UN intervention, and did nothing to preclude a referendum. Ever since 1972, Pakistan's diplomatic strategy has been to get India to admit that Kashmir remained "disputed" territory, and to involve the UN and friendly foreign powers in the issue. India has just as resolutely used its considerable diplomatic power to keep the United Nations and foreign powers out of the Kashmir dispute.

In effect, Simla resolved nothing. Unrest continued to flare up in the Kashmir Valley; Indian and Pakistani forces skirmished along the LOC. India continued a rapid increase of its armed forces, using new Soviet armor, artillery, and aircraft to develop a much-enhanced offensive capability against Pakistan.

Then, in 1974, India detonated a nuclear device in the Thar Desert, shaking Pakistan to its foundations and forcing Islamabad to embark on a long, covert, financially ruinous nuclear program. Pakistan's fiery leader, Zulfikar Ali Bhutto, announced his people would "eat grass" to pay for the arms race between two of the world's poorest nations. A very senior Pakistani diplomat, who attended a meeting between U.S. Secretary of State Henry Kissinger and Bhutto, told me that Kissinger had warned Bhutto the U.S. would "hold him personally responsible" if Pakistan went ahead with development of nuclear arms. Bhutto supporters were later to call his overthrow and execution by Gen. Zia ul-Haq "Kissinger's revenge." Coincidentally, in the summer of 1988, the USSR used precisely the same phrase, threatening to hold President Zia "personally responsible" for engineering a Soviet defeat in Afghanistan. Like Bhutto, Zia met an untimely end.

After Simla, India's leaders almost convinced themselves the Kashmir problem had been permanently resolved by Pakistan's defeat in 1971. They also believed that continuing opposition by Kashmir's majority to Indian rule was wholly the result of Pakistani intrigues and subversion. Bloody Pakistan's nose, the thinking went, and the Kashmir problem will go away.

But it did not. Behind a façade of tense calm, a spirit of revolt was surging among Kashmiri Muslims. On July 13, 1989, a march in Srinagar by Kashmiris to commemorate Islamic martyrs, including Muslim leaders executed by India, turned violent and was crushed, with heavy casualties. Five months later, Kashmiri militants kidnapped the daughter of the Home Minister; she was released in exchange for the freeing of five jailed Kashmiri leaders.

This bizarre incident released a wave of nationalist emotion, violent protests, and bloody rioting across Kashmir. Both India and Pakistan were completely surprised by the sudden Muslim "intifada," which, contrary to Delhi's mantras about foreign subversion, was in fact an indigenous, popular revolt by a people who could no longer bear Indian repression. Far from instigating the rebellion, Pakistan's intelligence service (ISI) was sharply rebuked by its political masters for failing to predict it.

On January 19, 1990, India proclaimed a state of siege in Kashmir: the compliant, pro-Indian Muslim Chief Minister, Farouk Abdullah, was forced to resign. Direct federal rule was imposed by Delhi, and the constitution and laws protecting individual rights were suspended in Kashmir. Delhi empowered its security forces to arrest and interrogate Kashmiris at will. Tens of thousands of troops and paramilitary police were rushed to Kashmir with orders to put down the rebellion by any means. Journalists were banned, so they could not report on what was to come.

Indian security forces had gained extensive experience in counter-insurgency and urban guerrilla warfare during the long, bitter battle that took place in the 1980s against Sikh secessionists in Punjab. Sikhs are followers of a warrior religion founded in the sixteenth century by Guru Nanak. Though only 2 percent of India's population, the industrious Sikhs of Punjab produce almost 50 percent of the nation's wheat, and fill many middle and senior positions in the armed forces and police.

In the early 1980s, groups of young Sikh fundamentalist militants began demanding independence from India and the creation of a Sikh state in Punjab, to be known as "Khalistan," which would border rebellious Kashmir to the southwest. Rebellion against Hindu rule spread quickly: Indian security forces were put on the defensive and seriously demoralized by increasingly effective Sikh guerrilla groups and urban street fighters. The militant Sikhs devoted as much energy to killing their own fellow Sikhs who wanted to stay within India as they did attacking Indian security forces.

Delhi was losing the battle against Sikh fundamentalists until Indira Gandhi put an utterly ruthless, highly skilled police general,

K.P.S. Gill, himself a Sikh, in charge of Punjab security. She gave Gill carte blanche, ordering him to smash the Sikh rebels, no questions asked. Gill reorganized the poorly led, disorganized, deeply demoralized security forces, and initiated a comprehensive intelligence program to understand, identify, and then penetrate the various Sikh secessionist factions.

Delhi chose the right man to crush the Sikh rebellion. The Sikh police general was tall, ferocious, and immensely impressive, with his perfectly wound turban, bristling mustache, neatly trimmed beard, and clipped, military speech. When I interviewed him, Gill answered politely enough, but his hard, fierce eyes bored into me, telegraphing the message that all journalists, particularly Western ones, were meddling scum. Gill spoke of eradicating the Sikh separatists as if he were casually discussing exterminating lice. Sikhs are renowned for their bravery, fierceness, tenacity, and love of revenge. Delhi had cleverly set a Sikh to catch its Sikh foes.

The only other man I had met who commanded such instant respect and fear was Pakistan's director general of intelligence, General Akhdar Rahman, who died in 1988 with President Zia in the mysterious crash of their c-130 transport aircraft. Akhdar made people tremble with fear; Gill looked as he was about to rip your skin off.

Gill counterattacked Sikh separatists, using summary executions and mass arrests; routine torture; intimidation of families; informers; and bribery. He flooded Punjab with regular army units and paramilitary police. Thousands of Sikh "miscreants" simply disappeared after being arrested "for questioning." Some were guilty of sedition; many others were innocent. Anyone denounced by informers, or whose name was uttered under torture, was arrested and, in turn, interrogated. Those suspected of being active militants were shot, and their bodies hidden.

In this manner, Gill and his men relentlessly broke each link in the chain of Sikh separatists. Indian security forces also used "false flag" agents, disguised as Sikh militants, to provoke factional battles by attacking other, genuine Sikh militants, or to commit atrocities that were then blamed by the media on the Sikh nationalists.

Gill finally crushed Sikh separatism, trampling on India's constitution, laws, and civil rights in the process. The outside world turned its back on this bloody drama. Canada, where there was a large, very militant Sikh expatriate community, became embroiled in a covert struggle between agents of India's intelligence service (RAW) and cells of Sikh extremists, one of which may have planted the bomb that destroyed an Air-India 747 aircraft in flight, killing hundreds of people. Canada's security services apparently shared considerable information on Sikh militants with RAW and allowed a large number of its agents to operate in Canada under cover.

But Sikhs, it is said, never forget a wrong, and will always have their vengeance. After the Sikhs' holiest place, the Golden Temple at Amritsar, was stormed by Indian troops, Indira Gandhi's own Sikh bodyguards shot her dead. Death was a fitting retribution, said Sikhs, for her cruel suppression of the Punjab.

Having only recently pacified the Sikhs in Punjab, Indian security forces and the military were totally surprised and dismayed by the 1989 explosion of protests by Muslims across Kashmir. But once over the initial shock, Delhi gradually marshaled its security forces and sent them to Kashmir, where the repressive methods perfected by General Gill in Punjab against Sikhs were immediately put to use against an even more dangerous foe: Muslims.

• • •

Though it was unseen by the outside world, the 1989 revolt in Kashmir had been brewing for decades. Delhi ruled Kashmir through a group of compliant Muslim politicians, just as Moscow ruled over Central Asia by means of local Communist satraps, or "Red sultans." Both ruling groups resembled traditional Mafia organizations, monopolizing illegal business, and subcontracting or franchising out areas of criminal and legal commercial activities. Corruption, extortion, and bribery were rampant, often surpassing even the outrageous levels common to lowland India. India's Muslim henchmen made themselves very rich and deeply hated.

Any Kashmiri who dared agitate for independence or union with Pakistan, including journalists and academics, was quickly jailed, often under the most brutal conditions. Occasional attempts by India to increase the Hindu population of Kashmir by moving settlers into Jammu inflamed Muslim passions, and brought attacks against the Hindu newcomers.

Blatantly rigged elections in 1987 further fanned outrage against Indian authorities. A year earlier, a handful of Kashmiri militants, grandly named the Jammu and Kashmir Liberation Front (JKLF), had taken to the mountains and begun a modest guerrilla insurrection. The JKLF's academic and intellectual leaders were deeply inspired by the Algerian war for independence against French rule, and sought to emulate the successful guerrilla warfare strategy and patriotic national mobilization achieved by the Algerian Front de Liberation Nationale (FLN).

Muslim Kashmiris were themselves a haughty lot, notoriously rich in self-esteem, and they found Indian hegemony intolerable. Kashmiri Hindus and the proconsular establishment from Delhi treated Muslim Kashmiris with contempt, rapacity, suspicion, and disdain. All the stereotypical hatreds between Muslims and Hindus common to the plains of India became inflated to twice life size in the rarefied mountain atmosphere of Kashmir, and eventually they exploded into violence.

The eruption was a genuine, spontaneous popular protest. Ill-trained Indian security forces panicked, opened fire on crowds, and savagely beat demonstrators. The inevitable result was renewed protests, this time with increased violence, as Muslims began fighting back with the few weapons they possessed.

Delhi rushed divisions of mountain troops and large numbers of paramilitary police to Kashmir. A new proconsul, Grish Saxena, seconded from the intelligence service RAW, was sent up from Delhi in the hope he would become a second K.P.S. Gill. A statewide crackdown began: thousands of Kashmiris were arrested, beaten, and tortured. Some, identified by informers as the protest's ringleaders, were summarily executed. Indian forces looted and burned, treating Kashmir like occupied enemy territory.

India's brutal reaction to popular protests in Kashmir sparked the formation of a number of resistance groups. At first, they amounted to no more than a handful of men, amateur fighters armed with bird guns, pistols, and knives. Some operated in Srinagar and the larger towns; others took to the wooded mountains. The Indian paramilitary forces were cowardly and undisciplined—little more than uniformed thugs; they committed growing outrages against the civilian population: rapes, robbery, arson, beatings. Their savage behavior, driven by anti-Muslim hatred, alienated more and more Kashmiris, causing many young men, and entire families, to flee across the Line of Control into Pakistani Kashmir.

Many Muslims stayed on in Azad Kashmir as permanent refugees; but a growing number of the young men took military training, and returned to fight Indian occupation forces. Veterans of the jihad in Afghanistan, both native Afghan mujahedin and foreign "Afghani" who had remained in and around Peshawar, went to Kashmir to train and assist the fighters of the new intifada. The Afghan veterans brought the Kashmiri mujahedin a wealth of combat experience and badly needed training in logistics, communications, and planning. Equally important, they infused the Kashmiris with Islamic fervor, and provided living proof that faith, courage, and determination could overcome seemingly overwhelming odds.

In the years from 1990 to 1995, Kashmiri resistance forces were estimated to number between 25,000 and 30,000 fighters, divided into a score of different groups. Some of the rebels received military train- ing in Pakistan from the ISI, and automatic weapons, mortars, and munitions were supplied to them across the border. This assistance, combined with help from Afghan mujahedin advisors, transformed the Kashmiris from a ragtag maquis into moderately effective guerrilla fighters, well able to put Indian security forces on the defensive.

The resistance ambushed Indian patrols, cut up convoys, killed stragglers, and staged frequent grenade and bomb attacks to make life miserable for Indian military personnel in the crowded cities and towns. Mountainous Kashmir was far better suited to guerrilla warfare than largely flat Punjab: its forested hills and high ground offered ample refuge for irregular forces, who easily eluded the slow-moving Indian forces pursuing them. Large-scale anti-guerrilla sweeps by pon- derous Indian regular forces proved equally ineffective.

Though India has gained the upper hand militarily in Kashmir, its repression, denounced without cease by Indian and international human rights organizations such as Amnesty International, Asia Watch, and Physicians for Human Rights, continues relentlessly. Indian authorities have banned many rights groups and journalists from Kashmir, using the excuse that "the time is not right for a visit." India simply does not want the world to see what it is doing in Kashmir.

Pakistan acted similarly in 1971 when its military proconsul, Gen. Tikka Khan, the "Butcher of Dacca," attempted to ruthlessly crush the Bengali nationalist movement in secessionist East Pakistan, later Bangladesh. Pakistan's brutality in Bangladesh was brief and erratic. India's savage behavior in Kashmir, by contrast, has been sustained and unwavering since late 1989.

Indian security forces have adopted the crude expedient of arresting, torturing, and killing anyone suspected of being a militant. Whenever mujahedin activity or unrest is reported in an area, Indian forces stage what they call a "crackdown." Indian troops cordon off an area, then parade its inhabitants before hooded informers. Men identified as militants by the informers are immediately taken away to Indian bases, where they are repeatedly tortured until they divulge information, real or made up. Then they are usually executed and their bodies returned to their families.

Detainees are routinely savagely beaten, often on the feet, a favorite Turkish punishment known as the "bastinado." Feet are a remarkably sensitive part of the body; repeated beating there produces intolerable pain after a short time that courses from the lower extremities to the head. Numerous detainees have had their feet amputated after post-beating gangrene set in.

Indian security also uses heavy wooden or metal rollers on the back of victims' backs and thighs. Muscles are crushed, and kidneys are damaged, releasing toxins into the bloodstream. Suspects are also given electric shock, brought to near drowning in tubs of filthy water; semi-suffocated by wet rags; constrained or suspended in excruciatingly painful positions; burned with cigarettes and lighters, and rectally violated with iron bars, bottles, or pieces of wood.

Suspected militants have been dragged from hospital beds, and even operating tables, by Indian forces. One doctor estimated that 60 percent of all hospitalized Kashmiris suffered from trauma caused by gunshots, explosions, or torture. Other injured suspects in jail are denied even basic medical attention. Many men arrested are simply shot at night and dumped into rivers; others have been doused with gasoline and burned alive.

The appalling brutality of India's security forces, notably the police and paramilitary gendarmes, is not unique to Kashmir, though it is far more intense and widespread in the mountain state. Human rights organizations have long accused police across India of torture, summary executions, and pervasive violence toward detainees, which has occasionally even included blinding. Muslims and other minorities in particular are victims of India's savage police, who are unconstrained by law, political control, or any notion of decency.

Arson has also become a favorite weapon of Indian security forces in Kashmir, where most dwellings are made of wood. Villages suspected of aiding or having harbored militants are frequently burned to the ground. Villagers suspected of aiding the intifada would be lined up, beaten, and robbed. Homes would be first looted, then burned. Domestic animals were slaughtered; wells were poisoned. Indian reporters and cameramen trying to document such cruelties have been beaten and, in a few reported cases, they, too, were doused with fuel and set alight.

Muslim women became the particular target of the paramilitary, and occasionally the regular forces. Rape became a constant feature of repression. In many cases, all of the young women of villages would be gang-raped, often repeatedly. The Indians understood full well that, in Muslim culture, rape is one of the most abominable crimes possible. A Muslim woman who has been raped is considered permanently defiled and unclean. In Bosnia and Kosovo, Serb forces raped thousands of Muslim women, sometimes even girls as young as nine, in an organized effort to break the Muslims' will to resist, or drive them from their homes. Rape was a double tragedy and curse for Muslim women: not only were they assaulted and brutalized, but afterwards they would be outcasts among their own people. Often, women who became pregnant from the rapes would commit suicide.

I spoke to a survivor of one of India's "crackdowns," a shy middle-aged woman with a deeply lined face and strikingly blue eyes, who had fled to Azad Kashmir after her small village was incinerated by Indian troops. "They took all of our men away and beat them," she told me in a trembling voice. "My husband and son were put into a truck and driven off. I have never heard from them since."

There was more, but her Muslim modesty and deep shame would not allow her tell me. A female journalist traveling with me took her aside and, through an interpreter, over many cups of tea, learned the woman's story. The Indian troops divided the younger women and girls from the older ones. They marched the younger women behind some stacks of fodder. The Indians, many of whom were drunk, tore off the women's clothing, threw the victims on the ground, and proceeded to gang-rape them repeatedly, including three girls under nine years of age. Those who resisted were beaten, and one was shot. After vaginally raping the women and girls, the Indian paramilitary police raped them again anally, spat on them, and called them "Muslim whores."

After relating her horrifying story, the woman, unable to face us, vanished into a tent, alone with her misery and shame. A Kashmiri man of the camp told me, "She is defiled. No man will ever touch her again after what the Hindus have done to her."

The relentless barbarities inflicted on Kashmiris by Indian troops have not provoked a national outcry in India. The public has ignored frequent reports of such savagery and the protests of Indian rights organizations. The Indian government and press have managed to demonize Muslim Kashmiris, branding them "subversives" and "terrorists." Kashmir is presented as a place where Indian troops bravely try to keep order under incessant attack by heavily armed, well-organized Muslim fanatics, armed and directed by Pakistan and a worldwide Islamic conspiracy. The killing of women and children by Indian forces is excused; these "unfortunates" are said to have been caught in the crossfire of gun battles initiated by terrorists making use of civilian cover. Kashmiri rebels have not helped their cause by detonating large car bombs in Srinagar and Jammu or murdering Hindu civilians.

In the west, the Kashmiri mujahedin groups have been ignored, or regarded as terrorists. The latter view came after a well-publicized incident in which four Westerners, oblivious to political events, went trekking in Kashmir. They were kidnapped by a then unknown mujahedin group, Al-Faran, and have never been seen since. The severed head of one of the unfortunate trekkers was later found on a rock, accompanied by a note from the shadowy Al-Faran. The British and Australian press had a field day with this grisly story and heaped abuse on Kashmiri Muslims. On July 4, 1998, another Kashmiri resistance group, Al-Fateh, told relatives the missing hikers were confirmed dead, and charged that the Al-Faran kidnappers were actually set up and run as a false-flag operation by Indian intelligence to blacken the name of the Islamic resistance.

It is impossible to reach a reliable count of civilian casualties in the Kashmiri intifada. Resistance groups claim at least 50,000 people have been killed by Indian forces since 1990. Delhi insists no more than a few thousand have died, mostly in crossfire, or, in many cases, at the hands of the "terrorists." Hundreds of Kashmiris deemed collaborators have been killed by the insurgents. In addition, some 200,000 Kashmiri Hindus, mainly from the Jammu region, have fled their homes for the safety of India. Indian military and police casualties are a closely guarded secret, though the number may exceed 10,000.

• • •

As the intifada in Kashmir intensified, Srinagar was transformed from a pleasant, easygoing lakeside vacation resort into a grim, dangerous place, where every alley and corner threatened Indian patrols with ambush or sniping. Indian soldiers and paramilitary troops guarded intersections and high ground from the safety of heavily sandbagged bunkers.

Indian regular troops, untrained in guerrilla warfare, conducted large, usually fruitless sweeps; alerted by civilian supporters, the guerrillas usually had time to slip away. When Indian soldiers managed to close with guerrillas, or encountered surprise attacks, the Indians responded by heavy, indiscriminate firing, often with heavy weapons, killing or wounding large numbers of civilians caught in the crossfire.

Delhi rushed more regular troops to Kashmir. By 1998, their number was to rise to over 300,000, or a third of the army's total force, putting a severe strain on logistics. Units were brought in from the Himalayan border with China and the eastern sectors, where rebellions simmered on in Assam and the remote eastern hill states neighboring Burma.

India's professional regular soldiers were fairly well disciplined and competently led (though as the revolt continued, they committed an increasing number of atrocities). But the large number of paramilitary forces also deployed in Kashmir, today about 300,000 men, became notorious for poor discipline, brutality, looting, and trigger-happy behavior. While regulars manned most checkpoints and guarded important installations, the Border Security Force, Central Reserve Police Force, Indo-Tibetan Border Police, and Jammu and Kashmir state police took the lead in rooting out rebels and punishing their civilian supporters, real or imagined.

Counter-insurgency operations are always a dirty business. Indian forces in Kashmir found themselves in an alien environment far from their home, surrounded by a hostile population, never knowing when they would be attacked. Demoralized and frightened, the Indians became ever more savage as their hatred for Muslim Kashmiris grew. Muslims who had not favored the intifada were driven into its arms by the increasing violence and ferocity of Indian repression.

Indian intelligence and security forces embarked on a campaign, patterned on operations against Sikh militants in Punjab, to identify, infiltrate, and destroy the urban networks of the various Kashmiri resistance groups. Informers, coerced by threats to their families, torture, or bribery, would single out resistance operatives. They would be arrested and subjected to the most brutal tortures. A favorite torture, developed in Punjab, was ramming a kilo of fiery hot chili powder up a victim's rectum. Children of suspected rebels would sometimes be tortured and raped in front of their parents.

In this manner, Indian security agents relentlessly uprooted the rebels' underground structure. Thousands of suspected militants, including journalists, academics, and intifada supporters, were arrested and many executed; their bodies were secretly buried. Amnesty International called, in March 1999, for India to end the "nightmare" of disappearances, which the London-based organization claimed had amounted to eight hundred people since 1990, including children, the elderly, and those with no known links to secessionist groups.

Indian human rights groups and international rights organizations vigorously protested the widespread abuses of human rights in Kashmir, but to no avail. India rejected all protests and refused to allow foreign observers into Kashmir. Journalists, both Indian and non-Indian, who wrote about India's rights violations were barred from Kashmir. India's widely disrespected judicial system bowed to political pressure, refusing to rule against the government's violation of the nation's constitution and laws.

By the end of 1995, the Indian Army had managed to seal the long Line of Control with Azad Kashmir by implanting dense belts of antipersonnel mines, listening devices, motion-detectors, and barbed wire along the border. Large numbers of troops were permanently stationed on the LOC in fortified positions. Israeli counter-insurgency advisors secretly aided the Indian Army in creating a lethal barrier along the entire length of the frontier, which reduced to a trickle the previous flow from Pakistani territory of fighters, munitions, and supplies. The mountainous, forested terrain still permitted some small mujahedin bands to slip across, but the fighting effectiveness of the resistance was seriously degraded by India's intensified security measures along the border with Pakistani Kashmir.

By 1996, the virtual sealing of the LOC, and ruthless repression inside Kashmir, brought the insurgency to its lowest ebb since 1990. According to the Indian Army, by then no more than four thousand insurgents were still active in the field, through the true figure was almost certainly higher. India maintained its exaggerated claims that most of the mujahedin in Kashmir are foreigners, meaning volunteers from other Islamic nations or Pakistani mercenaries.

Meanwhile, the various insurgent groups, some advocating continued struggle, others favoring a negotiated settlement, increasingly battled among themselves, and murdered Muslims deemed to be traitors. Indian intelligence agents, advised by KGB experts from Afghanistan, skillfully played on these divisions, as they had learned to do with feuding Sikh militants in Punjab, by staging false-flag attacks and spreading fake documents to provoke fighting between mujahedin factions. Indian casualties dropped sharply.

The state was literally blanketed by huge numbers of Indian security forces: in 1997, there was one Indian soldier or paramilitary policeman for every thirteen Kashmiris. The urban infrastructure of the various mujahedin groups had been shattered by torture, executions, and mass arrests. In the field, the Indian Army developed more effective and aggressive counter-insurgency techniques, abandoning mass, non-productive sweeps in favor of small-unit hunter-killer missions, supported by air surveillance and the extensive use of helicopters with night-vision devices. Indian military and security forces learned to cooperate and to share information. The mujahedin were everywhere on the defensive. By mid-1997, Delhi felt sufficiently confident to proclaim that the end of the insurgency was in sight.

But it was not.

8
The Afghani

It is thankless—and dangerous—to be a Muslim Kashmiri who wants to stay part of India, but a small minority of Kashmiris, mainly wealthy merchants and tourist operators who have seen their once-thriving businesses dwindle to nothing, distrust the mujahedin and prefer civic calm, even under Delhi's harsh rule, to endless insurrection or an independent state that they fear would be run by erratic Islamic radicals.

However, Muslim fundamentalists are a minority in the numerous resistance groups, and their political appeal to civilians is modest. Urbane Kashmiri Muslims have never been noted for fundamentalist ardor, and are a reasonably open-minded people.

Pro-Indian Muslims have gathered under the banner of Dr. Farouk Abdullah, a sixty-one-year-old doctor who is the son of the famed and often-jailed nationalist Sheik Abdullah, known as "the Lion of Kashmir," the leader of Kashmir's Muslims at the time of partition. The younger Abdullah lived for many years in England; he returned to Kashmir and was elected state prime minister in 1996 in an election that was crudely rigged by Indian authorities. However, India claimed the vote gave full legitimacy to the new government, and to Kashmir's future as an Indian state.

Most Kashmiris dismissed the vote as a fraud, and Dr. Abdullah as an Indian puppet. Algerians used to have a zesty expression for tame politicians who collaborated with the French: *beni-oui-ouis*. Even Delhi regards Abdullah and his government, who live and travel under constant heavy guard by Indian troops, with condescension.

Still, India and its local supporters keep insisting the choice was between Abdullah and malevolent Islamic radicals, who, if Kashmir ever attained real independence, would emulate Afghanistan's ultra-reactionary Taliban movement by imposing medieval Islam on the sophisticated Kashmiris. If India's *jawans* (soldiers) stop defending Kashmir, claims the pro-Indian faction, hordes of primitive Islamic warriors will sweep over Kashmir and down into India, like the Muslim Moguls of centuries past.

However, the idea that Taliban or any other Afghan group could invade Kashmir is preposterous. It would be impossible for Taliban's 20,000 tribal warriors to challenge India's military might in Kashmir by a direct attack across the Line of Control, or, for that matter, even move substantial forces thorough Pakistan. Islamabad would not stand for it. Such an act would trigger immediate war with India. While a few Taliban volunteer mujahedin may slip across the LOC, there is no real threat from Afghanistan.

For its part, Pakistan views the Taliban movement, which it helped create, as a double-edged sword. Inside Afghanistan it is useful; outside, a danger. Ever since independence in 1947, Pakistani leaders have worried about the threat of Pushtun nationalists, who called for creation of a Greater Pushtunistan, a state encompassing all the Pathan people straddling the Afghan-Pakistan border along the Durand Line, and including Pakistan's entire Northwest Frontier Province. Such a development could very well ignite separatist demands in two other Pakistani provinces, Baluchistan and Sind. Promoting the creation of an independent Pathan state was one of the options considered by the former Soviet Union during the 1980s in its campaign to dismember Pakistan.

A far more serious challenge to Indian rule over Kashmir is posed by the largest and one of the oldest Kashmiri resistance movements, the Jammu and Kashmir Liberation Front (JKLF). The party, based in England and Rawalpindi, Pakistan, is currently led by sixty-five-year-old Amanullah Khan, a veteran warhorse and Kashmiri nationalist who was born in the Gilgit-Baltistan region.

The hanging of JKLF leader Maqbool Butt in Delhi in 1984 enraged Kashmiris and was an important factor in the nationalist explosion of 1990. The JKLF advocates total independence for Kashmir and the formation of a federal state with a two-legislature parliamentary government. It would be a non-sectarian, secular state in which the members of parliament would be elected by direct representation, and the rights of all religions and ethnic groups were guaranteed. After five years of independence, the UN would organize and supervise a national referendum to determine whether Kashmir wished to remain independent, or to join India or Pakistan.

This sensible plan deeply worries both India and Pakistan. For Delhi, the moderate JKLF platform directly contradicts its claims that all the opposition are dangerous Muslim radicals bent on creating an Islamic theocracy under the influence of Afghanistan and Iran—the latter nation being cleverly thrown in by the Indians to set off alarm bells in Washington. The JKLF proposals also make Delhi very nervous because they sound too close to existing UN Security Council resolutions over Kashmir and could be adopted as a basis for an international settlement.

The JKLF makes Pakistan almost as nervous. The movement calls for independent Kashmir to be formed from the five provinces that more or less made up pre-1947 Kashmir: the Kashmir Valley (the Srinagar region); Jammu; Pakistan-held Azad Kashmir; Indian-held Ladakh; and Gilgit-Baltistan, which Pakistan calls its "Northern Territories."

Pakistan says it would immediately cede Azad Kashmir, a region of no intrinsic value, to an independent Kashmiri state. But Pakistan long ago grew deeply attached to the mountain region of Gilgit and Baltistan, which extends from Afghanistan to Ladakh and Tibet. The two great valleys are important earners of tourist income, and occupy a vital strategic location in the Himalayan-Karakoram system. Equally important, the Karakoram Highway, the sole road link between Pakistan and its principal ally, China, begins in Gilgit, and extends up the Hunza Valley over the Khunjerab Pass, into Chinese Sinkiang.

If an independent Kashmir were to reclaim Gilgit-Baltistan, a large section of Pakistan's beautiful north—its own version of Kashmir—would be wrenched away. Islamabad has sought since the 1950s to erase the region's image as part of Kashmir, and recast it as an extension of Pakistan. The JKLF's troublesome leader, Amanullah Khan, has found himself thrown into Pakistani jails more than once for raising this contentious issue.

In 1990, the JKLF declared itself a government in exile, which led to a serious split in its ranks. Amanullah Khan's attempts to stage two marches of JKLF civilians across the LOC in February and March 1992, which could easily have sparked war with India, enormously annoyed Islamabad, which very nearly proscribed his movement. The Pakistanis cannot seem to decide whether the JKLF is more of a threat to them, or to India. Meanwhile, JKLF claims Islamabad is secretly in cahoots with Delhi to maintain the status quo by sabotaging Kashmiri independence.

There may be substance to this cynical view. India and Pakistan have grown used to the status quo of Kashmir, which, if not comfortable is at least familiar. Any change would unleash unpredictable forces and threaten to upset the region's political geography. The situation has been frozen since 1947, and states, like people, do not like change. Listening to the disgruntled Kashmiris reminded me of similar statements by Palestinians, who claimed their Arab brothers were secretly conspiring with Israel to deny them a state that would, inevitably, alter the Mideast map. Similarly, India and Pakistan, for all their recriminations, have grown accustomed to the existing order of things.

Islamabad much prefers other pro-Pakistani Kashmiri resistance groups: such as the Harakatul Ansar, the Hizbullah (no relation to Lebanon's Hizbullah), the Harakatul Mujahedin, Jihad Islami, Gujjar Tigers, Al-Barq, and eighteen other colorfully named organizations. Most of these number no more than a few hundred to a few thousand active supporters, and even many of these are split into inimical factions that occasionally fight among themselves over territory, money, and personal or ideological rivalries. Some of these Kashmiri resistance groups represent bourgeois, urban elements; others call for creation of an Islamic state in Kashmir run under Sharia law. The only thing all have in common is their intense hatred of India.

One thing is certain. India will never relinquish its portion of Kashmir without ensuring that Pakistan must give up its part, the Northern Territories, as well. Cynical Indians are counting on equally cynical Pakistanis never to do this.

• • •

India constantly claims that Pakistan finances, trains, and arms the Kashmiri resistance organizations, which it always brands "terrorist groups." India has long blamed Islamabad's machinations for the revolt in Kashmir. In truth, Pakistan does discreetly sustain some, though certainly not all, of the Kashmiri resistance forces, though of late its support has been somewhat reduced. Pakistan's intelligence agency, Inter-Service Intelligence (ISI), the most effective Third World spy organization, has aided and armed at least eight of the Kashmiri freedom groups, including, at various times, the problematic JKLF.

As recounted in the first part of this book, ISI managed the long war in Afghanistan against Soviet occupation, in close cooperation with the CIA, providing logistical support, training, arms, communications, and staff planning to the seven Afghan mujahedin groups. ISI officers served in the field, leading attacks and conducting sabotage missions against Soviet forces. Without ISI support, and its provision of U.S.-supplied Stinger missiles, the medieval bands of Afghan warriors could never have fought the Red Army to a bloody stalemate.

Just as Indian security forces mastered counter-insurgency tactics in rebellious Punjab, the ISI has drawn on its long, successful experience in the Afghan war to assist and, at times, direct the Kashmiri resistance. A small number of combat-hardened Afghan mujahedin and volunteers from other Islamic nations, the remnants of the Islamic Foreign Legion who battled in Afghanistan—including the by now notorious Osama bin Ladeen—joined the Kashmiri resistance as advisors and fighters. However, Indian claims that nearly all Kashmiri resistance fighters are foreigners—mainly Afghans, or Arab mercenaries—are simply untrue: most of the insurgents are native Kashmiris, though a cadre of foreign holy warriors has played a key role, and ISI supplies key logistic support.

In one of the refugee camps along the Jhelum River, I was greeted by an old comrade-in-arms, Commander Nadji. Tall, skinny, and bearded, he wore the knitted, round Chitral hat beloved of all Afghans that has become a badge of honor worn by veterans of the Great Jihad. We had met in Peshawar, Pakistan, in 1986, while the war raged in neighboring Afghanistan.

Nadji was an Egyptian descended from the band of six hundred Albanian soldiers of fortune who, in 1805, had conquered Egypt under their chief, the great Mehmet Ali Pasha. He gave up his engineering studies in Cairo, and went to join the Islamic International Brigade in the great Afghan Jihad.

Nadji and his fellow legionnaires had been discreetly financed by the Saudi royal family, which was always ready to fund Islamic militancy, provided it was as far away as possible from their kingdom. The Saudis also saw in the Islamic Legion a useful counter to the growing influence of their bitter rival Iran, which was intriguing among the Shia Hazara tribes of central and western Afghanistan.

Nadji fought for three years in central Afghanistan, and was wounded in the leg by shellfire shortly before the Soviet withdrawal. By the time he recovered, civil war between the Afghan factions had replaced Soviet occupation. Like most other members of the Islamic Legion, Nadji soon grew disgusted by the sordid tribal mêlée that replaced the once glorious jihad. Embittered and disillusioned, like so many other past youthful revolutionaries, he returned to Egypt. But there he became a wanted man: the Egyptian government regarded the Afghan veterans, or "Afghani," as dangerous troublemakers who were training the growing Islamic underground in Egypt in urban guerrilla warfare.

Soon after we first met in Peshawar, Nadji had told me, "When we have liberated Afghanistan from Soviet imperialism, we will go on to free Egypt from American imperialism." Why not? In the eyes of Islamic militants, Egypt's military ruler-turned-president, General Husni Mubarak, was no less a puppet of the Americans than the Afghan military dictator, General Najibullah, was of the Soviets. There was no difference, in their eyes, between Soviet and American imperialism. But neo-colonial powers were bent on occupying the Muslim world and exploiting its rich resources. Commander Nadji's words to me were to be repeated, almost verbatim, in 1998 by the militant anti-American *mujahid*, Osama bin Ladeen.

When rebellion erupted in Kashmir, Nadji fled Egypt and returned to Peshawar. He and hundreds of other "Afghani" rushed to Azad Kashmir to offer their services to the neophyte Kashmiri guerrillas. The ISI eagerly encouraged the restless Afghan veterans to leave Peshawar and betake themselves to Azad Kashmir. The "Afghani" had joined local Islamic fundamentalist parties in loudly accusing Benazir Bhutto's government of being American stooges. These charges made Islamabad very nervous, not least because they held a good measure of truth. The American government made no secret that it far preferred the malleable Bhutto to the iron-fisted Zia ul-Haq. Bhutto had no pan-Islamist or Greater Pakistan pretensions; she was content to cooperate at all times with American policy, repress Islamic forces, "modernize" Pakistan, and maintain "stability." These were Western code words for keeping Pakistan firmly in America's strategic orbit and responsive to Washington's diktat.

The U.S. strongly backed the Western-educated Bhutto as a "moderate" and—that famous term of approval for cooperative Third World leaders—"someone we can do business with." Yet, while overtly supporting the deeply corrupt Bhutto regime, Washington was getting ready to scupper Pakistan. The powerful Israel lobby, Washington's most effective special-interest organization, had grown alarmed by Islamabad's nuclear potential, fearing Pakistani nuclear weapons might find their way into the hands of Israel's Arab enemies, such as Syria, Iraq, or Libya. Though there was absolutely no evidence of this happening, Israel and its Washington lobby engineered a change in U.S. policy toward Pakistan.

Pakistan, once hailed in the U.S. as a heroic ally during the Afghan conflict, was swiftly and ruthlessly downgraded to the status of "Islamic threat," and summarily denied by Congress, through the Pressler Amendment, the military and economic aid that had long sustained it.

The cutoff of U.S. military aid, spare parts, new weapons, and economic assistance brought Pakistan close to economic collapse, and caused a very serious decline in its military power just at a time when India was issuing increasing threats and beefing up its offensive forces on the border. Ironically, the U.S. embargo of conventional arms to former loyal ally Pakistan had the counterproductive result of compelling Islamabad to accelerate its covert nuclear program and rely increasingly on nuclear weapons for defense against India.

• • •

Nadji chain-smoked and coughed as we spoke, his lanky, gaunt frame shaken by chronic bronchitis brought on by endless cigarettes, stress, the dust in Egypt, and now Kashmir's cold, damp climate. "At first, we could move across the LOC easily. We'd go over at night, and attack Indian patrols or watch posts with mortars, RPGs (rocket-propelled grenades), and automatic weapons. The Indians usually panicked, and fired everywhere.

"The Hindus made the Afghan Communist soldiers look brave." He laughed scornfully. "We killed a lot of them. Many just ran away." News that fierce Afghan mujahedin veterans, who showed no mercy and took no prisoners, were operating in Kashmir, demoralized Indian troops and kept them hunkered down in their fortified positions.

"But you know, my friend, the same evil thing happened here as in Afghanistan," Nadji continued. "The many resistance groups each ended up with a different sponsor, and they spent as much time fighting each other as they did the infidel. We cursed Muslims are always better at fighting our brothers than the unbelievers." His body shook from a spasm of coughing.

"By now," he continued bitterly, "the Indians have learned to fight better. They are more aggressive. Kashmiris are becoming afraid to help us, or they even inform on the mujahedin—to prevent their villages from being burned down and their women raped." Nadji shrugged, and stroked his uneven beard. "We don't have enough men, or arms. This time, there are no Stinger missiles to use against Indian helicopters. The war, my old friend, is getting very difficult. We are really alone."

But what about support from the Islamic world? I asked. Nadji spat on the ground and lit another cigarette. "Support? We have been abandoned. Only Pakistan gives us any real help. A little 'baksheesh' [money, tips] comes from the Gulf emirates—less, for sure, than the money the emirs spend each week on their European whores. Other than that, the Muslim world completely ignores the Kashmir intifada.

"Those bastard Muslim sons of dogs won't even give us diplomatic support. And the Indians are clever, very clever at buying off the Arab states and other Muslim nations. Some trade, vacations to Bombay, gold rings and jewels, that's all it takes. Muslims can be bought for very little."

Nadji was right. India's skillful diplomacy, and its sheer size, made even Islamic nations unwilling to support the Kashmiri struggle for independence. What benefit could be gained by antagonizing mighty India for the sake of a little-known people who seemed unlikely to ever gain independence? Delhi cleverly played another diplomatic card by making it very clear to Arab states that its long-time support of Palestinian rights would depend on their silence over Kashmir. Delhi apparently saw no contradiction in steadfastly advocating self-determination and statehood for Palestinians on one hand, while denying the same right to Kashmiris on the other—or by regularly condemning Israel in the UN for its repression in Palestine, while insisting the UN had no business whatsoever in Kashmir.

We sat and sipped tea, watching the steam from our dented tin mugs rise up in the cool, moist air. We had drunk tea many times before in Peshawar, and inside Afghanistan as well. Those days seemed very distant: we young optimists had hoped the brutal Russians and their local Communist henchmen would be driven from Afghanistan and replaced by an Islamic government, guided by the Koran's principles of equal justice, social welfare, equality, and the active democracy practiced during the early, golden days of Islam.

"We killed Afghanistan to make it free. Maybe we'll do the same for Kashmir," observed Nadji dejectedly. "By God, we beat Russia, the world's biggest military power, and now we're being asked to go beat India, with almost one billion people. How many miracles can we do in one lifetime, in the name of Allah. How many?"

More tea and cigarettes brightened Nadji's mood. "But what else can we do? The Holy Koran tells us it's the duty of all good Muslims to go fight injustice wherever it occurs. Every man must fight his own jihad, both against his own internal devils, and against the world's wrongs."

Such earnest and pious professions may sound romantic, even theatrical, to Western ears. In our world, consumerism and movie-star worship long ago replaced religion. But among Muslims it is still common to "live by the book" and be guided by its commands. Young, militant Muslims, like Nadji, reject Western values, and have sought to rebuild a psychological foundation for themselves in the rediscovery of their grandfathers' beliefs and customs. There must have been many young men in the International Brigades during the Spanish Civil War who spoke just like Nadji, their hearts filled with the fresh optimism of youth and the incandescent passion of certainty and faith.

Nadji stood, embraced me repeatedly, and put his hand over my heart, in the manner of the Afghans. He waved farewell as our jeep departed. I looked back at him as we bounced away along the dirt track, a lone holy warrior from distant Egypt, waging his own lonely struggle against the world's second most populous nation for the sake of oppressed fellow Muslims, whose alien Indo-European language he could not even speak.

A year later, I learned that my old friend Nadji had been *shaheed*, martyred. He had been killed in action against Indian forces during a nighttime firefight. His men had to leave his body on the field. Commander Nadji's jihad was over. The news of his death shook me. I recalled the Koranic phrase, "Those who fall in the holy struggle are not dead, but live on," and I prayed that it was true.

9
Deconstructing South Asia

Kashmir's troubles have been a long, painful headache for India's leaders, offering their assorted political opponents an endless supply of ready ammunition. In the turgid world of Indian domestic politics, accusations of being "soft on terrorism"—code for seeking accommodation with Kashmiri secessionists—or "caving in to Pakistan" can be an electoral kiss of death. Kashmir has become the pre-eminent symbol of the long struggle with hated Pakistan, and a constant reminder to Hindu nationalists of real and imagined historical wrongs inflicted on India by past Muslim rulers.

Over the past decade a new political party, the Bharatiya Janata Party (BJP), quickly emerged from relative obscurity as a regional movement to become India's second national party, and the sole challenger of the once mighty but now decrepit Congress Party. The BJP, which dominated the last coalition government in Delhi until the spring of 1999, rose to power on a platform of extreme Hindu chauvinism, advocating ruthless and total repression of the independence movement in Kashmir, revocation of special civil legal rights of India's 120 million Muslim minority, and the eradication of Pakistan.

In spite of ostensibly moderate positions on some issues, the BJP emits a potent aura of anti-Muslim, anti-Christian, anti-Pakistan, and anti-Western prejudice that plays well among India's illiterates, who readily welcome identifiable scapegoats for their many daily miseries.

In the darkest recesses of the BJP, far from the light of public or media scrutiny, is the Rashtriya Swayamsewak Sangh (RSS) a sinister group of Hindu extremists, some of whose views are startlingly close to Nazi race ideology. The RSS was founded in the 1930s as a Hindu revivalist movement influenced by Germany's Nazis and Mussolini's Fascists. Some Indian critics call the RSS "Hindu brownshirts." An RSS gunman, Nathuram Godse, assassinated modern India's greatest man, Mohandas Gandhi, for advocating coexistence with Muslims.

The RSS and two other Hindu extremist movements, the Vishwa Hindu Parishad (VHP) and the Shiv Sena, advocate a "Great Hindu awakening" that will produce a reborn Hindu state dedicated to

"Hindutva," or total Hindu cultural and political domination of society. Any among India's 200 million non-Hindus who object, or fail to conform, will be "disciplined." The BJP has repeatedly vowed to "cleanse" India of all historical remnants of its Muslim Mogul conquerors. As a harbinger of this *Kulturkampf*, mobs of BJP fanatics tore down an ancient mosque at Ayodhya in 1992, an act of vandalism that ignited murderous riots across India, in which some two thousand people, mostly Muslims, were killed.

BJP leaders also vowed to revoke separate domestic laws for Muslims and other groups. "Stop pampering Muslims" is a favorite BJP war-cry, and code for ultimately eradicating Islamic identity and imposing Hinduism on India's non-Hindus. The Bombay-based Shiv Sena goes further. Its demagogic leader, Bal Thackery, an outspoken admirer of Hitler, demands that India be purged of all "foreign" (i.e. non-Hindu) religious, cultural, commercial, and linguistic influences.

Most Indians reject such Hindu extremism, yet despite the RSS fanatics who lurk in the BJP's darkest closets, many fed-up voters were repeatedly drawn to the BJP because it had not been as fouled by pervasive corruption, nor as corroded by cynicism, as the too-long-ruling Congress Party. Muslims and many lower-caste Hindus are, of course, terrified of the racist, Brahmin-dominated BJP.

India's neighbors were equally dismayed by the BJP's abrupt rise to power from almost nowhere. BJP leaders had long preached India must become "Bharat Hind"—Great India, successor to the British Indian Raj. Many BJP firebrands call for Pakistan to be "crushed" and reabsorbed into India; Bangladesh, Sri Lanka, and Nepal may be added to Greater India at a convenient later date.

India's manifest destiny, proclaims the BJP, is to make the entire Indian Ocean a Hindu lake, from East Africa to Australia. India's sphere of influence, according to BJP grand strategists, extends all the way south to the icy wastes of Antarctica, eastward from Iran to Thailand, and deep into Central Asia. Soon, predict some BJP seers, India must inevitably come into conflict with the U.S. and China for possession of Mideast oil. India must be militarily prepared.

Whether the BJP can realize its geopolitical dreams of Indian Empire, or even regain and maintain political power, remains uncertain. But BJP does keep its word. For at least two years before forming the national government in March 1998, BJP leaders had been promising that, if elected, they would bring India's nuclear arsenal out of hiding, and flex India's strategic muscles to prove that Hindu India was the world's newest superpower.

Western observers dismissed such threats as empty gasconading, but, soon after assuming office, BJP did precisely what it had promised. India detonated a series of five nuclear explosions in May 1998, an event that jolted the world and gave Indians a giant shot of nuclear Viagra.

While India's nuclear breast-beating elated many Indians and gave the BJP a short-term political boost, the explosions had the unintended consequence of focusing international attention on the long-forgotten Kashmir dispute. Suddenly, the world realized that it might trigger a general nuclear war in South Asia. Diplomatically, the BJP had just shot itself in the foot.

Once nuclear euphoria had worn off, the shaky BJP-led coalition began to fragment over regional and personal issues. In the spring of 1999, Prime Minister Vajpayee's government finally collapsed when a junior coalition partner pulled out in a huff. New national elections were called for the fall of 1999, with the BJP government staying on in a care-taker role. The news was not all bad for the BJP: its principal rival, the Congress Party, was shaken by internal squabbling and deficient in strong leadership. New elections might even bring a clear majority that would give the BJP a free hand to fully implement its nationalistic agenda.

• • •

Kashmir also evokes deep existential fears in Delhi that go far beyond concerns of day-to-day politics, or even the swollen nationalist preten-sions of the BJP. Though India's exquisitely rich culture and history date back more than four thousand years, it has been a nation for only the past fifty-one years. As a political entity, modern India was the cre-ation of British imperialism, a bittersweet legacy to which Indians cling as a source of national legitimacy and cohesiveness—as well as a totem of foreign oppression on which they blame many of their ills.

Though few Indian leaders will ever admit to it, their darkest unspoken fear is that the complex, fragile, often maddening diversity of modern India will some day unravel, just as another great, cosmopolitan, multiethnic empire, the late Soviet Union, did in 1991.

That India functions at all as a unified state is something of a daily political miracle. Its 970 million people speak some two hundred languages and major dialects, follow eight major religions and myriad cults, and represent a bewildering jumble of races and ethnic groups. The languages of north and south India are mutually incomprehensible, necessitating the use of English as a national lingua franca. India has the world's third-largest Muslim population, after Indonesia and Pakistan. Poor land communications, vast distances, and natural obstacles combine to divide, and then subdivide, India into semi-isolated regions.

Economically, India, with nearly a billion people, looks like an Asian colossus. But on closer scrutiny one discovers the amazing fact that India's economy is slightly smaller than that of Holland, which has a mere 15.5 million people. The misapprehension by Western politicians and businessmen that India's newly opened markets promise an Asian gold rush led the U.S. government to wink at India's nuclear program, thus avoiding confrontation with Delhi.

India is really an agglomeration of diverse nations held together from the center, at Delhi; this feat is achieved by a vast bureaucracy, powerful security forces, political inertia, and sheer deadweight—rather what a united Europe might one day aspire to resemble. Even India's much-vaunted democratic system is being relentlessly eroded by endemic corruption, graft, and violence.

Local warlords, powerful feudal landowners, caste-based party bosses, and gangsters known as *goondas* have come to dominate the political process. India's huge internal paramilitary security forces (some 1.1 million strong) and its local police are notorious for extortion, corruption, and brutal misconduct.

India has been afflicted by secessionist movements ever since independence. The Kashmir independence movement and Sikh separatism in Punjab have been the greatest challenge to a united India.

But other, more obscure independence movements have flared for decades in the northeastern state of Assam, in the hill tracts of India's far east (abutting Burma), and in the Andaman Islands of the Indian Ocean.

From time to time, there are rumblings of potential secession in the twenty-five states that make up the Indian union, notably the southern state of Tamil Nadu, whose population outnumbers that of France. Some Indians even believe that all of predominantly Dravidian South India may one day decide to escape what is seen as economic, political, and cultural domination by the Hindi-speaking north.

India's leaders have long worried that the secession from the union of either Indian-ruled Kashmir or Sikh Punjab could trigger a process of gradual national dissolution. The dramatic disintegration of the Soviet Empire in Eastern Europe, and then the collapse of the USSR itself, horrified India's political establishment. They were all too well aware that the Soviet Union's final demise was begun by miners' strikes in Poland, followed by the Afghan war, and, finally, popular uprisings in East Germany. None of these events taken separately appeared to threaten the existence of the Soviet imperium; but together they combined to break the sinews of Soviet power, producing an earthshaking, historical revolution.

Thus, for most thinking Indians, Kashmiri independence or, worse, its accession to Pakistan is an intolerable, mortal threat to the integrity of their nation. To Hindu nationalists, even the continued existence of Pakistan constitutes a threat to the Indian union, as well as a painful affront to their sense of national importance and a galling reminder of their hated historical enemy, the Muslim Mogul Empire.

Pakistan reflects the mirror image of these deeply ingrained political and psychological fears. India's ceaseless fulminations and blood-curdling threats against Pakistan, its growing anti-Islamic rhetoric, frequent pogroms against Indian Muslims, and the steady growth of Indian military power deployed against Pakistan have convinced most Pakistanis that India is a mortal danger, and intends to dismember their nation.

Pakistanis fear, with some reason, that India's repression of Kashmiri Muslims and Sikh nationalists is an evil foretoken of what awaits them if their nation is ever reabsorbed into Greater India.

India's invasion of East Pakistan, and attempts by agents of India's powerful intelligence service, the Research and Analysis Wing (RAW), to destabilize Pakistan's Sind Province and Northwest Frontier by fomenting communal violence are seen by Pakistanis as final proof of India's determination to dismember their nation.

Ironically, Pakistan's leaders have tried to promote the same policy of destabilization in India. The ISI, Pakistan's intelligence service, has been intermittently active in aiding secessionist rebellions in Kashmir, Punjab, and, to a far lesser degree, rebels in eastern India. Though they would never say so publicly, Pakistan's strategists have long held the view their nation's sole salvation would be the breakup of India, an event that would also leave Pakistan the dominant military power on the subcontinent.

China, India's other powerful rival, would be no less happy to see the Indian union dissolve into a patchwork of weak, feuding states. China's cautious official position has been that long-strained relations with India are gradually improving. But in private, China regards India's growing military capability with mounting concern. India, for its part, has raised alarms over the alleged threat of strategic encirclement by China, and used the issue to justify its nuclear tests.

Chinese military intelligence expressed just such concerns about India in deep background talks with me in 1983, at a time when China was principally focused on the strategic threat from the Soviet Union. I had been invited to Beijing to exchange views with Chinese strategic analysts because of my close relations with the Afghan mujahedin, who were resisting the Soviet occupation of Afghanistan. In exchange for my assessment of the various Afghan resistance groups and the general course of the war, the Chinese shared with me some of their strategic thinking about India and the Soviet Union. Shortly after, China began discreetly supplying weapons and munitions to the Afghan resistance.

The Chinese security officials told me that they anticipated a military clash with India in the Himalayas or Karakorams early in the twenty-first century, or perhaps even sooner, as part of either an Indo-Pakistani war or a struggle to control Tibet or Burma.

Chinese strategists, who take a far longer view than their Western counterparts, believe India will eventually come under serious centrifugal strains that may cause it to splinter. China's leadership is probably torn between encouraging this process, with all the risks that involves, and attempting to postpone what they see as an inevitable clash with India until after Beijing has completed its lengthy process of military modernization at the end of the first decade of the twenty-first century.

The view expressed to me in Beijing, and subsequently repeated by other Chinese military sources, is that the growing power of India and China will be unlikely to coexist in harmony. The two great powers, divided by an uncertain mountain border and small, unstable states, must eventually fight for mastery of Asia.

10
The World's Most Dangerous Border

hokoti, the last village on the Pakistani side of the Line of Control, was a cluster of dilapidated wooden buildings, shacks, and teahouses that bore evident scars of frequent Indian shelling. The LOC lies a couple of miles east of Chokoti. The invisible line snakes between heights held by entrenched Pakistani and Indian forces, their ultimate positions when the 1949 ceasefire came into effect. The Jhelum River, heedless of politics or war, cuts a right angle across the LOC, flowing east toward the city of Barmula, just behind Indian lines, and then, a mere 25 miles (40 km) farther east, to Srinagar.

At first, the mighty Jhelum Gorge, surrounded by steep, scrub-clad hills and clumps of trees, was silent save for the rushing of the gray waters below. A vast panorama of mountains with distant snow-capped crags beyond them offered a tourist-brochure scene of idyllic Kashmir. A Pakistani army camp in a sheltered depression was the only sign of human habitation. A group of subalterns of the 180th mountain brigade sat around a green table, playing bridge, sipping lemonade, and complaining in clipped English accents about the terrible heat. They could have been bored young officers of the British Raj in the Queen Empress's army a century ago.

"Be careful," they warned cheerily, "the bloody Indians are shooting again. Keep your heads down!"

We climbed up a very steep ridge over broken rocks and scree, sweating profusely in the blistering 120° F (49° C) weather. A heat wave had struck northern Indian and Pakistan, killing hundreds on the plains below. Our military escort ordered us to keep low and stay alert. As we reached the top of the ridge, a series of sharp reports echoed around the valley, sending flocks of birds into panicked flight. A stream of tracer bullets sprayed over our heads. From somewhere across the valley, a medium machine gun had opened up on our position.

"Take cover, take cover," yelled the Pakistani captain who was guiding us. We dove into a line of sandbagged trenches, and headed into the shelter of a large bunker. Mortars on the Indian side began firing at our position, and other points along the LOC. Pakistani machine guns and mortars returned fire.

The heavy exchange continued for about five minutes. After the guns fell silent we observed the Indian bunkers and trenches across the valley through field glasses, but detected no sign of movement. Off to our right, beyond our field of vision in the direction of Poonch, Pakistani and Indian artillery began to exchange salvos of 122mm and 155mm shells. Two of the world's poorest nations had just expended tens of thousands of dollars' worth of ammunition, for no better purpose than to vent the hatred, frustration, and boredom of the frontline soldiers on either side.

Indian and Pakistani troops have been skirmishing along the LOC since 1949. They usually snipe at one another's positions and lob occasional shells. But, from time to time, particularly when tensions rise sharply between Delhi and Islamabad, the fighting becomes generalized along the LOC, as brigade- or even division-sized units go into action. When this occurs neither side knows for certain whether the bombardment is merely another demonstration or the opening of a major offensive. As a result, nerves stay frayed; both sides keep their forces on the alert along the LOC, and supporting divisions in a state of high combat-readiness farther behind the front.

I watched the two sides trade fire, wondering if the exchange marked the beginning on an all-out Indian invasion of Azad Kashmir. Tensions between India and Pakistan were running high in the spring and summer of 1992. Both sides were at hair-trigger readiness after two months of mounting threats. India had massed a number of new divisions in Kashmir behind the LOC. Just south of Kashmir, in Northern Punjab, elements of two Indian armored "strike corps" were concentrating between Pathankot and Amritsar for what could become a major offensive against the strategic Pakistani city of Sialkot, the gateway to southern Azad Kashmir.

Frustrated and enraged by the rebellion in Kashmir, India was loudly threatening to "teach Pakistan a lesson." Reserve units were being activated and mobilized in India and Pakistan. Troops were moving into forward positions, and behind them long truck convoys of war supplies, Indian armor, and artillery had left their cantonments and adopted offensive deployments. Indian and Pakistani airbases were on high alert, with aircraft armed and fueled up, many prepared to take off on two or three minutes' notice. Both air forces had gone to war-readiness reconnaissance and combat air patrols.

Reports were coming from South Asia and abroad that India had deployed a number of nuclear weapons to forward airbases near the Pakistani border for its precision-strike Jaguar fighter-bombers. Pakistan, it was rumored, had a number of F-16s with nuclear bombs ready to take off at a moment's notice at Chaklala airbase. Though Delhi and Islamabad denied they had nuclear weapons, and thus had not gone to full nuclear alert, the U.S. Central Intelligence Agency was later to report to Congress that the two foes had in fact been activating their nuclear arsenals.

This confrontation over Kashmir was the closest the world had come to a full-scale nuclear war since 1973, when Israel had armed and deployed its top-secret arsenal of nuclear-tipped missiles and nuclear bombs, and was getting ready to use them to destroy advancing Syrian and Egyptian armored divisions on the Golan Heights and in Sinai. Fortunately, the Egyptian and Syrian attacks both petered out before the panicky Israelis had unleashed their nuclear weapons. The Syrians, in fact, deliberately halted their advance just before reaching the western edge of the Golan Heights, not wishing to give Israel any excuse to launch a nuclear attack.

Standing in a bunker in the middle of what might become a general, or even a nuclear war, was not a comfortable feeling. Having covered some ten wars or conflicts, I was used to being under fire. From the relative safety of a bunker, it was even rather entertaining. But the idea that a nuclear war might actually occur, with me sitting at ground zero, was unsettling. Wars often begin as much by mischance and miscalculation as by plan. Localized clashes that got out of control could quickly escalate into division-level, then corps-level fighting, then to all-out war along the 1,000-mile (1,600-km) front from the Arabian Sea to Tibet. And, according to the CIA, the Indo-Pakistani border, on which I was currently positioned, was the most likely place for a nuclear war to erupt.

Fortunately, India decided not to attack Pakistan. The highly professional generals of India's armed forces restrained the war fever of their civilian masters, who, like politicians everywhere, misjudged or misunderstood the implications, conduct, and true costs of war. Fighting in Kashmir's mountainous terrain would be primarily infantry combat, and much of it World War I-style frontal attack, allowing the defending Pakistanis to fight from strong, prepared positions on high ground. India would not be able to make use of its considerable advantage in armor, artillery, and aircraft. A stalemate was likely to ensue after bloody, inconclusive combat.

But even a military stalemate presented great danger, for Indian generals would then be driven to seek victory by broadening the scope of their operations to other sectors, where India's mobile forces could be used to better profit. To decisively defeat Pakistan, India would have to attack farther south on the plains of Punjab, and strike across the great Thar Desert of Rajastan into Sind, just north of the great port city of Karachi. This would mean a total war between the two huge nations, with the possible threat of a nuclear exchange. India's leaders wisely declined the battle. Still, it was a close-run thing, and a harbinger of what might come in the future.

Movements by Kashmiri rebels across the LOC heightened these simmering tensions. Pakistani forces often give mujahedin units covering fire when they run into Indian patrols, or come under fire from Indian positions. Indian generals repeatedly warn they may exercise the right of hot pursuit to follow the mujahedin back to their bases in Azad Kashmir, or even launch offensives to destroy the insurgents' bases there. The widely held belief among Indians that the Kashmiri intifada would crumble if its roots in Pakistan were torn out constantly tempts Delhi to launch a punitive attack into Azad Kashmir, just as Turkey's generals have considerably degraded the combat-effectiveness of Kurdish PKK (Kurdish Workers' Party) guerrillas by repeatedly mounting air and ground offensives against their operating bases in northern Iraq.

Hot pursuit of rebels into Azad Kashmir by the Indian Army could quickly escalate into a bigger war, particularly if the attackers were threatened with Pakistani counterattacks. To rescue the stalled attacking force, Indian commanders would have to rush in reinforcements, initiate diversionary assaults at other points on the line, or, if these measures failed, open a broader offensive in northern Punjab. Such actions could spark an all-out war along the entire 1,000-mile (1,600-km) front from the Siachen Glacier to the Arabian Sea.

Pentagon war-gamers consider this possibility to be the most likely scenario for triggering a major Indo-Pakistani conflict, one that neither side wants, but from which they could not withdraw without serious political and military loss. One senior Pentagon official described the hot-pursuit scenario as "our constant nightmare."

A full-scale war with India would threaten Pakistan's very existence, and present its general staff with the almost impossible task of defending their strategically vulnerable nation. Pakistan resembles Egypt: a great river flows down from remote mountains, on whose banks, and great southern delta, live the majority of the population. On the map, both nations look large; but when desert, arid land, and unpopulated areas are deducted from the picture, what remains is a relatively small nation clinging precariously to a narrow river valley.

Pakistan's population and defenses are concentrated in two important provinces, Sind in the south, and Punjab in the north. Its other regions—the Northwest Frontier, the Northern Territories, and Baluchistan—are geographically remote. Between the southern port of Karachi and the Punjab's most important northern metropolis, Lahore, lies about 600 miles (1,000 km) of desert and scrub on either side of the Indus valley.

Halfway between these two cities is a large salient that juts into Pakistan. From this point, Indian mobile forces need race over only 50 miles (80 km) of flat terrain to reach the cities of Sukkur, Rahimyar Khan, or, farther north, the important Bawalalpur-Multan nexus, in order to sever the road and rail lines that link Punjab and Sind. If these vital spinal communications were cut, Pakistan would be divided, isolated, and paralyzed. Indian forces could isolate Punjab, preventing Pakistani reinforcements from moving south, while they conquered Karachi and Hyderabad at their leisure.

Keenly aware of Pakistan's strategic weakness, India's defense planners have created a group of highly mobile "strike corps," composed of powerful armored and mechanized units, supported by mobile artillery and highly capable units of engineers. Much of the army's strength—1,400 modern T-72 tanks, BMP-1/2 armored fighting vehicles, and modern, self-propelled or mobile guns—is concentrated in these strike corps, which are deployed in Punjab, the Thar Desert, and above the marshy Rann of Kutch, just north of the Arabian Sea coast. Their mission, in time of war, is to penetrate deeply into Pakistan, sever its communications, and defeat the divided Pakistani army.

On paper, India's forces on its western front appear to be only slightly stronger than Pakistan's. While confronting Pakistan, India must also maintain large numbers of troops on the borders with Chinese-ruled Tibet, and garrison rebellious Kashmir, Assam, and the tribal states of India's far eastern border with Burma. In wartime, India's huge, million-man paramilitary forces could perform some of these functions, relieving army troops for duty on the front with Pakistan. But the very real threat that China might threaten India's northern borders in support of its ally, Pakistan, forces India's high command to maintain substantial air and ground forces to cover the remote north.

This strategic drain on troops leaves India with a significant but hardly overwhelming superiority on its western front. There, India deploys three armored, four mechanized, and thirteen or so infantry divisions or division equivalents (two of them armored), as well as large numbers of artillery formations. In Kashmir, India fields at least five of its nine mountain divisions.

Pakistan, by contrast, need only use light infantry units to watch its borders with Afghanistan and Iran, concentrating its best forces on the Indian front. Pakistan can deploy two armored divisions, and about fourteen or fifteen infantry divisions or division equivalents.

In armor, Pakistan is outnumbered 3 to 2 by India; in artillery, 3 to 1. Pakistan's artillery is less modern, and has a shorter range than India's. The bulk of Pakistan's tanks, old U.S. M48s and Chinese Type-59s/69s/ and 85s, are obsolescent, undergunned, and poorly equipped, particularly compared with India's more modern family of Soviet-supplied T-72 tanks. The three hundred modern T-80UD tanks Pakistan bought from Ukraine have been offset by equally effective new armor that India has been acquiring from Russia.

In the air, India long ago outclassed Pakistan's air force, which has been crippled by a long, punishing American embargo of arms and spare parts. India not only outnumbers Pakistan's air force by nearly 2 to 1, its state-of-the-art Russian MiG-29s and SU-30s and French Mirage 2000s technologically outclass Pakistan's only fairly modern fighters, a handful of 32 F-16s. The rest of Pakistan's 410-combat aircraft force consists of elderly French Mirages, and a collection of obsolescent J-6 and J-7 Chinese fighters, modernized versions of the venerable MiG-21, and Chinese Q-5 ground attack aircraft, based on the late '50s model MiG-19.

The military embargo imposed on Pakistan by the United States at the end of the Afghan war in 1989–90 seriously weakened Pakistan's air force: it could not obtain the new F-16s it badly needed, spare parts for its existing American-made equipment, or AWACS capability for the command and control of modern air combat. As a result, the combat capability of the once formidable Pakistan Air Force was cut in half. Pakistan was compelled to shop the world's arms markets for used equipment, finally acquiring from France, after many delays, a batch of old, refurbished, 1960s-vintage Mirage-Vs.

Pakistan's air force still produces better pilots than India's air arm, which has one of the world's highest accident rates, but modern Russian equipment, advanced electronics and radars, and improved command and control have lessened Pakistan's once substantial qualitative edge.

India's other advantage is that its economy is almost six times larger than Pakistan's. In three previous Indo-Pakistani wars, both sides quickly ran out of munitions and war supplies, but over the past twenty years India has ensured this failure will not happen again by developing a powerful military-industrial base and an extensive chain of well-stocked military depots close to the Pakistani border, designed to support sustained offensive operations by its mobile strike corps.

By contrast, Pakistan lacks this strategic logistic base, and must import from abroad many of its war stocks, spares, and basic supplies. In time of war, this grave imbalance means Pakistani forces would soon run low on armor, aircraft, missiles, engines, electronics, spare parts, and heavy munitions, while Indian forces would be able to sustain combat for a considerably longer period—perhaps long enough to attain decisive victory. In fact, India's logistic supplies and spare parts reserves give it the capability of fighting for eight to twelve weeks longer than Pakistan.

Once hostilities began, India's powerful navy, which includes modern submarines and one aircraft carrier (with a second under order), would immediately blockade Pakistan's only two seaports at Karachi and Gwadar in Baluchistan, cutting off all of Pakistan's maritime trade. The only way beleaguered Pakistan could obtain strategic supplies of oil, heavy weapons, and munitions would be from Iran, by means of a vulnerable, extremely difficult, 1,000-mile (1,600-km) supply route across the vast deserts and mountains of Baluchistan. In time of war, once Pakistan had exhausted its reserves of fuel and munitions, it would be unable to replenish its vital war stocks because of an effective blockade by the Indian Navy. Pakistan's smaller navy would challenge the Indian blockade, but would be unlikely to actually break it and reopen maritime trade.

India also has the advantage of size. With few targets of strategic importance in the border areas, India could comfortably withdraw before any Pakistani offensive without risking defeat, then counterattack, and cut off over-extending Pakistani forces. India, like Russia, is simply too large to conquer. The only way for Pakistan to win a strategic victory would be to surround and destroy all of India's mobile strike corps along the border in under ten days of sustained combat. But such an outcome is most unlikely, given Pakistan's weakness in armor, logistic support, and air cover.

In a war with India, Pakistan would be much more likely to remain on the strategic defensive: its best hope would be to grab and hold portions of Indian territory along the border to be used as bargaining chips when the war had ended. However, Pakistan's logistical weakness means that, in a lengthy war of attrition, India would be bound to win. Delhi's refusal to be intimidated by the U.S. embargo imposed after its nuclear tests suggests strongly that India might be equally resistant to foreign diplomatic and economic pressure to quickly end a war against Pakistan.

For Pakistan, in the event of a major war, simply defending the long line from Kashmir to Karachi will be an almost impossible task. All of Pakistan's cities, large towns, and communications between Islamabad and Karachi are compressed into the Indus Valley. Modern, mechanized warfare demands ample maneuver space, and fluid defense in depth. Having the advantage of the strategic offensive, Indian can choose where and when to launch its powerful strike corps, concentrating them for inevitable breakthroughs where Pakistani forces are stretched thin, or are absent. After slicing through brittle Pakistani defenses, India's mechanized forces could then defeat the Pakistanis in detail, opening the way to the great port city of Karachi, and to Lahore.

India has another important advantage that becomes crucial in desert warfare: spy satellites that can deliver fairly rapid data on the location of Pakistani forces to the Indian high command in Delhi. During the Iran-Iraq War, data secretly supplied to Baghdad by U.S.

reconnaissance satellites played a decisive role in the conflict. According to reliable intelligence sources, the U.S. actually gave Saddam Hussein's regime a ground station through which it could receive real-time downlinked data from American recon satellites.

In the 1991 Gulf War, Iraqi units in Kuwait's deserts were under constant microscopic examination by U.S. spy satellites. Thanks to its fast-developing space program and growing high-tech computing technology, India too will soon be able to monitor from space all Pakistani military movements. Pakistan has no satellites and, at least for now, no access to space recon data from friendly nations. India's spy satellites will not, however, be able to detect Pakistani missile launches.

If a full-scale war erupts, and Pakistan is unable to prevent its defenses from being torn open, Islamabad's last recourse may be to fire tactical nuclear weapons at the advancing Indian armored corps, and the logistic bases that support them. This, of course, would cause India to retaliate, possibly with a nuclear attack on cities such as Lahore, Multan, Karachi, and Islamabad. Pakistan would use its new medium-range ballistic missiles to strike Delhi, Amritsar, Bombay, Jaipur, Ahmadabad, and even as far south as Bangalore.

As previously noted, a Rand Corp. study estimated that an India-Pakistan nuclear exchange would cause 2 million immediate casualties, and a further 100 million in ensuing weeks.

Adding to the risk of nuclear war, India has repeatedly threatened air and missile strikes against Pakistan's nuclear reactors, weapons assembly facilities, and bases from which nuclear-armed aircraft or missiles can be launched. Indian strategists were greatly impressed by Israel's destruction of Iraq's Osirak reactor in 1981, and have reportedly been encouraged by Israeli advisors to "surgically" remove Pakistan's nuclear capability. Israel has been actively aiding India's secret nuclear program since the 1980s, and sending counter-insurgency specialists to aid Indian forces in Kashmir.

Any Indian attacks on Pakistani nuclear plants would invite immediate retaliation by Pakistan. Even without the danger of enemy attack, India's eleven reactors devoted to production of weapons-grade uranium-233 and plutonium-239 are ticking time bombs, often denounced by critics as little Chernobyls, because of their poor maintenance and a shoddy safety record.

An attack on Pakistani or Indian reactors would release clouds of radioactive dust and debris that would blanket southern Asia, spreading, eventually, around the globe. The explosion of just one nuclear reactor would pollute the groundwater and food chain in the region for many decades. The proximity of Indian and Pakistani reactors to heavily populated areas makes a potential "reactor war" all the more dangerous.

The recent introduction by India and Pakistan of short- and medium-range ballistic missiles configured to carry nuclear warheads sharply increases the reach of any potential nuclear exchange. The missiles have a flight time to target of as little as three minutes. Recent nuclear tests conducted in India in the Thar Desert were designed to validate new tactical nuclear warheads for its missiles, air-delivered bombs, and 155mm artillery, as well as a precursor thermonuclear, or hydrogen, bomb.

India's acceleration of development of an intermediate version of the Agni-II is clearly designed to strike targets on the Tibet Plateau and deep into western China, including the important industrial cities of Chengdu, Wuhan, Kunming, and Chongqing—and even Hong Kong and Shanghai. In April 1999, India tested the new, solid-fueled, two-stage Agni-II, which can deliver a one-ton conventional or nuclear warhead over a distance of 1,554 miles (2,500 km), making it a true intermediate-range ballistic missile (IRBM). Indian defense officials claimed Agni-II would eventually be deployed on rail cars.

Pakistan responded only three days later by test-firing its 1,430-mile (2,300-km) Ghauri-II IRBM, and a new, single-stage missile, the 466-mile- (750-km-) range Shaheen.

While Delhi and Islamabad rattled their missiles, India's then defense minister, George Fernandes, warned, "With today's launch, we have reached a point where no one from anywhere will dare threaten us." "Anywhere" clearly meant China and even the United States.

Development of strategic arms by India's Defense Research and Development Organization will not end with Agni-II. The DRDO is expected to introduce the 2,175-mile- (3,500-km-) range Agni-III in the year 2000, a version capable of striking targets anywhere in China.

India is also developing a true intercontinental ballistic missile (ICBM), likely by adding a third solid-fuel stage to Agni-III. This 3,728–4,350-mile (6,000–7,000-km) missile will be capable of reaching parts of North America, Japan, and Europe. In addition, DRDO is working on a submarine-launched ballistic missile, Sagarika, and an air-breathing cruise missile. These long-range systems have alarmed not only China, but all of Asia and even American defense planners.

Equally worrying, neither India nor Pakistan has effective surveillance systems capable of giving early warning of enemy missile launches. As a result, their new ballistic missiles create a hair-trigger, use-them-or-lose-them situation—meaning that they might be launched on warning, under fear enemy missiles were incoming, or after a false report of nuclear attack. The necessary civilian and military command-and-control authority to effectively handle nuclear weapons and, in extremis, to decide on their use or non-use, are lacking in both India and Pakistan, though the two nations are working to create such strategic organizations.

Right now, the nuclear arsenals of India and Pakistan are under a complex, even uncertain, chain of command that could break down in a crisis, or even produce a false warning of an enemy nuclear attack.

Chronically poor telecommunications and frequent breakdowns in command-and-control on both sides create a further threat of unauthorized or mistaken launches. Agreement by India and Pakistan to advise their neighbor of test launches has in no way lessened this danger. In South Asia, telephone communications are so poor, most senior government officials rely on cell phones. In the event of war, even primitive jamming techniques by the enemy would disrupt the radio transmitters and relay stations on which cell phones depend to function, as well as other radio and microwave transmissions. The fog of war would thicken, then grow opaque: in this dangerous miasma, Indian and Pakistani leaders might have to make nearly instant decisions that could mean death for millions of their citizens and a catastrophe for the entire Earth.

A more dangerous situation cannot be imagined—and Kashmir could very well be the fuse that ignites a nuclear holocaust on the continent.

11
Paradise Lost

SRINAGAR

After the usual harrowing flight north from Delhi, I arrived at fabled Srinagar. Kashmir may be the jewel of the subcontinent, but Srinagar is rather disappointing. In spite of its legendary lakeside setting, quaint wooden buildings, clusters of houseboats, and Mogul gardens, Srinagar has the same overcrowded, scruffy, haphazard air as most other South Asian cities. Traffic jams, heaps of refuse, and a miasma of polluted air belie the beauty that surrounds this city of 450,000. Spoiled by the steady influx of tourists for the past century, Srinagar's natives have gained a well-deserved reputation for fleecing, harassing, and abusing visitors. Even the famous houseboats that ply Dal Lake are infested with rats and armies of roaches that are almost as aggressive and annoying as the swarms of touts that incessantly cajole and importune tourists.

Before the uprising, Srinagar's narrow streets, dark, winding alleys, and colorful bazaars offering spices, fruits, and handicrafts had some exotic charm. But the intifada turned the once vibrant, colorful city into a semi-ghost town. As I walked through the grim, deserted streets I met wary patrols of Indian Army, police and paramilitary troops. Sandbagged Indian checkpoints, manned by nervous, trigger-happy troops, guarded important intersections and government buildings. I had seen a similar pall of fear and raw tension fall over other cities at war: Beirut, Luanda, Algiers, San Salvador, Bogota, Kabul. Srinagar was clearly a city under siege.

At dusk, a curfew went into effect, leaving the streets empty and sinister. Indian troops in jeeps and light trucks scanned the wooden buildings, their automatic weapons at the ready, on the alert for any movement on the roofs that might mean snipers. The Indians never knew when a grenade would be tossed at them or, worse, an RPG rocket fired at one of their vehicles. Any unusual or unexpected activities after dusk could trigger volleys of fire from the edgy Indian soldiers; they would shoot first and investigate later. The large number of innocent civilians shot by accident were simply classified as "terrorists," or "caught in crossfire."

Outside Srinagar, security was even more tenuous. Roads to the once-popular tourist resorts at Gulmarg and Pahalgam were often closed by small bands of mujahedin. Military and police vehicles were routinely ambushed, forcing the Indians to travel in large convoys. The heavily wooded slopes along the roads and narrow defiles provided ideal guerrilla cover, where even the amateur fighters of the various mujahedin groups could operate with some measure of effectiveness.

Wars fought among civilian populations are always a dirty, bloody business. Guerrilla wars, in which the insurgents often receive support from the local populace, are even more so. As the French discovered four decades ago in Algeria, the most effective way to crush guerrilla forces is to separate them from the civilians who sustain them.

$$\bullet \quad \bullet \quad \bullet$$

Is there a solution to the problem of Kashmir? Half a century of wrangling between India and Pakistan, two wars, and a national uprising have so far changed nothing. Until 1998, the outside world was content to regard Kashmir as a festering, but strategically contained bilateral dispute between India and Pakistan. Like Afghanistan, the area was so remote, so little known, that it was impossible to rouse international public opinion over its travails, even among Islamic nations. Even the United Nations, which had originally called for a referendum to settle the state's future, lost interest in the seemingly intractable issue, and skillful Indian diplomacy thwarted Pakistan's attempts to internationalize the problem.

While other remote conflicts, like East Timor or Tibet, attracted enough media attention to cause popular indignation in the West, the suffering and aspirations of Kashmir's people were largely ignored. The distorted but widely held view that all Muslim liberation movements are terrorists, or at least dangerous troublemakers, contributed to the general lack of concern for Kashmir. Human rights groups that raised the issue received scant attention. Desultory efforts by the United States, Britain, and the Soviet Union to resolve Kashmir soon petered out after being overtaken by more pressing matters. Leave bad enough alone was the world's view of Kashmir.

This international nonchalance abruptly changed in mid-1998 when India detonated five nuclear devices. The nuclear tests, intended to bolster India's security, backfired on Delhi by shocking the outside world and focusing its attention on long-neglected Kashmir. The immediate result for India was opprobrium and temporary financial sanctions. Badly needed foreign investors were scared off, China and Pakistan were deeply alarmed, and the world was furious at India. Pakistan's riposte—a nuclear test of its own—deepened international concern and forced the entire matter of Indo-Pakistani relations and Kashmir onto the diplomatic docket—precisely what India had so long labored to avoid.

Alarm bells began to go off from Washington to Tokyo, as strategists who had previously written off Southwest Asia as an unimportant geopolitical backwater abruptly realized that two deeply inimical nuclear powers, at scimitars drawn over Kashmir, could very easily get themselves into an advertent, or accidental, nuclear war that would kill millions and pollute the planet with radioactive fallout. The dirty secret everyone had chosen to ignore was suddenly out in the open.

Delhi, stunned by unexpected international condemnation, attempted to furiously backpedal, claiming its nuclear explosions were merely a response to threats from China, a contention few believed. India's conditional offers to sign the Non-Proliferation Treaty did little to allay concern that the subcontinent was at the edge of a nuclear abyss.

Kashmir could no longer be safely forgotten. Without a settlement of the dispute, which focuses and magnifies all the historical, religious and political hatreds between the two estranged sister-nations, the dangerous impasse would persist indefinitely, subject to perilous escalation at any time.

The confrontation came just as the United States was rapidly expanding its influence into energy- and resource-rich Central Asia. A second Great Game was afoot in the vast steppe and mountain region stretching from China to the Caucasus. Whereas in the nineteenth century, railroads had been the conduits of trade and empire building, at the very end of the twentieth century, oil and gas pipelines had become the new arteries of geostrategic power projection and economic exploitation. A long list of countries, including Russia, the United States, Pakistan, India, China, Iran, Turkey, Saudi Arabia, Japan, South Korea, and Europe were all vying to grab a portion of the new oil and gas reserves in the Caspian Basin and, further west, in the semi-independent former Soviet republics. It looked like the world's next gold rush.

The festering civil war in Afghanistan blocked the shortest pipeline routes south and forced the U.S. to alter its bitterly hostile policy toward Tehran and seek accommodation with Iran, through whose territory lay the next best export route for Central Asia's riches. Just as a laboriously achieved détente was beginning to develop between the U.S. and Iran, there was a new upsurge of hostility between nuclear-armed India and Pakistan; Kashmir, the focus of Indo-Pakistani rivalry, suddenly intruded into the Central Asian issue, threatening to create a second Afghanistan and possibly draw China and India into direct conflict.

While the need for a comprehensive settlement is evident, the means remain elusive. Neither India nor Pakistan will allow the other to dominate a unified Kashmir, and the majority of Kashmir's people, for their part, strongly reject Indian domination and aspire to the right of self-determination enshrined in the United Nations Charter. After the bloody intifada, and India's ruthless repression, it seems unlikely most Kashmiris would voluntarily consent to continued direct rule by India.

India insists that the resolution of the Jammu and Kashmir problem is an internal matter, in which outside powers and the UN have no business. (The Jammu portion of Kashmir has a Hindu majority and thus will opt for continued union with India.) Pakistan has never been troubled by outsiders questioning its continued possession of the Northern Territories, but that may change if the Kashmir issue comes under international arbitration. In fact, it could open a diplomatic Pandora's box, raising the vexing questions not only of the Northern Territories, but also of Gilgit-Baltistan, Indian-held Ladakh, and the Chinese annexation of Aksai Chin.

In spite of these daunting diplomatic rigidities, the original fifty-year-old UN plan for a supervised referendum in Kashmir still remains the best possible solution. There is no political, demographic, or economic reason why Kashmir could not exist as a viable independent state, with the proviso that, as a buffer between India and Pakistan, it would have to establish and maintain absolute neutrality.

An honest vote in a referendum, of course, would produce a majority in favor of accession to Pakistan or independence. India has long understood this fact, and, accordingly, is determined at all costs to block any vote it cannot control and, inevitably, rig. Only intense international political and economic pressure, or a massive upsurge in the insurrection, could change Delhi's mind, though even this seems unlikely. India's politicians, particularly the BJP's Hindu chauvinists, have staked their fortunes on crushing the revolt in Kashmir, and would be turfed out of office by angry Indian voters who would see any settlement over Kashmir as a sellout to the hated Muslims, and even more fiercely hated Pakistan. Losing Kashmir would fly in the face of the BJP's loudly stated ambitions to re-create the old Raj under Hindu rule, and negate the party's very *raison d'être* as the spear-point of Hindu revivalism.

If independence is unachievable, and union with Pakistan impossible, what about genuine autonomy within the Indian union? Delhi claims Kashmir already has full autonomy under the local state government run by Dr. Farouk Abdullah. Few believe this canard, not even apparently Dr. Abdullah, who is reportedly considering giving up being an Indian satrap and returning to his residence in the peaceful English countryside. Real autonomy would imply a right to secede from India; or at least, to elect a state government that is closely aligned to Pakistan. Delhi would accept neither. A truly autonomous government in Kashmir might quickly spark calls for more autonomy from other restive regions that chafe at Delhi's controls and taxation, such as Assam, Mizoram, Nagaland, or worse, even big states like Tamil Nadu and Karnataka, which might choose to emulate independent-minded Russian regions like Tatarstan, Krasnoyarsk, or Udmurtia, by keeping their taxes at home, selling resources and exports directly to foreigners, and refusing to any longer subsidize poor regions of the country.

Every potential solution is replete with problems and dangers. But Kashmiris have made plain they will no longer accept the status quo. Their efforts to cast off Indian rule, and India's savage response, threaten war daily between India and Pakistan. A way of cutting through this modern Gordian knot must be found before the world's most populous region stumbles into nuclear conflict. The world can no longer afford to close its eyes to this half-century-old dispute.

India's ambition to attain a seat on the UN Security Council, and gain international respectability as a democratic, mature great power, is being undermined by its continued repression in Kashmir, one of the worst examples of human rights violations. Ironically, while the world condemns China for its harsh repression in Tibet over the past decade, India has been responsible for even more political killings and tortures during the same period in Kashmir.

India would probably be better off without its portion of strife-torn Kashmir. Keeping the mountain state in the union by force is costing Delhi huge sums of money it can ill afford, wearing down the Indian army, and damaging India's reputation.

But the Indian government has got itself stuck in the mountains of Kashmir: it is unable to go either forward or backward, as the voices of its moderate politicians are increasingly drowned out by the rising clamor of Hindu fundamentalism and chauvinism. No Indian politician dares risk being accused of having surrendered the glorious earthly paradise of Kashmir to the hated Muslim enemy. Muslim Kashmiris cannot abide Indian rule. Everything must change; but nothing, it seems, will.

In April 1999, a new and ghastly potential solution to the endless Kashmir dispute became suddenly and horrifyingly apparent. Half a world away, the Serb regime of Slobodan Milošević chose to solve a similar, seemingly intractable problem—Kosovo—by first unleashing ethnic and religious warfare against its restive Albanian citizens, then expelling them from the country.

The ethnic terrorism Serbs had inflicted on Croatia and Bosnia was only a prelude to the full-scale horror of the depopulation of Kosovo, the worst crime against humanity in Europe since World War II.

Like some of India's more extreme Hindu fundamentalists, Serbia's latter-day ethnic Fascists were determined to restore the ethnic Slav purity of their region, to "drive the Muslim hordes back to Mecca" and exact pitiless revenge for historical grievances that dated back five hundred years or more. The Serb Orthodox Church played a major role in whipping up anti-Muslim, anti-Albanian hatred, just as some of India's extremist Hindu priests incited violence against Muslims and Christians. To Serbs, the Kosovar Albanians and the Slav Muslims of Bosnia were "Turks"; to Hindu fundamentalists, the Muslims of Kashmir, of India itself, and of Pakistan were all latter-day "Moguls" who defiled the sanctity of Mother India.

Serbia, a small but fanatically determined nation of only ten million, defied the world community and the wrath of NATO. In a matter of weeks, Serbs drove one million Albanians out of Kosovo, dumping them like human garbage in Albania, Macedonia, and Montenegro, putting the rest into internal flight. Kosovo was made Albanian-*rein*, or purified of the Muslim *Untermensch*.

Hindu fundamentalists and even some senior Indian leaders cannot but have noted Milošević's attempt to inflict a "final solution" on the Muslims of Kosovo, not to mention the West's dilatory and tardy response to this monstrous crime.

What if India unleashed its army of paramilitary thugs against the recalcitrant, rebellious Muslim civilians of Kashmir? The idea is horrifying to contemplate. Driving a large portion of Muslim Kashmiris over the border into neighboring Pakistan would rid India once and for all of their vexing presence, crush the intifada, and conclusively cement India's rule over Kashmir. India would then be free to import Hindu settlers to repopulate Kashmir. What could Pakistan do to prevent a tidal wave of refugees from being driven across the Line of Control? Its only option would be an all-out war against far more powerful India, a war that it would surely lose. The example of Kosovo also provides a lesson to India in how it might destabilize hated Pakistan by sending a flood of millions of Kashmiri refugees across the border. It could even lead to Pakistan's collapse.

The bestial actions of a faraway Balkan dictator had suddenly introduced an ominous new element into the already explosive crisis over Kashmir.

PART THREE

War in the

Death Zone

12
The Road to Siachen

My third journey into the war zone at the top of the world took me to one of the strangest conflicts in history. Over the years, I had heard reports that India and Pakistan were engaged in a bitter struggle over a vast glacier called Siachen, somewhere deep in the frozen mountain wastes between northern Kashmir and Tibet. It would be extraordinarily difficult to find a remoter or more hostile place on Earth.

"It's madness. Total madness," a Pakistani commando officer told me one night in Peshawar. "Siachen is Hell on Earth. We're fighting the bloody Indians to prevent them from grabbing what we say is our rightful part of Hell. That's how much we hate each other."

As I was later to discover, the major was right. The Siachen Glacier was a frozen hell. What else but burning hatred could drive men to battle over an alien, airless wilderness, so high and forbidding that even skilled mountain climbers spoke of it with awe and fear? Yet the Indians and Pakistanis had been fighting over this icy massif for a decade, and showed no sign of relenting.

It was madness on a grand, militarized scale. I determined to go and see this highest war in history.

• • •

The Pakistan Airways Boeing 737 took off smartly from Islamabad and headed northeast over Azad Kashmir. I sat in the cockpit, chatting with the captain and first officer, both veterans of the crack Pakistani Air Force. At first, the mountains of Kashmir offered a splendid panorama beneath us, but soon a heavy layer of thick, low-hanging clouds hid the ground. We flew for about an hour in the bright sunshine, swapping aviation stories and jokes about the infinite perils of India's internal airlines.

Ahead of us, slightly to our right, an enormous peak rose out of the clouds. "That's Nanga Parbat," the first officer announced. "Eight thousand, one hundred and twenty-six meters [26,660 feet]."

We turned right around Nanga Parbat and began to descend over the Gilgit Valley. To our left another great snow-crowned peak, mighty Rakaposhi, rose 25,545 feet (7,786 m) into the sky. Scores of climbers had died on its treacherous, icy, crumbling slopes. The twin peaks were avoided by all save the most accomplished and experienced climbers.

Now the captain's mood abruptly changed; he became serious, focused, and tense. "I've got to get to work," he said, scanning his flight instruments. He put the 737 into a steep descent toward the clouds, then slowed. Minutes later we left the safe, sunlit upper world and entered the menacing sea of cloud that hung between Rakaposhi and Nanga Parbat. Darkness enveloped us.

"We will be going through the mountains in one minute," the captain announced tersely. Below and around us, concealed behind blankets of gray cumulus clouds, were jagged peaks. I peered nervously into the thick gloom, expecting to see a wall of black rock come flying at us. Ten very long, tense minutes later, we broke through the clouds to find ourselves flying down a long, treeless valley, dotted with small lakes and moraines of glacial rock. To our left and right, mountains rose almost vertically until they disappeared into the mist and clouds.

As we flew onward, the valley grew narrower. Rising air currents buffeted the heavy jet. The ground appeared to be closing in on the belly of the aircraft, and its wingtips seemed close enough to touch the sides of the snow-covered mountains that pressed in on either side of us. This is what it must be like, I mused, to fly at 100 feet (30 m) down Park Avenue in a big passenger jet on a stormy night. The experience was both thrilling and extremely frightening. One false move and our plane, hurtling down a funnel of rock at 350 miles an hour (560 km/h), would either hit the ground or clip a mountainside, sending us cartwheeling to disaster.

After a short eternity of tension, the pilot threw the 737 into a sharp, 90-degree right turn down another valley that intersected the one we had been following. We stood on our side: I was looking out the window directly down into a rushing stream. Our right wingtip dropped to within what appeared a few feet of the ground. The aircraft jolted and shuddered alarmingly as the turn bled off speed.

Abruptly, the pilot righted the 737, and we emerged from the narrow valley over a broad, sandy plain, through which flowed a wide, dark river. We had reached Baltistan, Pakistan's other northern province, and sometime part of Kashmir. On the far side of the plain, some 15 miles (24 km) distant, rose mountains, and behind this scarp rose another and another, forming a gigantic wall of vertiginous, snow-capped peaks that thrust their jagged tors into the clouds: these were the Karakorams, or Black Mountains, the western extension of the high Himalayas. In the midst of this majestic panorama, which filled my entire visual horizon, one titanic white peak soared above all the others, shining jewel-bright in the hard, high-altitude sunlight. "Look." The captain pointed. "K-2."

Mighty K-2 rises 28,251 ft. (8,611 meters) over on the mountain border between Baltistan and the Chinese province of Sinkiang, formerly known as Eastern Turkestan. Though slightly lower than Mt. Everest, whose summit is at 29,028 ft. (8,848 meters), K-2 is much less accessible, far harder to climb, subject to more violent weather, and more notorious as a killer of climbers. Just south of K-2, three other towering mountains with raw, serrated peaks stood like attending giants on either side of it: Masherbrun-1 at 25,659 ft. (7,821 meters), Gasherbrun-1 at 26,469 ft. (8,068 meters), and Mt. Goodwin-Austen, 28,265 ft. (8,615 meters). All three have an evil reputation among professional climbers. The groups of "tourist" or "dude" climbers who take package tours to poor, defiled Everest, leaving behind heaps of garbage, drained batteries, and frozen feces, do not venture into the wild region of K-2 or its guardians. Just to reach their bases requires at least twelve days' difficult mountain trek from Skardu, the capital of Baltistan.

K-2, Gasherbrun-1, Masherbrun-1, Rakaposhi, Nanga Parbat, and Lhotse are also called the Great Sacred Mountains, along with the mysterious, 28,208-ft. (8,598-meter) Kangchenjunga, farther to the east in the Himalayas, which appears only rarely from its veil of clouds (it has always done so to mark the coronation of the royal family of Sikkim). I am not a particularly religious person, but to me these wild, regal mountains are cathedrals that fill me with the deepest reverence and awe; I am certain they are sacred, though to which gods I do not know. Perhaps they are gods themselves: great frozen tors of adamantine power and majesty, crowned by swirling clouds and wreaths of blowing snow, glowing deep gold and russet in the rarefied, frigid air.

We landed at Baltistan's main city, Skardu, at 7,700 ft. (2,347 meters), a miserable collection of concrete buildings, huts, stalls, and tea rooms, with six thousand most uninspiring inhabitants.

Skardu was an important stop on the ancient caravan route between India, China, and Central Asia. From Srinagar in Kashmir, the caravan route heads north, crossing the Himalayas at the Burzil Pass; it continues to Astor, just below the massif of Nanga Parbat, and thence northeast along the Indus valley to Skardu.

From Skardu, caravans would follow the Indus northwest to Gilgit, then up over the treacherous passes leading into Turkestan—the same famed Silk Road taken by Marco Polo. A second important caravan route ran 260 difficult miles (420 km) from Srinagar up over the Himalayas at Zoji La, down into Ladakh to Kargil, then east along the Indus to Leh, or "Little Tibet." From Leh, the caravans would strike north over the next mountain range to the Shyok River Valley, then north again around the base of the Siachen Glacier to the Karakoram Pass that debouches onto the plains of Turkestan. From there, they would follow the ancient Silk Road to the legendary oasis trading cities of the oases Yarkand and Kashgar.

Today, Skardu is the jumping-off point for major mountaineering expeditions to K-2 and its sister peaks. Though 10,000 square miles (25,900 sq km) in area, Baltistan is thinly populated, with a total population of only 224,000 people, some of whom are nomads. The region is sandwiched between three of the world's highest mountain ranges—the Himalayas, Karakorams, and Hindu Kush—and Tibet. In winter all the passes into Baltistan are totally closed by snow, isolating the valley for five or six months annually from the outside world. The only way to reach Baltistan in winter is by air; however, even in spring and summer, Skardu airport is frequently closed by snow, storms, or thick clouds.

Skardu lies on a rise above the great, 1,900-mile- (3,057-km-) long Indus River, whose headwaters rise on the Tibetan Plateau, flow westward across Baltistan, into the Gilgit Valley, and then south the length of Pakistan, emptying into the Arabian Sea at the port of Karachi. Without the Indus and its tributaries, most of Pakistan would be lifeless desert.

The Indus is a big, brawny river, dark brown in some places, gray in others, a torrent of frigid water filled with tumbling rocks, boulders, trees, rich mud and gravel. Like the Nile, it brings down precious alluvium from the mountains to the flood plains of the south. With its five major tributaries—Sutlej, Jhelum, Chenab, Ravi, and Beas—the Indus is the Mother of Pakistan, supporting some 100 million people. Along the Indus's banks in the third millennium BC rose the Mohenjodaro civilization, which flourished in the region when the ancient Egyptian culture was also at its height.

• • •

Skardu's seedy bazaar was filled with heaps of dark, wooly, brown yak hides, mountain-climbing gear, cheap Chinese fans and TV sets, sacks filled with spices of every color and aroma, huge jute bags of rice and wheat from the south, rusting auto parts, worn tires, cases of tinned milk, and buckets of ghee, or clarified butter.

Dust blew through the streets, propelled by a relentless wind. The sun beat down hard in the thin, dry air, immediately parching the skin and throat. Rainclouds from the south were trapped by the Pir Panjal range and Himalayas, leaving the long Baltistan Valley arid and barren, like the neighboring Tibetan plateau to the northeast. Arriving in this vast, lonely desert at the roof of the world, after leaving green, wooded Kashmir made for a dramatic and disturbing contrast. Cross the col of Zoji La and you suddenly find yourself in one of the bleakest wastes in Central Asia, where there is almost no rainfall and even the winter's snows on the loftiest peaks are but a thin dusting of white. Ladakh and Baltistan resemble their geographic sister, Tibet: an arid plateau of granite dust, devoid of trees or pastures, encircled by dark crags and cut by broad couloirs of broken rock.

Baltis, a small people with marked Tibetan-Mongol features, mingled in the Skardu bazaar with fair Kashmiris and Gilgitis as well as darker-hued Pakistanis from the south. Most Baltis are Shia Muslims. Sunni Muslim tribes to the south consider the Baltis heretics, and used to regularly wage war against them, further isolating the valley from contact with India.

The dilapidated center of Skardu was also a meeting-place for the inevitable latter-day hippies from Europe one always finds in remote mountain towns. Unwashed Dutch girls in blue saris and beads, scruffy young Germans with scraggly blond beards, wearing dirty parkas and Chitral hats, and a gaggle of coarse, nomadic Australians sat about in little groups, smoking hash, and trying, without much success, to look like the locals, who rewarded their efforts with polite disdain. A mountain expedition was purchasing canned milk, wooden boxes of tea, and large jute bags of rice.

That night, I left the spartan government guest house where I had lodged, and walked down to the river. I was completely alone; the only sound came from the rushing water and wind. The light of the full moon hanging just above the valley reflected off the snowy mountains above and bathed the river in a flat, soft luminescence. I took a few steps into the icy water, bent over and picked up a rock worn smooth and rounded by the rushing waters. Where had it come from, I wondered? Probably somewhere high up in mysterious Tibet, a land I had never seen. The gray-green basalt rock, which dried quickly in the arid air, felt strangely warm; it molded into my hand. I stood in the moonlight, experiencing a magical moment of communion with the hidden gods of the roof of the world.

I said a brief prayer for my mother, father, and distant friends.

The next day I arose at dawn and went to breakfast. A cheery Pakistani army officer marched into the dining room, introduced himself with fine courtesy as Captain Aziz, drank a cup of milky tea with me, and announced, "Come, Mr. Eric, it is time to go to Siachen." The Pakistani military had laid on a jeep to take me to the glacier, which was a closed, highly sensitive military zone, and the theater of active combat operations. Had I known what ordeals lay in wait, my enthusiasm to embark on this adventure would have been somewhat more restrained.

Baltistan lies on a northwest axis between the world's two highest mountain ranges, the Himalayas to the south and the Karakorams to the north. The Karakorams extend 250 miles (400 km) from the Hunza Valley above Gilgit to the western borders of Tibet, an unbroken chain of soaring peaks and glacier-filled valleys that, unlike the Himalayas, has no intersecting passes, and is thus virtually inaccessible to travelers or commerce. In the nineteenth century, a few hardy British surveyors had roughly mapped the western end of the Karakorams; aside from these tentative efforts, the forbidding mountains remained almost entirely uncharted and unknown.

Two vast glaciers, Baltoro and Siachen, the highest and largest outside of the Arctic and Antarctic regions, extend along the northern flank of Baltistan. These huge seas of ice and deep, lethal crevasses rise to altitudes of over 22,965 ft. (7,000 meters). Siachen, which means "wild rose" in the Balti language, is the higher of the two.

Siachen marks the eastern end of Baltistan. Here the borders of Chinese Sinkiang, Tibet, and Indian-held Ladakh meet in one of the world's most remote, inhospitable places. Just to the north, an ancient caravan route leads over the 18,290-foot (5,575-meter) Karakoram Pass into Chinese-held Aksai Chin. From there, the unpaved track continues to the desert oasis of Haji Langar, where it connects to the major military road built by China that runs northwest from Tibet, through the icy wastes of Aksai Chin, to Yarkand and Kashgar in Sinkiang.

The Karachi Agreement, signed by Pakistan and India at the end of their 1947 war, demarcated the ceasefire line up to a point on the Shyok River near the southern end of the Siachen Glacier. During the 1947 fighting, Muslim Baltistani forces had advanced to the foot of the glacier, clearing the entire valley of Indian forces. North of the Khaplau region and Nubra Valley, however, the ceasefire line was left undemarcated and notional.

At the time, the region's mountainous geography was only poorly mapped, even less understood, and rightly deemed of no earthly use to anyone. Pakistan was later to claim the border should have extended northeast from the Nubra Valley to the Karakoram Pass, but did not press this point after the 1947 ceasefire. The Indian and Pakistani governments had little interest in the area, and were preoccupied with their violent dispute over Kashmir.

So the situation remained until 1950, when China invaded and occupied Tibet. India was initially alarmed by the Chinese invasion, but was unable to confront both China and Pakistan at the same time. India's leader, Prime Minister Jawaharlal Nehru, was an ardent socialist and leading advocate of Third World political unity against the "imperialist" powers. Nehru much admired Mao Tse-tung and his Chinese revolution; he believed India and China should cooperate closely to dominate and guide Asia. Equally important, Nehru's Fabian socialism held that territorial disputes—the evil fruits of capitalism and imperialism—could not occur between "fraternal socialist nations." India had nothing to fear from China, insisted Nehru.

Nehru's remarkably naïve view of China became official government policy. Delhi simply closed its eyes to China's occupation of

Tibet, hoping the entire nasty business would somehow go away. Nehru seemed to believe that once China had reasserted its ancient political "patronage" over Tibet, Mao would withdraw his troops and allow the remote Himalayan kingdom to slip back into its traditional peaceful obscurity. The 2,500-mile (4,000-km) frontier between China and India was, in Nehru's optimistic phrase, to be "a border of peace."

To Nehru's surprise and chagrin, China did not withdraw its troops, but set about converting Tibet into a Chinese province. Chinese field armies were permanently based in Tibet, supported by new military roads, depots, and airfields, and Han Chinese settlers were brought into Tibet by Beijing. A flood of immigrants followed, eventually turning Tibetans into a minority within their own nation. A brief, abortive effort by the U.S. Central Intelligence Agency and India's intelligence service to mount a rebellion against China's occupation of Tibet was ruthlessly crushed.

Nevertheless, India proclaimed the era of good relations and brotherhood between Delhi and Beijing, known under the charming slogan "Hindi-Chini-Bhai-Bhai," would prevail over mundane questions of borders and territory. Much of India's leadership had only the vaguest notion of the geography of the Himalayas and Karakorams, a region as alien to most Indian plains dwellers as Alaska's mountain ranges would be to residents of southern Alabama.

India's mood of false optimism and the era of Hindi-Chini-Bhai-Bhai was shattered in late 1959 when Chinese troops based in Tibet began to edge into northern Ladakh and disputed regions of Arunachal Pradesh (then called the North Eastern Frontier Agency, or NEFA) along the high, mountainous frontier above East Pakistan and Burma. Beijing claimed it was merely asserting sovereignty over territory that had always belonged to the Chinese Empire. Delhi finally raised the alarm, accused China of illegally occupying 34,740 sq. mi. (90,000 square kilometers) of its territory in Arunachal Pradesh, and began rushing troops to the endangered northern fronts. China forcefully reasserted its claim to the disputed border region above Assam.

Almost unnoticed by Delhi, China also occupied the barren, uninhabited, but strategically important 15,440 sq. mi. (40,000-square-kilometer) region of Aksai Chin near the end of its western border, which had been historically considered part of Ladakh. India claimed that Pakistan had facilitated the Chinese takeover, in return for diplomatic and military support, which is likely true. Delhi became acutely alarmed when it learned China had been building a highly strategic military road for the past three years through Aksai Chin, linking Tibet with Chinese Sinkiang to the west.

As in so many of the Third World's modern territorial disputes, much of the fault for the growing Indian-Chinese border crisis lay with imperial Britain. The British Raj had demarcated India's northern borders with Tibet and Turkestan (now Chinese Sinkiang) in a haphazard and often slipshod manner. Neither region was deemed a threat to India. The British Raj had no commercial interests in Tibet or Central Asia, so both regions were largely ignored, though a wary eye was kept on the Russian Empire, which was slowly expanding south toward the Himalayas and Afghanistan. As a result, the rulers of the British Raj decided to leave the wild mountain ranges and deep valleys of the eastern Himalayas and Ladakh as a sort of no-man's-land between the two rival empires.

In 1914 Sir Henry McMahon, representing Lord Curzon, the viceroy of India, negotiated a treaty with Tibet that delineated the border between the British Raj, Burma, Tibet, and the lands of the local Muslim rulers of Eastern Turkestan. Chinese representatives only observed these negotiations, and refused to sign the resulting agreement. This abstention allowed them to maintain later that the McMahon Line was invalid, had no legal basis, and was an act of colonial arrogance imposed by British imperialists on Tibet's weak religious leadership—which, in any event (according to China), had no authority to negotiate over borders that were rightfully under the mandate of Beijing, the historic overlord of Tibet.

The McMahon Line was roughly drawn and often geographically vague. Legend has it McMahon used a thick-nibbed pen whose broad strokes left many border regions in question. The British-demarcated frontier failed, in many instances, to follow the region's natural topographical divisions of valleys, watersheds, and ridge lines, creating a confused, ill-defined, and fragmented border, a sort of geographical limbo. India and China subsequently published maps that showed large areas of territory claimed by the other side within their own borders. Both nations claimed that what had previously been mutually accepted as a forgotten no-man's-land had actually been under their active administration. It was thus inevitable the two great powers of

Asia that succeeded the British Raj would eventually clash over the poorly demarcated roof of the world.

Nehru, under pressure from his Defense Minister, V.K. Krishna Menon, and his cousin Lt. Gen. B.M. Kaul, and increasingly hard pressed by noisy opposition parties and the jingoistic Indian media, decided in 1960 to confront China. Menon and Kaul proposed a "forward strategy" to solidify Indian claims on the northern border. This hasty, ill-conceived plan called for Indian troops to advance boldly into the disputed territory, edge around Chinese forward posts, and isolate them from their supply lines.

The Indian Army's swift, bloodless 1961 success in taking over the former Portuguese colony of Goa had emboldened the generals of the high command. Furthermore, Menon claimed China was diplomatically isolated, locked in confrontation with both the United States and the Soviet Union, and reeling from the disaster of Mao's Great Leap Forward, in which up to 30 million Chinese peasants died of starvation. China was in no position to resist India, Menon argued, and would fall back without a real fight. Nehru finally gave in to the pressure, deciding the time was ripe to challenge a weakened China.

China's brilliant Foreign Minister Zhou Enlai sought to head off a clash with India by offering to accept India's claims along the eastern end of the McMahon Line in Arunachal Pradesh, a region of little value to China, in return for India's acceptance of China's claims to all of Aksai Chin. In addition, China proposed to drop its historic claim to 40,000 square miles (103,600 sq km) of territory between the McMahon Line and the foothills of the Himalayas above Assam. Delhi, confident in its own military prowess, rejected Zhou's proposal out of hand.

Indian patrols began skirmishing with Chinese units in the high, misty valleys of the North East Frontier Agency (NEFA). In spite of Delhi's decision to go on the offensive, its military buildup was desultory. Some army units, including the famous Fourth Infantry Division, of North Africa fame, were moved up into the mountains. A single division was not enough to defend the long NEFA border, a task that demanded, at the very least, four divisions. Similarly, a single brigade was sent up to Ladakh, when five would have been the minimum for successful offensive operations.

The Indian troops deployed north had few radios capable of

operating in the mountains, were poorly provisioned, lacked warm clothing, and were indifferently led. Worse, the Indians had no accurate military maps of the mountain region. Some Indian units were forced to use old British tourist maps and guidebooks. The Indian troops, or jawans, most of whom were lowlanders, quickly became disoriented and depressed at altitudes of 18,000 feet (5,486 m), and often got lost in the twisting, cloud-shrouded Himalayan valleys as they tried to outflank or envelop Chinese positions.

India's lackadaisical attitude contrasted sharply with China's determination to maintain control of the crest of the Himalayas and cement control of Tibet. The People's Liberation Army (PLA) drove new roads from Lhasa to Ladakh, hard on India's border, established supply dumps, and set up regular communication links to military units deployed along the Himalayan Line of Control. Chinese mountain troops were supplied with accurate maps, and, unlike their Indian opponents, given detailed briefings on the topography around them. The Indians knew almost nothing of what the Chinese were doing; most of Delhi's scant information came from sporadic patrols along the LOC, nomads, and from misinformed diplomats in far-off Beijing.

By contrast, the diligent Chinese had built a network of spies among local mountain tribesmen, who provided accurate information about Indian deployments in forward and rear areas. According to the Indian writer Rajesk Kadian, the Chinese, with admirable Maoist thoroughness, even built prisoner-of-war camps designed to hold 3,000 captives, which he says was a "remarkably accurate assessment as after the war, 3,587 Indian soldiers were taken prisoner."

In one amusing incident, the Chinese set up a little hut of pleasure near the border, in which two attractive Mompa tribeswomen played the role of Himalayan Mata Haris by eliciting military information through pillow-talk from lonely, garrulous Indian officers.

By the fall of 1962, tensions between India and China were at the boiling point; clashes and skirmishes were occurring almost daily at both ends of the Himalayas. India's feisty press and the political opposition beat the war drums, demanding Nehru's government take action to "stop Chinese aggression." Nehru was still loath to jeopardize relations with Mao Tse-tung, but wavered in the face of his general's warnings and rising public clamor for military action. Krishna Menon finally made up Nehru's mind.

The cadaverous and intensely nervous Menon bore a remarkable physical resemblance to Pakistan's consumptive founder, Mohammed Ali Jinnah. Menon was a fiery left-winger who bitterly hated the West and believed India was destined to lead the Third World. Unfortunately, his bombastic oratorical skills far exceeded his knowledge or intelligence. Nehru always put far too much faith in Menon, allowed his erratic and spiteful defense minister to convince him that it was time to launch a full-scale offensive, one the Chinese and would not be able to resist or even react to militarily. India's professional generals thought Menon was a loud-mouthed fool; Menon returned the favor by refusing to listen to their views on the Himalayas, or even the information they gave him about the army's glaring lack of combat-preparedness and logistical weakness.

Krishna Menon assured Nehru the Indian Army was ready and able to evict the Chinese from their encroachments in the NEFA and Ladakh. In September 1962, Nehru reluctantly ordered the army to occupy Indian-claimed areas. Nehru and Menon assumed such action would be the work of only a few days. Indian astrologers consulted the stars and assured Menon the offensive would be a triumphant success. Neither the politicians in Delhi nor the Indian general staff understood the military situation. In fact, very few Indians knew anything about the remote Himalayan border, other than the fact that it was being threatened by China.

The Chinese, of course, did not see themselves as aggressors, but as the liberators of territory that was rightfully Chinese. In truth, some of the areas and border posts claimed by India actually lay, according to nineteenth-century British Raj maps, within Tibetan and Chinese territory.

At first, India's offensive advanced without serious challenge. Chinese forces fell back steadily. But a month after Indian troops had occupied substantial portions of the disputed border zones, the Chinese counterattacked. On October 20, 1962, four Chinese mountain divisions attacked points along the eastern border, and in Ladakh. The Indians quickly found themselves outgunned, outmaneuvered, and outsmarted by the veteran Chinese troops. India's jawans had not been trained in mountain warfare, their equipment was obsolete, and their officers were out of their depth.

The Chinese People's Liberation Army (PLA) employed the same tactics in the Himalayas and Ladakh that had proven so successful against U.S. troops in the mountains of Korea. Chinese troops were trained to pin down heavily defended hilltop positions by frontal attacks, then edge around the enemy flanks, and attack from the rear. Thanks to redoubtable marching skill and a light logistical tail that was not dependent on roads, Chinese infantry could cover great distances over rough terrain that would be considered impassable by heavily laden Western armies.

The PLA's ability to move men and supplies swiftly over broken ground by day or night gave it remarkable flexibility and mobility, allowing the Chinese to avoid or bypass enemy strongpoints. In Korea, mountains proved ideal tactical topography for China's fluid infantry tactics. Time after time, PLA units worked around dug-in UN units, or drove deep into U.S. defense lines by crossing unguarded mountain ridges where road-bound American troops could not follow or operate.

After heavy fighting, Indian forces at both ends of the frontier were thrown into full retreat. In the second week of November, Chinese troops launched a major offensive against Indian positions around the key strongpoint of Bomdi La, the gateway from the high mountains to the wide plains of Assam. Indian units were battered by artillery, pinned down, then outflanked by Chinese thrusts over the mountains. In Ladakh, the PLA assaulted the Indians on a 250-mile (400-km) front. There, however, unlike in the NEFA, the Chinese made slower progress, though they again pushed the defending Indians steadily back.

By the third week of November 1962, Indian defense lines in the NEFA were broken. After the battle of Bomdi La the victorious Chinese were poised to debouch from the Himalayas into Assam. Calcutta lay only 300 undefended miles (480 km) to the south. Panic erupted in Delhi. A deeply humiliated Nehru abandoned his most cherished beliefs in anti-imperialism, swallowed his considerable pride, and begged the United States to send aircraft to bomb the advancing Chinese, with nuclear weapons if necessary, he pointedly added.

Then, on November 21, China stunned everyone by announcing a unilateral ceasefire, and a withdrawal of its troops behind the disputed Line of Control: in other words, a return to the prewar status quo. Chairman Mao, ever the artful psychologist, thus added humiliation to India's military debacle. Beijing announced its army had "taught India a lesson." Indeed it had. The defeat left India reeling in shock, and unwilling to challenge China in the Himalayas or Ladakh for the next thirty years.

Nehru was stunned and emotionally shattered. The disaster left him a broken man, and his health began to fail. He was as devastated as his friend and ally Gamal Abdel Nasser had been by the calamitous defeat inflicted on Egypt by Israel in 1967. Nehru died less than two years later.

The 1962 disaster led India to quickly expand and rearm its military forces. New mountain divisions were formed, and accurate surveys were begun of the hitherto uncharted Himalayan and Ladakh border regions. Disputed Kashmir suddenly assumed heightened strategic importance as Delhi worried that China had designs on the mountain state, or that it might join Pakistan in a coordinated assault on northern India. Most important, India's leaders became convinced China represented a long-term territorial rival. In 1963, India began secret development of a nuclear weapons program.

For the next twenty years, India steadily shored up its defenses in the Himalayas and Ladakh. When Pakistan and China agreed to begin construction of an all-weather road, the Karakoram Highway (not to be confused with the Karakoram Pass), linking Gilgit with Sinkiang, alarm bells began to ring in Delhi. India feared that in time of war Chinese troops would be able to reinforce northern Pakistan via this route, even though the narrow, perilous highway snaked over high mountains and was often blocked by landslides or snow, and could be easily interdicted by bombing or commando raids.

Construction of the Karakoram Highway and Indian anger over the loss of Aksai Chin to China spurred Delhi to begin expanding its military influence in the remote, undemarcated mountain regions north of Ladakh, and around the Siachen Glacier.

In the late 1970s, a series of mountaineering expeditions led by Indian Army officers began exploring and surveying the peaks in the Siachen-Baltoro-Kangri region. At first, Pakistan accepted these expeditions as purely scientific and did not react. But in 1983 the Indians lifted an entire mountain battalion by helicopter onto the eastern side of the Siachen Glacier. A series of permanent military posts were constructed there in April 1984, generally at elevations of 8,000 to 16,000 feet (2,438 to 4,876 m). That same year Indian forces deployed forward, digging in atop the glacier, commanding its highest points and most important features. This gave the Indians an important tactical advantage, but made the task of supplying them extremely arduous and hazardous.

India's military intrusion into what had been an undemarcated no-man's-land deeply alarmed Islamabad. Pakistan became convinced the Indians were embarked on a grand strategy to advance westward into Baltistan and occupy Skardu. Using Skardu and its large airfield as a main operating base, the Indians, it was feared, would then drive into the Gilgit Valley, thus severing the Karakoram Highway, Pakistan's sole land link to its most important ally, China. Some Pakistani strategists, deeply concerned by India's fast-growing strategic alliance with the USSR, even claimed India was bent on invading Chinese Sinkiang, capturing the vital road junction of Kashgar, and then linking up in the Pamirs with Soviet forces in the Soviet Socialist Republic of Kirgiz.

As a result, Pakistan rushed troops to Siachen, and began building bases in the Khapalu Valley to support them. The glacier, 50 miles (80 km) long, and rising to an average altitude of 20,000 feet (6,096 m), quickly became the world's most improbable and difficult battlefield. Indian and Pakistani mountain units began a dramatic race to occupy the remaining peaks commanding the glacier. Infantry battles, with machine guns, mortars, rockets, and artillery, raged between the two sides in a desperate effort to deny the enemy superior ground. By 1984, the two foes had deployed a total of some 10,000 troops at Siachen. That same year, they fought one of the largest battles on Siachen, supported by heavy artillery and rocket batteries, each suffering losses of around one hundred dead.

The Pakistanis held one important tactical advantage at Siachen. Their troops on the glacier, dug in at elevations from 9,000 to 15,000 feet (2,743–4,572 m), could be supplied by a land route from Skardu to the Khapalu Valley. From bases and depots at Khapalu, men and supplies could be brought up to the glacier by jeep or truck, then moved to forward positions by mule, or on porters' backs. The Pakistanis were able to move 130mm guns onto the glacier, bringing many of the Indians' positions atop and behind Siachen within range.

By contrast, the Indians had no land route to their generally higher positions on the glacier: the terrain on the Indian-controlled side was too rough and steep to allow vehicular traffic. The Indians were forced to move men and supplies north from their main operational base in

Ladakh at Kargil, up to camps in the Nubra Valley at the foot of the Siachen Glacier. From there, every soldier, bullet and shell had to be laboriously transported by porter, pack animal, or helicopter onto the glacier. Indian artillery was forced to locate at the base of the glacier, putting the guns out of range of the Pakistani logistics bases at Khapalu. Supplying the three Indian battalions deployed at Siachen with ammunition and combat supplies became an arduous and enormously costly operation. Expenditure of heavy-artillery ammunition alone by the two sides at Siachen amounted to some 80,000 rounds annually.

In early 1999, India began work on a road from its forward supply bases to the glacier, a route that had to cross numerous 18,000-foot (5,486-m) passes frequently blocked by landslides and avalanches. The cost of such an undertaking is huge, particularly for a nation in which a third of the citizens subsist in dire poverty, but India seemed determined to dominate Siachen at all costs and, just as important, deny it to the hated Pakistanis.

The air at Siachen's altitude is only half as dense as at sea level. This meant helicopters were able to lift only a quarter of their normal load—or even less, depending on the altitude to which they sought to fly. In many cases, Indian helicopters could only carry one or two soldiers or a few boxes of ammunition or food to the glacier's top. Resupply for the Indians, and to a somewhat lesser but still painful degree for the Pakistanis, became an agonizingly slow, tedious process that put men and machines under enormous, punishing strain. Frequent severe weather and violent storms made all air and ground movement extremely risky and unreliable. Accidents killed as many men as enemy fire.

It was, as one Indian officer told me, "like fighting a war on the moon." And that was just the problem of logistics. The terrible cold and extreme altitude atop the glacier was equally and undiscriminatingly murderous to soldiers and journalists alike, as I would shortly discover.

13
Musa the Warrior

Captain Aziz and I set off at dawn from Skardu in a green Toyota Land Cruiser. Aziz was a thin, wiry Punjabi from Multan, in the south, with a ready smile, a cheerful disposition, and (I happily noted) well-developed driving skills. We followed the mighty Indus for some hours, skirting its banks and its gravelly alluvial plain, over what purported to be a road, at least on the military map he provided me with, but which was in truth no better than a rough dirt track, with occasional patches of gravel where water flowed down, pitted with deep, treacherous holes that seemed designed to break axles. Shaky bridges of wooden planking crossed dry water courses, or *nullahs*, that intersected the track. Land Cruisers are not built for creature comforts; their dour Japanese designers seemed to have forgotten, or never learned, the use of springs.

The view along the Indus was magnificent. To our left extended the unbroken wall of the snow-clad Karakorams, a gigantic maze of peaks stretching to the far horizon. The thin air and strong sun etched the mountains in sharp detail. Above us, the cloudless sky was an intense cobalt blue. Birds wheeled in rising currents of air as the morning cool dissipated and the day grew warmer.

At Gol, we crossed a swaying wooden plank bridge suspended, from concrete pillars at either end, over the boiling, dark waters of the Indus. Every 10 miles (16 km) or so, a small, decrepit village of mud bricks stood by the side of the track. As we passed, villagers waved to us, or stared in curiosity. All about, the dun-colored land was parched and sere, a high-altitude desert set beneath the radiant snows of the distant mountains.

After Gol, we continued on a southeast bearing for Khapalu along the wide banks of the Indus. Khapalu is described as the most important town in the region, but it turned out to be no more than another miserable collection of shacks and warehouses, a sort of miniature version of Skardu. A large wooden suspension bridge moored to two imposing concrete arches spanned another, almost equally turbulent river, the Shyok. After clattering over it, Aziz and I stopped to admire the view of the rushing river, then continued our arduous drive, heading in the general direction of the narrow valley of the Saltoro River, which flows down from the Siachen Glacier.

What had been a dirt road along the Shyok soon degenerated into a pitted rock track that seemed to be shaking the life out of the jeep and its riders. We could drive at no more than 10 miles per hour (16 km/h) for fear of breaking an axle; even so, clouds of dust and grit covered us, filling our mouths, ears, and eyes. I held on for dear life as the jeep jolted and swayed violently.

At numerous points, landslides or large boulders obstructed the route. Somehow, the intrepid Capt. Aziz managed to maneuver the jeep over or around them, sometimes with only an inch to spare. We had occasionally to fill deep holes in the track with rocks. Aziz warned me to keep a constant watch for rockslides. It would take only a one or two falling chunks of rock to push us into the river below.

In the afternoon, we entered a fairly flat region with broad, green fields of wheat that offered a welcome contrast to the arid wastes we had lately crossed. Balti women, clothed in gaily colored yellow and blue robes, were working in the lush fields.

"We are coming to an oasis village I call 'the little paradise,'" announced Captain Aziz. Indeed, after the near-desert landscapes we had seen, the hamlet did seem rather magical. It looked, I thought, like the Holy Koran's vision of paradise, a place of running water, greenery, orchards, and handsome women. Waterfalls cascaded down the sides of a steep cliff bordering the village, becoming rivulets of bubbling silver that coursed around its humble mud-brick buildings, and copses of slender trees. The little cultivated plots were intersected by a chessboard of irrigation ditches carrying streams of cold, clear mountain water. Birds and butterflies from many miles around flocked to the oasis, congregating noisily in its fruit trees and willows.

A British adventurer of the last century described the oasis villages of Baltistan as looking like "bits of some other country cut out with a pair of scissors and dropped into a desert: a cloudless region, always burning or freezing, under the clear blue sky."

We reclined and lunched beside a brook, beneath tall, leafy trees that offered shelter from the sun, gratefully relaxing in the cool, moist air. I went to the waterfall and washed off the dust that covered me from head to foot. A group of smiling Balti villagers came to offer us fruits from their orchards, bowls of nuts, and milky-white tea. The women, I noted, were far taller and more attractive than the ones I had seen in seedy Skardu. Children eyed us shyly, pointing at the strange farangi who had come to their little paradise. I drank hungrily and deeply from the waterfall, whose cold, clear waters tasted delicious, an extremely rare luxury in a part of the world where groundwater is almost always perilous to all but the most inured natives.

I wondered if the writer James Hilton had used this village, or one much like it, as the setting of his famed novel, *Lost Horizon*, in which a British diplomat crash-lands somewhere in the Himalayas, and discovers the lost valley of Shangri-La, an Eden whose kind, gentle people never grow old. There must be hidden valleys here in Baltistan, I mused, places no Westerners had ever visited, where the arcane secrets and magic of Tibet's red-hat lamas were still preserved. In some lost lamasery of Baltistan there had to be a sacred text explaining how the legendary high priests of Tibet were able to live for hundreds of years. Still pondering these thoughts, I fell into a deep, gentle sleep beside the banks of the rushing stream.

An hour later we set off again along the bank of the river. After two more hours of driving we left the track, and worked our way up a long slope. Capt. Aziz halted the jeep, got out, and motioned me to follow him. We climbed up a steep ridge that rose to our right. Just below the crest, Aziz ordered, "Stay low."

I cautiously stuck my head above the ridge and had a quite sudden and horrible attack of vertigo. We were on the edge of an enormous precipice that fell at least 1¼ miles (2 km) straight down into a distant valley below. It was the kind of terrifying drop about which I'd had recurrent nightmares over the years: clinging by my fingernails to the edge of a cliff, slowly loosing my grip, and then falling screaming into the abyss.

We had reached the crest of the Ladakh mountain range, which extends from northwest to southeast along Tibet's western border—and the Line of Control between Indian Ladakh and Pakistani territory. Before us lay a panorama of snow-capped mountains, forested hills, and glittering rivers that reminded me of the glorious vistas of Switzerland's Bernese Oberland—magnified by a factor of ten. From where we crouched, the vast sweep of Kashmir and Ladakh extended below us, framed, to the south, by the soaring range of the Zanskar

Mountains. Beyond the Zanskar lay the vale of Kashmir, and below that the flat, endless, steamy plains of northern India. In the thin, dry air, distant objects appear close. One's sense of distance and proportion becomes confused. Yaks on a far-off slope seem but a few minutes' walk away. A single tree that is plainly visible may be a day's walk distant. Sound, too, distorts in the mountains, playing strange tricks on the ears.

"Look, there. Kargil." Aziz pointed to a town at the confluence of three rivers in the valley below us. "Keep your head down," he warned. "The Indians watch this ridge."

Kargil was Ladakh's second-largest town after the capital, Leh, and the main operating and logistics base for Indian Army units at the Siachen Glacier. Even from afar, Kargil was unprepossessing, a haphazard collection of wooden buildings and storehouses with a small bazaar in the middle that bore evident signs of occasional shelling by Pakistani artillery during periodic border flare-ups. From Kargil, a narrow Indian military road followed the old caravan route, winding northeast up into the Nubra Valley to the foot of the Indian side of the Siachen Glacier.

In May 1999, some 800 Kashmiri mujahedin crossed the LOC and seized the 16,000-foot ridge line from which we were peering down on Kargil. From their vantage points, the mujihadin were able to bring down fire, and target Pakistani artillery, on the strategic Kargil-Leh military road. India's main ammunition dump near Kargil was blown up, destroying 80,000 howitzer shells.

India launched a series of violet counter-offensives to regain the heights above Kargil, Drass Batalik, and the Mushkoh Valley, employing up to two mountain divisions, Gurkhas, heavy artillery, and round-the-clock air strikes. As Delhi and Islamabad traded threats of war, and Indian generals threatened to attack Pakistan south of Kashmir, Indian strike corps in Punjab and the Thar Desert moved to offensive deployments. Pakistani forces went on full alert. India and Pakistan were within hours of full-scale war. There were reports that both sides had armed and deployed some of their nuclear weapons.

The heavy fighting raged for eight weeks, costing India at least 1,200 casualties, two warplanes, and a helicopter. The worst fighting between India and Pakistan in thirty years deeply alarmed the U.S., which brought intensive pressure to bear on Pakistan to pull back the *mujahedin*, who could not have gone into action without logistic and artillery support from the Pakistani army. Prime Minister Nawaz Sharif was forced to order the *mujahedin* back; Pakistan was widely blamed around the world for starting the fighting. But as a result of the surprise attack, the Kashmir dispute had suddenly become internationalized, and it dominated international headlines for two months.

We left our lookout and resumed driving. The rising terrain became more alpine, dotted with dark boulders, runnels of gray gravel, and heaps of glacial rock. As we struggled over the terrible, tooth-rattling rock track, I held on grimly as each jolt sent spasms of pain through my tensed, aching back muscles. Once again, we were covered in dust and blasted by the fierce, unfiltered sunlight. The road led up, and then further up the side of a huge massif of dark, striated rock.

After more agony, we reached the top of the Bilafond Pass at 15,609 feet (4,757 m). Before me, a wall of sheer, light gray peaks rose about 10 miles (16 km) from our position, raw, serrated and jagged, set against the backdrop of an intensely blue sky and thin wisps of cloud. A vast, utterly still lake, perhaps 6 miles (10 km) in length and 3 miles (5 km) in width, lay at the foot of the mountain wall, reflecting with mirror-like clarity the sharp peaks behind. I had never seen such wild mountains. They bore none of the rounded, weathered maturity of America's or Europe's peaks: they were young, powerful, menacing. Witch's peaks, I thought, a setting that reminded me of Mussorgsky's sinister tone poem *St. John's Night on the Bare Mountain*.

We skirted along a huge mountain that formed the right flank of the motionless lake, edging along the increasingly narrow track that had been hewn into the cliffside. The track was just wide enough for the jeep: one side was a wall of crumbling rock, on the other a sheer, almost vertical drop some thousands of feet into the water below. There was no guardrail or any sort of barrier to prevent us flying over the precipice. From time to time, the track narrowed. I watched with fascinated horror as we half projected over the void. Captain Aziz inched forward, his knuckles white on the steering wheel.

A boulder lay on the track. We stopped to study the new obstacle. We felt tiny, like ants struggling up the side of an alp. I could see the track as it extended ahead for many miles: it looked like a thread laid halfway up the side of a mountain. Vertigo and agoraphobia—the fear of open space—gripped me. I felt insignificant, minute, a speck of dust in a landscape of titans. There was no sign that any other humans had ever been in this land of the gods.

The dauntless Aziz managed to circumvent the boulder, but not before our jeep had first the front wheel, then the rear, hanging in the air. "Be ready to jump if we start going over," he cried. At least, I thought ruefully, I will have the world's most beautiful view as I die.

A half-mile (1 km) farther on, a shower of small rocks peppered us. Soon after, an avalanche of boulders came crashing down in front of the jeep. There was no shelter. We could not turn around. "Allah keep us safe," exclaimed Aziz. I heartily concurred, as we bounced grimly onward. An hour later, we had to shoo a reluctant bovine, half yak, half cow, off the track where it had decided to spend the afternoon.

We descended into a steep valley, worked our way up over a col between two peaks, then down into another long, narrow valley covered with broken rocks. The air was getting thinner; there was a rising chill. "We are getting close to the border with Tibet," Aziz told me. "It's just there, over that next range of mountains." Mysterious, forbidden Tibet, which I had so longed to visit, lay hidden from our view only by a single range of mountains. We could have hiked there in a few days, I mused.

Darkness was falling. Night always comes early in high mountain valleys. The rapidly setting sun tinged the soaring peaks above us with ocher, a ribbon of gold, magenta, and then red. After another hour of laborious driving, we came to a small village built on either side of a fast-flowing mountain stream. A group of low, evil-looking mud huts with wooden plank roofs held down by large rocks clustered together. Skinny, cranky goats and a few chickens milled about. Faces peered out at us from unlit doorways. An air of abandon and misery hung over this grim little hamlet, lost in the darkening mountains.

Aziz led me into a large hut. An overpowering stink of smoke, sweat, rotting refuse, and goat fat filled the squalid enclosure. It was very dark inside, illuminated only by a single kerosene lantern and a large fire in the stone hearth in the middle of the hovel. At first, I thought we were alone, but as my eyes grew accustomed to the darkness, I discerned six or seven figures standing in the darkness beyond the pool of light thrown off by the fire and flickering kerosene lantern.

The figures lurched and stumbled toward us. They were very small men, none over 5 feet 2 inches (1.6 m) in height, terribly scrawny, and obviously malnourished, with features typical of the Tibetan high-lands: broad foreheads; limp, dirty hair; almond eyes; and sallow, yel-low skins. The villagers wore an assortment of rags and threadbare shawls. Their faces and hands were covered with dirt and grime.

I was introduced to the village elders, who greeted us fairly warmly, offering thick, oily tea in battered tin cups that had obviously never been washed. As we sat and talked through Aziz, who knew some Balti, I noted other figures, boys and a few women, crouching in the shad-ows, staring with rapt fascination at the strange visitors from another planet. The fire made the air inside hot and fetid. I longed to escape but could not, as we were being served dinner, an experience that I knew would prove both ghastly and potentially lethal.

A tin bowl of some unidentifiable brown, malodorous sludge was put into my hands, along with a small wheel of flat barley bread. I pushed the Balti stew around in the bowl, pretending to eat it—a trick I had learned in Africa when confronted with "bush stew," and devoured the bread. Soon after we finished, three more figures emerged from the gloom beyond the firelight. They stumbled forward and gib-bered at us, faces contorted, eyes empty of reason, saliva running from their toothless, gaping mouths. One came up and put a filthy hand on my face. I was revolted, but steeled myself lest I insult our hosts and provoke an angry response from these strange Balti mountain people.

Aziz explained to me that this village was notorious for its high number of mental defectives. "But most of the villages here are like this," he said. "There is no iodine in their food or water, and the vil-lagers become crazy or sick as a result."

Iodine deficiency is the curse of high mountain dwellers. Decades earlier, I had seen the same malady in some of Switzerland's remote val-leys. Lack of dietary iodine caused thyroid deficiencies and Down's syndrome. Iodized salt had eliminated this affliction in Europe, but here in Tibet, and across the wide sweep of the Himalayas and Karakorams, lack of iodine and other vital nutrients—notably vitamins A, B, and C—caused a wide variety of easily preventable disorders, and a generalized weakening of immune systems that left the mountain dwellers vulnerable to other diseases, both acute and debilitating. Virtually all of the inhabitants of the mountain regions from Afghanistan to Burma also suffer from endemic parasites that further weaken them and curtail their short, brutish lives.

After dinner, we crawled into sleeping bags and huddled close to the dwindling fire. From the darkness came strange grunts and scurryings. I wondered if we would be murdered in our sleep for our possessions, and forced myself to sleep with one eye open—or so I thought. In fact, I fell into a deep sleep. Suddenly, I was awakened by a hand on my face. Another of the village defectives was stroking my face. He had never seen a European or North American and was fascinated, I subsequently learned, by my fair skin.

We left the village before dawn, eager to be well away from this pestilential place. For most of a day, we jolted and bumped over a rock track that led ever upward toward the mountain ridges above. The air became thinner still, cold and crisp. At least the clouds of gritty dust that had previously engulfed us were gone. There was almost no vegetation save lichens and green-gray moss. Water poured down the steep slopes of the Saltoro Pass, collecting into frigid pools, splashing around boulders, spraying into the air. I saw almost no sign of animal life but an occasional herd of wooly yaks grazing on high pastures, and, twice, mountain goats on the edge of the snowfields above us.

Toward dusk, we saw the twinkle of electric lights in the distance. They seemed a quite magical apparition in this primitive wilderness. Darkness fell just as we picked our way down into another valley, over which towered an enormous massif of rock, snow, and ice. We had finally reached Dansum, elevation 8,400 feet (2,560 m), the foot of the mighty Siachen Glacier, a 50-mile (80-km) river of ice that flowed imperceptibly down from the massifs of Masherbrun and mighty K-2.

The Pakistani army's main operating base for the Siachen campaign was a collection of whitewashed buildings with metal roofs, barracks, storehouses, munitions depot, a field hospital, and a landing pad for helicopters. A flagpole, neatly surrounded by white stones, stood at the center of the camp, a cheery reminder of the outside world that we had left so far behind. The camp was a tiny dot of civilization utterly lost in a vast wilderness of mountains and unexplored valleys; it reminded me more of an isolated scientific station on the coast of Antarctica than an army base.

After showering off layers of grime and dust, we went to the officers' mess for dinner. A cheery fire burned and crackled in a large stone fireplace, on whose mantelpiece reposed numerous regimental trophies and plates. A long table filled most of the room, and around it sat about twenty army officers. Military pictures and unit pennants hung on the whitewashed walls. It could have been a British Army regimental mess on the wild Northwest Frontier a century ago. The only difference was the location, and the darker-hued faces of the trim, tough-looking Pakistani officers.

I was introduced to the colonel commanding the base and to his subordinates. All appeared quite delighted to have some company in this outpost at the very end of the world. Suddenly, a tall officer I had not previously seen came up from behind me, put his hand on my shoulder, and said, "My dear Eric, how nice to see you again. We meet in such strange places!"

Indeed. The first time I met Colonel Youssef was in Peshawar, on the Northwest Frontier. The second was inside Afghanistan, when the wiry, 6-foot-4-inch (1.9-m) Pathan officer had been seconded to Pakistan's Inter-Service Intelligence and was busy directing Afghan mujahedin in the great *jihad* against the Communists. A few years later, we met again in Peshawar, this time with his chief, the courageous soldier and fierce Islamic warrior Lt. Gen. Javid Nasser, director general of ISI, Inter-Service Intelligence, Pakistan's military intelligence service. Upon my return from Afghanistan, General Nasser had touched me deeply by giving me his personal, annotated copy of the Holy Koran, a mark of the highest respect and affection among observant Muslims.

Colonel Youssef now bore the silver insignia of the Black Panthers, Pakistan's elite commando unit that was employed in especially dangerous or politically sensitive operations. We joked, swapped war stories, and laughed our way through dinner. I told Youssef and his fellow officers about wars I had seen in other mountain regions: Lebanon, eastern Anatolia, Abkhazia in the majestic Caucasus, northern Yemen, Burma, and Iraqi Kurdistan. All mountain wars, we concluded, were the same: all that mattered was holding the highest ground and ridge lines—and getting adequate supplies up to the troops. Armies that knew how to fight on foot, and march—like the Chinese—were superior to round-bound armies, spoiled by always riding to war on wheels.

Youssef surprised me by recalling an offhand remark I'd made years before in Peshawar. My mother, who was born in northern Greece, grew up in Albania, a tiny, mountainous Balkan land that much resembled in topography, tribal customs, and warlike spirit the uplands of Scotland, and the bellicose Pathans of Pakistan's Northwest Frontier. I have no doubt whatsoever that my love for fierce mountaineers and sympathy with their hopeless struggles against invading lowlanders was genetic in origin.

"I've studied the campaigns against the Turks of the great Albanian hero, Skenderbeg," Youssef continued, to my amazement. "He was one of history's finest mountain warriors."

Casually discussing fifteenth-century Albania in a lost valley next to the border of Tibet! It seemed hallucinatory. As I explained how Skenderbeg and his mountaineers had ambushed and annihilated the Sultan's armies in the mountain defiles of Albania, firelight played over the dark walls of the mess. To these modern warriors, battles fought five hundred years ago had as much to teach, as much importance and passion, as those conducted a year before. War was war. Technology and equipment might change, but the laws and conduct of the art of war are immutable. The campaigns of Skenderbeg and Xenophon held as much relevance for these professional soldiers as Vietnam, or their last war with India.

I recalled the dictum that, compared to war, all man's other efforts seem trivial. Here I was, happily among comrades who were not afraid to avow their love of combat and the profession of arms. We in the West can no longer openly admit the potent appeal war holds for many men. Instead, we hide behind the justification that war is a necessary evil, forced upon our reluctant selves purely for the sake of self-defense.

I finally took my leave of the officers, returned to my simple room, and gratefully crawled into my sleeping bag. It was very cold. My nose clogged up; my breathing grew shallow; and my heart seemed to beat with abnormal force. I had a minor headache. These were the early signs of altitude stress. I'd first experienced these symptoms in Cuzco, Peru, at about 9,000 feet (2,743 m) in the Andes. We were at roughly the same elevation, exactly the altitude at which oxygen deprivation begins to be felt. It had probably been coming on all afternoon and evening, but our slow ascent, the excitement of the adventure, and the cheery evening in the mess had masked the symptoms from me until now.

High altitude also causes insomnia. I tossed and turned in my sleeping bag for what seemed hours, struggling to take deep breaths of air, and aching all over from the punishing jeep ride. I drank half a pint (280 ml) of vodka that I had secreted in my bag. Drinking is contraindicated at altitude, but the spirit finally helped send me off to a troubled, fitful sleep. I dreamed of Albania, mountains, and more mountains.

At dawn, Captain Aziz and I breakfasted on hearty porridge and mugs of sweet chai, bade farewell to our last evening's companions, and set off in our trusty Land Cruiser. We immediately began ascending a steep rock track that began near the camp, zigzagging up the side of the Siachen massif. The jeep struggled in the thin air over what seemed an endless, mind-numbing series of sharp switchbacks. Soon, the barracks of the camp we had left below appeared the size of matchboxes. Higher and higher we climbed, clinging precariously to the narrow track chiseled into the side of the massif.

Late in the morning, we finally reached our destination. The gray crags opened up, forming a small, flat valley nestled among snow-capped peaks. Clustered in the middle were four low buildings and numerous supply bunkers. A Pakistani flag whipped in the stiff breeze. We had reached Al-Badr Camp, the base of the 25th Punjabi Regiment's "Siachen Angels."

Five officers stood waiting for me. All were burned black by the powerful sun and strong winds. They wore heavy brown sweaters, berets or knitted mountain caps, thick black beards, and mountaineer's sunglasses with one-way, silvered lenses and side flaps. After saluting, the shortest of the officers, a stocky broad-chested man, stepped forward to greet me. He beamed a radiant smile that revealed from the undergrowth of his formidable beard a set of pure white teeth. "Greeting, Mr. Eric, be welcome! You are our honored guest. I am Colonel Musa of the 25th Punjabis."

I took an immediate liking to Colonel Musa. He had an infectious smile and a cheerful warmth that seemed not at all in conflict with the awe and fearful respect he inspired in his men. Musa radiated fierce energy. He proudly showed me around his small base, introduced me to the rest of his officers, then took me for a quick lunch of pungent goat curry and tea in the unit's spartan mess.

Musa's men put on demonstrations of rock-climbing, crossing streams on ropes, and live-firing exercises, during which I blasted a distant pile of rock with a medium machine gun, earning praise from the beaming Colonel Musa for my tight, accurate tracer bursts, an art I had learned as a infantryman and combat engineer in the U.S. Army. I also fired a Chinese 12.7mm pedestal-mounted heavy machine gun, watching the big shells sail through the air to their target.

Soon after, we marched forward about half a mile (1 km) to another flat open area, where two Chinese-made 130mm guns were positioned under camouflage netting. Their crews stood at the ready. That morning, Indian artillery on the opposite side of the Siachen massif had been shelling Pakistani positions. Colonel Musa had thoughtfully delayed his riposte until I arrived.

Higher up, and farther forward on the glacier, a Pakistani artillery spotter was radioing in the coordinates of the Indian guns. An officer listened intently on headphones, noting the fire coordinates on a grid map, and performing calculations of temperature, wind speed, and humidity. He barked orders. The guns were elevated, and adjusted in azimuth. I looked at the long-barreled, green-painted 130s with a certain awe. Originally produced by the Soviet Union and later copied by China, these were the notoriously deadly pieces that had so often routed South Vietnamese army units during the Vietnam War. They were greatly feared by American troops who, until the 130s arrived, had never had to face artillery more powerful than mortars. The guns were old, but deadly accurate, long-range, and fast to reload; they could even fire on a flat trajectory, making them useful for direct combat support and antitank defense.

A corporal waved a red flag, giving the order to fire. I was standing about 20 feet (6 km) behind the first gun. When it was fired, I was blown off my feet. The air atop Siachen was too thin to buffer the concussion of the exploding propellant charges. As I struggled to my feet, the second 130mm fired. The shock waves again knocked me over. The Pakistani gun crews laughed uproariously. I backed off and braced myself for the next volley.

The 130mm shells arced up and away from our position, disappearing over a ridge. About thirty seconds later came a dull report as the shells exploded, then echoes and more echoes, and echoes of echoes, bouncing off the sides of the mountains. "In winter, when the snows are thick," explained a gunnery officer, "we must be careful when we fire that we don't cause an avalanche onto our own positions."

The big 130s loosed another dozen rounds, then ceased fire. The officer who had been manning the radio spoke intently to the forward artillery observers on the ridge above. He then jumped up with a big smile, calling out the ancient Islamic battle cry, "Allah Akbar!" God is great! The forward observer reported five direct hits on the Indian artillery positions, causing two secondary explosions and silencing the enemy guns. Everyone cheered lustily and cried, "Allah Akbar!" Today, Pakistan had won a small skirmish in the long, bitter struggle to control the world's highest battlefield.

The next morning, after a semi-sleepless night induced by the high altitude, I climbed higher up the glacier with Colonel Musa and a party of his men. The ascent over broken, wet rock was extremely steep, and at times perilous. While filming, I accidentally stepped into a deep pool of frigid water. I then had the extremely curious experience of being soaking wet and extremely cold from the waist down while the rest of me was baking in the hot sun.

Above us, the sky was an intense blue. Snow-clad mountain peaks surrounded us on every side. The high-altitude cold was kept at bay by the power of the unfiltered sunlight. As we passed 14,000 feet (4,267 m), each step became more and more laborious. My heart pounded alarmingly. I gasped for breath and my head began to throb with pain. We stopped often to drink water. High altitudes, like deserts, are lethally dehydrating. Unless one consumes large quantities of water, the kidneys seize up and may cease functioning. Fighter pilots and mountaineers are almost always very thin: they exist in a constant state of semi-dehydration caused by strong sun, heat, and high altitude.

By noon, we arrived at a broad, flat plain of pure white snow. It reminded me of Greenland seen from the air at 33,000 feet (10,000 m), an enormous, white, featureless nothingness extending away into a hazy infinity. We had finally reached the area of the Conway Saddle, at about 16,000 feet (4,876 m) one of the higher Pakistani positions on Siachen. The air was extremely thin, bone-dry, and bitterly cold, rather like dry ice. The azure sky above seemed close enough to grasp in my hands. A wave of vertigo overcame me. I felt I might fly upward at any moment and be lost in the blue sea above. The world seemed to spin. I wanted to lie down and cling to the ground with my hands and feet. The altitude and lack of oxygen were numbing my body and brain. It was a beautiful but terrifying place. Never in my life had I climbed so high on foot. The summit of great Everest, the world's highest mountain, was only 13,000 feet (3,962 m) higher than where we stood.

My Pakistani companions knelt down in the snow and said their midday prayers. I thought how very odd it was to see men in thick, quilted Arctic parkas and sunglasses bowing down in the snow and praying to the god of the distant Arabian desert, 16,000 feet (4,876 m) below us and 1,800 miles (2,896 km) away to the west. Colonel Musa led the prayers at the top of the world....."Bismillah, ar-Rahman, ar-Rahim...in the name of Allah, the most gracious, the most merciful, praise be to Allah, the cherisher and sustainer of the worlds, most gracious, most merciful, master of the Day of Judgement, Thee do we worship, And Thine aid we seek...."

We had tea at a sandbagged Pakistani forward post atop an icy knoll. A half-mile (1 km) farther on lay Indian positions. During periodic flare-ups, the heavily armed Indians and Pakistanis would use mortars and anti-aircraft weapons, such as 14.5mm, 37mm, and 57mm guns, to fire at one another's positions. The big 37mm and 57mm shells were particularly devastating against sandbagged positions, and could chew their way through thick concrete.

Colonel Musa showed me a commanding peak for which the Pakistanis and Indians had fought bitterly. "We spotted a group of Indian soldiers trying to reach the peak, which looks down on our positions and makes a perfect artillery observation post," the colonel explained. "We had to stop them." He told me the story.

A Pakistani helicopter took off from Dansum. However, the contested peak atop Siachen was so high, the helicopter could carry only one soldier up into the thin air. A lone Pakistani commando with a light machine gun was lifted up to the top of the peak. He rappeled down a rope from the helicopter, which was struggling to hover in the thin air and gusty winds. Just as the Indians reached the top of the peak, the Pakistani officer opened fire, killing some, and driving off the rest. They fired at him and threw grenades, wounding him severely. But the Pakistani held on until another soldier was brought up, then another. Thanks to this little Thermopylae, the Pakistanis managed to retain control of the strategic peak, and thus prevent the Indians from directing artillery fire onto their vulnerable rear areas.

The forward Pakistani positions that cover the 48-mile (77-km) front, or line of contact, consisted of snow-covered bunkers and trenches, reinforced by sandbags and piles of rock. Each was garrisoned by a squad of mountain troops whose principal task was to keep watch on the no-man's-land between them and the Indian advance posts. These front-line posts had to be reinforced and provisioned under cover of darkness. Because of the mountainous terrain, most of the fortified posts were isolated, unable to support their neighboring positions or join other strongpoints in delivering interlocking fire.

For the soldiers, staring for hours out across the white, snowy wastes was tedious, mind-numbing work that often produced visual distortions and snow-blindness. In spite of the dark snow-goggles worn by everyone at this altitude, retinal and corneal damage from the intense, searing sunlight and lack of filtering ozone was common. Some soldiers had gone permanently blind on Siachen.

The altitude, terrible cold, searing wind, and lack of humidity inflicted a host of ailments on the Pakistani and Indian combatants. Frostbite constantly threatened soldiers who had to remain immobile for long periods in forward positions. In the winter the temperature, driven down by intense wind chill, could drop to minus 60°F (minus 51°C). Exposed skin would freeze in less than one minute: fingertips, noses, cheeks, and earlobes were particularly vulnerable. Even in the short, more clement summer months, the cold could come unexpectedly, brought by frequent, but unpredictable storms. Heavy-duty lubricants in small arms and artillery would freeze, forcing soldiers to keep the actions of their rifles under their thick parkas.

Howling winds that never seemed to cease produced a deep psychological depression in the soldiers; it was an eerie wailing that distorted sound and frayed the taut nerves of even the hardiest veterans, relentlessly sapping their vitality. Soldiers on Siachen claimed they heard strange, spectral voices on the wind, or cries of agony and torment. Some said these were the calls of the yeti, or abominable snowmen, that by legend roamed the wild heights of Siachen; others that ghosts of the dead, or mountain *djinns*, wailed their blood-chilling cries in the frozen night.

The effects of high altitude were at least better understood. At 10,000 feet (3,048 m), the oxygen content of air is only half that of sea level. Physical exertion at this level—about the height of the highest ski slopes at Aspen or St. Moritz—produces breathlessness and rapid heartbeat. Many people experience stuffed nose, a sharp metallic taste in the mouth, headaches, and insomnia. Two or three days of rest is generally enough to acclimatize most people. In the high Andes, new arrivals are given frequent cups of coca-leaf tea to help assuage the effects of altitude.

Newly arrived Pakistani troops spend a week acclimatizing at the 10,000-foot level, doing light duty before moving to higher positions, up to 15,000 feet (4,572 m). Above 10,000 feet, the altitude begins to seriously stress the body and alter its chemistry.

At 18,000 to 22,000 feet (5,486–6,706 m), the highest elevations at Siachen, climbers enter what is known as the "death zone." Physical exertion becomes extremely difficult and labored. The body constantly gasps for air. The heart furiously pumps blood but cannot adequately nourish the body's extremities. Low oxygen produces growing disorientation and confusion, making even simple physical or mental tasks excruciatingly slow and tiresome. Hearing and vision become distorted. Dehydration caused by the thin, arid air and strong sunlight further stresses the body, and causes severe constipation. The skin can feel as if ants are running over it. Even eating becomes an ordeal.

Most climbers can acclimatize to the higher elevations, but certain people are particularly susceptible to the two scourges of the mountains: high-altitude pulmonary edema (HAPE), and high-altitude cerebral edema (HACE). In the former, body fluids are driven by high pressure into the lungs. The sufferer quite literally begins to drown in his own fluids. Blood fills the sputum. HAPE comes swiftly and can produce death within hours. The only remedy is rapid descent. There is much wisdom in the old mountain maxim: "Climb high, sleep low."

Cerebral edema is rarer, but equally deadly. Body fluids rush into the brain, causing it to swell against the skull, producing intense pain, hallucinations, stupor, dementia, and then death. Again, rapid descent is the only way to save the sufferer. Both conditions seem to affect men more than women, and middle-aged men, as I was later to discover, in particular. Even those who have become acclimatized to high altitude can suddenly be stricken by either sickness. In effect, both HAPE and HACE are similar to the bends, the deadly condition experienced by divers who go too deep, or ascend and depressurize too quickly.

Altitude sickness on Siachen causes almost as many Pakistani and Indian casualties as enemy action. Ironically, natives to the high valleys of Baltistan, Ladakh, and Tibet often fall ill to a variety of disorders and fevers when they descend to lower altitudes or the plains of northern India. As a final scourge, many of the soldiers stationed for long periods at Siachen also experienced impotence, often lasting for months, after they returned to low altitude.

For Pakistani and Indian troops, most of whom came from the distant, torrid lowlands far to the south, Siachen was a terrifying and demoralizing place unfit for human habitation. Men and machines routinely broke down in the punishing cold and lethal altitude. Logistics dominated combat: every bullet and shell, each container of water or food had to be laboriously transported from distant supply depots. Loneliness and boredom afflicted everyone; it was, as one Pakistani officer told me, "the worst place on Earth to fight a war."

I stood with Colonel Musa, looking out over the sea of peaks that surrounded us, comparing our experiences under fire. He asked me about the wars I had seen—in Angola, the Mideast, Central America, and Indochina. I asked him about the places he had fought in during his long military career. He had seen combat against India in the mountains of Kashmir, the plains of northern Punjab, the desert of Rajastan, and far to the south in the salt marshes of the Rann of Kutch.

"Where, as a professional soldier," I inquired, "do you prefer to fight—mountains, hills, or lowlands?"

Musa looked at me for a moment, deeply serious. I could see my reflection in his one-way sunglasses. Then a big, ferocious smile and a phalanx of perfect white teeth erupted from behind his beard. I was instantly reminded of G.K. Chesterton's marvelous lines about the Ottoman sultan in his poem "Lepanto":

There is laughter like the fountains in that face of all men feared;
It stirs the forest darkness, the darkness of his beard;
It curls the blood-red crescent, the crescent of his lips...

"My dear Eric, I like to fight wherever there are Indians!" he exclaimed, throwing back his head and roaring with laughter.

Musa was a true mujahid, or soldier of Allah. He and his fellow mujahedin were performing their duty before God of defending Islam anywhere it was attacked by *kufir*, or unbelievers. The Holy Koran says, "Fight in the way of Allah against those who fight against you, but do not yourselves be aggressors; for, verily, Allah does not love aggressors.... Fight against them until there is no longer oppression and all men are free to worship God. But if they [the enemy] desist, all hostility shall cease...."

And of those martyrs, or *shaheed*, who have fallen in the sacred struggle known as jihad, the Koran teaches, "Speak not of those who are slain in the way of God as dead: for they are alive...."

To Colonel Musa, India was the deadliest enemy of his faith, Islam, and also of his beloved homeland, Pakistan.

Across the snowy no-man's-land were three battalions of Indian *jawans* who bore the same passionate animosity against Islam and Pakistan. What else but incandescent hatred would drive sensible, civilized men to fight for a decade over uninhabitable, desolate wastes that were of no earthly value to anyone save yetis and yaks?

I have seen human hatred expressed in many places over the decades, from the Mideast to Africa and Asia. Growing up in New York, and later living in the Mideast, I was steeped in the bitter struggle between Jews and Arabs. I had experienced the mindless, primitive tribal hatred between Greeks and Turks, Armenians and Turks, Koreans and Japanese. I had seen the heaps of bodies caused by racial hatred between black and white Africans, or between Bantu Africans and non-Negroid Somalis, Ethiopians, and Tutsis.

But no hatred I have ever encountered, save that held by Serbs and Greeks for Muslims, equaled the vitriolic detestation between Indians and Pakistanis, two related peoples who to most outsiders are virtually indistinguishable from one another. The fiercest form of hatred, it seems, is that between brothers and cousins.

Until recently, the bitter animosity between India and Pakistan was considered by Westerners a bizarre curiosity of an unimportant part of the world. But now that both old foes have nuclear weapons, and the means to deliver them at long range within minutes, the Indo-Pakistani feud, which focuses on Kashmir and Siachen, has suddenly become a major international concern and a threat to all mankind.

14
The Hatred of Brothers

The roots of the remarkable hatred between India and Pakistan, Hindu and Muslim, lie buried deep in the past. India is one of the world's greatest and oldest civilizations. During the centuries of high Hindu civilization, India was never a unified political entity, but a dizzying patchwork of princely states and kingdoms that devoted much of their energy and treasure to doing battle with their neighbors.

In AD 713, Muslim armies advanced from Arabia and Iran into India's westernmost regions, Sind and Punjab, permanently implanting their religion and establishing a number of Muslim-dominated states. Islam then spread down the west coast of India, as far as the Deccan, and established pockets of believers across northern and central India.

In spite of partial Islamic penetration of India, Hindu culture and religion continued to dominate the subcontinent, and largely shaped its identity. Like China, Hindu India believed itself to be the center of the civilized world, and all outsiders barbarians. Ironically, it was one such barbarian people, the invading British, who would eventually lay the foundation of a truly united India, and preside over this historic birth in 1947.

Hindu civilization flourished and dominated India until the tenth century AD, when successive waves of Turks, Persians, and Afghans invaded the north. During the ensuing three centuries, India was progressively weakened by feudal warfare, dynasty conflicts, and endless political intrigues. But guarded by the seas in the south, and a nearly impassable wall of mountains on the north, India remained largely immune to outside interference, save in Sind, Punjab, and the region around Delhi and Agra.

India was extremely fortunate to escape the greatest earthquake of the Middle Ages, the twelfth-century conquests of Genghis Khan and his Mongol hordes. This warrior king created history's largest empire, which at its zenith extended from China to Palestine and Eastern Europe. The Mongol armies also occupied Tibet, where they were welcomed, but they failed to penetrate farther south.

By contrast, Islamic civilization, which had reached its glittering apogee in the late thirteenth century, was doomed by the advance of the Mongol hordes. The great eastern Muslim cities of Samarkand, Bokhara, Khiva, and Merv, and then the magnificent cities of Iran, were taken by storm and laid waste, one after the other. The inhabitants were slaughtered; pyramids of 100,000 human heads were erected. Irrigation systems were destroyed, and salt plowed into fields.

Muslim civilization, which led the world in science, mathematics, medicine, architecture, and literature at a time when London was a village of 15,000 unwashed people, was almost erased from the map.

In 1258, the Mongols stormed and razed Islam's greatest city, Baghdad, massacring its million inhabitants. For the Muslim world the Mongol invasions were a catastrophe that could be compared only to nuclear war. Entire nations were exterminated, leaving behind nothing but rubble, fallow fields, and bones. Even today Islamic civilization has not recovered; for example, modern Baghdad is smaller than the thirteenth-century city of Haroun al-Rashid.

The nomadic Mongols did not want cities or captive populations, so they utterly destroyed everything before them to make more pasturelands for their horse armies and flocks. The Great Khans set out to kill until there were no people left on Earth except Mongols.

The Himalayas saved India from this nightmare.

India's self-absorbed isolation ended abruptly in 1498, five years after Columbus landed in the West Indies, when the Portuguese explorer Vasco da Gama landed at Calicut on India's southern coast, an event that was to have profound historic consequences for the subcontinent. European powers, having learned to circumnavigate Africa, began to descend on the southern coasts of India and the East Indies in pursuit of the lucrative spice trade. The British East India Company seized Surat in 1612, Bombay in 1661, and Calcutta in 1698, driving out its Portuguese and Dutch competitors. The French established a garrison at Pondicherry, south of Madras.

Equally important, and more immediate, a Chaghatai Turkish-Mongol khan from Central Asia, Zahiruddin Babur, fashioned a large empire north of the Himalayas and the Hindu Kush. Babur's ambition was to follow in the footsteps of his fourteenth-century predecessor, the great Mongol conqueror Timur the Lame, or Tamerlane, who had occupied parts of northern India, including Delhi. By the fifteenth century, however, Genghis Khan's successors had lost much of their primitive ferocity, developing a powerful civilization under the tutelage of Chinese administrators. Islam became the official religion of the Turkish-Mongol khans and many of their subjects, supplanting shamanism and Tibetan Buddhism.

Assembling a large army, Babur marched down the traditional invasion route: through Afghanistan, across the Khyber Pass, and onto the plains of Punjab. On April 21, 1526, at Panipat, just north of Delhi, Babur met and defeated a far larger army of the local Muslim ruler. Babur moved his court to Agra, laying the foundation for the subsequent Mogul dynasty that was to rule much of India for the next three centuries.

Weak and debauched, India's feuding Hindu rulers could not withstand the advance of Babur's artillery and Turkic-Mongol horse armies. Within a few years most of northern India fell to Babur's rule; his famed successors, Akbar and Jahangir, Shah Jahan, and Aurangzeb, conquered much of central and southern India, establishing one of history's greatest and certainly most sumptuous empires.

The Turkic-Mongols—who became known in India as Moguls—quickly established a civilization of enormous vitality, strength, and cultural richness. Islam, already well entrenched in the western regions of Sind and Punjab, spread across northern India into Bengal, and down into the south. India's new iconoclastic Muslim rulers destroyed Hindu temples and Buddhist shrines alike, or converted many sacred Hindu places into Muslim shrines and mosques.

For India's Hindu Brahmin élite, the Mogul conquest was a devastating political, cultural, and psychological defeat. India's rigidly structured Hindu social order was undermined by the liberating forces of egalitarian Islam. Hindus were left with a sense of powerlessness, second-class citizens in realms they once ruled. Many Hindu maharajas and rajas soon became lieges of India's Muslim rulers, though other Hindus, such as the warlike Rajputs, Marathas, and Jats, resisted fiercely. So, too, did Sikhs in Punjab. From the Red Fort in Delhi and from Agra, the Great Moguls held sway over a rich and vast Indian Empire. The fusion of Muslim energy and politico-military power with Indian culture produced one of history's greatest explosions of art, literature, and architecture.

The Mogul Empire was gradually undermined, then finally overthrown, in the early nineteenth century by a new maritime power, Great Britain, the first major occupier of India to invade from the sea. Once again the proud, haughty Hindus were conquered by a foreign people, who brought yet another robust religion to further vitiate Hinduism. In Punjab, the breadbasket of India, the decline and decadence of Hinduism had sparked the birth of a new warrior faith, Sikhism, three centuries earlier.

The British, following their policy of divide and rule, deftly played India's princely Hindu and Muslim rulers off against each other. In doing so, they often favored the minority Muslims, whom the British considered more honest, reliable, and industrious than the "shifty" Hindus. Furthermore, the British, who had no doubt whatsoever of their racial superiority, were offended and angered by the pretensions of the "little brown men" of the old Hindu aristocracy, who had the audacity to see themselves as superior to the intruding British.

Equally significant, India's British overlords strongly favored the warlike "martial races" of the north—Pathans, Punjabis, Sikhs, Rajputs, and Gurkhas—over other Indian peoples, creating a military caste system that persists to this day in both India and Pakistan. The British considered the Hindus of the plains and the Muslims of Sind to be weak, cowardly, and eminently untrustworthy. By contrast, they judged India's light-skinned, Indo-European frontier peoples to be racially, morally, and intellectually superior.

As a result, the ranks of the British Indian Army were filled by mountain races from the north, who returned the favor by adopting the ethos and habits of their British masters. British racism against darker-skinned Indians fitted neatly with similar prejudices held by light-complexioned, high-caste Hindus, who, not infrequently, dismiss dark-skinned Dravidians of the south as "niggers."

A prime goal of Nehru and the other fathers of Indian independence, many of whom were high-caste Brahmins, was to restore the faded greatness of Hindu civilization, which had been so long eclipsed, first by the Mogul Empire, and then the British Raj. Though the Congress Party founded by Gandhi and Nehru encompassed a sizeable number of Muslims, and was officially dedicated to multiculturalism and religious tolerance, strong currents of Hindu nationalism coursed below its ecumenical surface. To many Indian nationalists, particularly extremists of the RSS (Rashtriya Swayamsemak Saugh), the VHP (Vishwa Hindu Parishad) and other Hindu chauvinist groups (who would later unite under the banner of the Bharatiya Janata Party [BJP]) India could only be reborn when pernicious foreign influences, notably Islam, but also Christianity and even capitalism, were either suppressed or entirely eradicated.

Hindu nationalists were raised believing their once-glittering civilization had been raped, pillaged, defiled, and permanently debased by foreign oppressors. The British were gone, but 120 million Muslims remained, "like an asp coiled in the bosom of Mother India," according to one RSS pundit. The Muslim minority was a constant, everyday reminder of historical defeat, shame, and failure. The granting of special civil rights based on Islamic law to India's Muslim community further convinced Hindu extremists that their Islamic neighbors were a subversive foreign people, a fifth column whose loyalty to the nation was at best uncertain, and an ever-present danger to the Hindu polity.

The decline of Hindu civilization, invasions by the Moguls and British, and the subsequent colonial period, left many Indians, and particularly Hindus, with a deep sense of national, cultural, and ethnic inferiority. The British have long been grand masters of snobbery, class distinction, and the fine art of making other people feel inferior. The new British rulers convinced most Indians in ways both overt and subtle that they were a lesser breed, incompetent and morally unfit to govern their own affairs; Hindu India was backward, dirty, steeped in primitive superstition, corrupt, deceitful, and cowardly.

Many upper-class Hindus, educated by the British, came to believe these slanders, and not surprisingly sought refuge from them by trying to become more British than the British—or, as Indians put it, to become *pukka* like the great white sahibs who ruled them. Mohandas Gandhi in his youth and early career as a lawyer sought to be one of these "brown Englishmen." Even so, Winston Churchill, the quintessential imperialist, would later describe this great moral leader and noble thinker, with typical British racism, as a "half-naked fakir."

How else could imperial Britain have ruled 300 million Indians with a garrison that never exceeded 100,000 white troops (usually far smaller), thinly spread over the vastness of India? Divide and rule played a major role, but inculcation in the Indian mind of the natural superiority of whites was equally potent as a dominating force. This legacy of inferiority still afflicts India today. Indians have an overriding desire to be taken seriously by the outside world, to be seen as the clever, educated, talented people that they are, rather than as a teeming mass of unwashed, hungry beggars or silly, comical "babus," speaking singsong English and putting on airs. The pomposity and arrogance so often displayed by upper-caste Hindus, which makes Indians widely unpopular and the constant butt of jokes by foreigners, is in good part a reflection of their deep psychological craving for respect.

India wants to be seen and treated by the world as a major military, political, economic, and technological power, instead of a quaint, exotic Third World derelict. This urgent desire for respect was the prime force that drove the nationalist BJP-dominated government in 1998 to detonate five nuclear weapons. India's atomic explosions were mighty affirmations of Great India and Hindu national-cultural power, known as Hindutva. In the Indian view, its nuclear tests blew open the door of the exclusionary white man's club of superpowers. India was sending the message it would shortly be the world's newest great power, and the dominant force in South Asia. Delhi thundered it would no longer accept "nuclear apartheid." The time had come to restore India's lost greatness.

The spread of Islam in India had also posed another threat: it undermined the traditional caste system, the power base of the ruling Hindu élite. Caste established an unchanging social order, in which large parts of India's huge population were condemned to perpetual servitude to their betters. In many ways, India's caste system resembles both the serfdom of medieval Europe, by keeping agricultural laborers in permanent thrall to landowners and nobles, and South Africa's former apartheid system, by strictly segregating races, tribes, and social groups.

Indian governments have been committed ever since independence to eliminating the caste system. In spite of massive efforts, education, and creation of special reserved jobs, caste still holds much of rural India in its pernicious grasp. Caste is too deeply ingrained in Indian culture and society to be swept away by government fiat. Besides, caste provides a pliant industrial and agricultural lumpenproletariat for factory and landowners. A combination of Hinduism and tradition teaches that it is impossible for a person to leave his caste and move to a higher one during a lifetime. A soul achieves gradual improvement only through reincarnation. This religious belief, which cements passivity, social immobility, and servitude, provides a potent opiate that numbs the masses into acceptance of their condition. Marx would have found a rich lode to mine in today's India (and, for that matter, Pakistan), two-thirds of whose illiterate, superstition-ridden people still live in semi-feudal conditions.

The advent of Islam to India directly threatened the caste system, and thus the socio-economic order. Over the centuries since the introduction of Islam to India, millions of untouchables and other low castes have embraced egalitarian Islam to escape the prison of caste. Islam offered upward social and physical mobility, the chance to escape the fetters of the past, and even to marry into a higher group. The defection of large numbers of Hindus to Islam not only upset the social order, it menaced the domination of India's ruling Hindu political and landowning élite.

Interestingly, Islam played much the same revolutionary role in Eastern Europe from the thirteenth to the fifteenth century. The invading Ottoman armies overturned the medieval feudal system and freed large numbers of serfs in what was to become Romania, Bulgaria, Greece, Serbia, Hungary, and Albania. Persecuted religious sects, such as the Bogomils of Bosnia and Serbia, converted en masse to Islam to escape savage persecution by their fellow Catholics or members of Orthodox churches. While Christians were busy slaughtering and burning one another, the Muslim Ottomans adopted the more sensible and rewarding expedient of simply levying a special head tax on infidels, and welcoming with favor converts to Islam. The Turks were always a minority within their cosmopolitan, polyglot Ottoman Empire, as were the Moguls in India.

The military prowess of the warlike Moguls and, later, Britain's promotion of the martial races left India with a deeply imbued belief that Muslims far excelled Hindus in the art of war. Muslims were fiercer, braver, better fighters, went the widely held belief among Hindus, a feeling that was reinforced by Britain's not-so-subtle repetition of the notion that Hindus were soft, unreliable, and very poor fighters. Even within the post-Independence Indian Army, there was a widespread feeling that one Muslim Pakistani soldier was worth three Hindu Indian jawans. Pakistan magnified such notions by constantly trumpeting the martial superiority of its soldiers and pilots over the Indians. The only units of the Indian Army considered a match for the

Pakistanis, many of whose generals and soldiers were warlike Pathans from the wild Northwest Frontier, were the equally ferocious warrior Sikhs and Gurkhas. India's victory in the 1971 war against Pakistan did much to erase the notion of Muslim military superiority, but to this day many Indians remain deeply intimidated by their warlike Muslim neighbors, and fear the sword of Islam.

Muslims also represented a subtler psychological threat to Hindus, though one rarely sensed by outsiders. In spite of India's pornographic temples and the famed *Kama Sutra*, modern India is a far cry sexually from the hedonistic days of the lascivious Hindu courts. Indian society is highly conservative and strict, even puritanical, when it comes to matters of sex. Only in recent years has the growth of urban life, the emergence of a strong middle class, and the ubiquitous intrusion of Western pop culture introduced a measure of sexual liberation and moral laxity to Indian society. Sexual dysfunctions are a common complaint in India, the legacy of puritanical Hindu upbringing, youthful marriages, and lack of sex education. As a result, Delhi, Bombay, and other major cities sport a wide number of well-advertised "sex doctors" and marital specialists.

India's Muslims, by contrast, do not seem to suffer from such problems. Islam encourages a robust sex life, albeit strictly within the bounds of matrimony. Muslims tend to have somewhat more offspring than Hindus, a fact that causes great alarm among Hindu extremists who claim, preposterously, that their Muslim neighbors are about to swamp India with floods of Islamic children. Serbs in the Balkans make the very same lurid claims about Muslim Bosnians and Albanians (the latter do have Europe's highest birth rate). The supposed demographic "green peril" and Islam's easygoing attitude toward sex have given Muslims the undeserved but prevalent reputation of being both over-sexed, and better lovers than Hindus. Some Indians believe Muslims are more sexually potent because they are circumcised. There seems everywhere to be a curiously strong animosity between men who are circumcised and those who are not. This canard stokes the always smoldering fires of anti-Muslim resentment or hatred.

A far more important source of anti-Muslim feeling in India comes from economic and social stress. At least a third, and perhaps as much as 40 percent of India's population of 983 million lives below even Delhi's meager definition of the poverty level. Fewer than 25 percent of

Indians are literate; functional literacy may be closer to 10 percent. The literacy rate in Pakistan is similar.

Everyday life for most poor Indians still borders on the intolerable, in spite of successful campaigns by post-independence Indian governments to eradicate the famines and pestilence that killed millions in the past. Subsistence farming and gruesome industrial working conditions expose malnourished Indian laborers to hunger, sickness, and daily misery. At least 300,000 children die each year of diarrhea. India's infant mortality rate is double that of China.

Only 2.5 percent of India's population has an annual household income of more than US$2,500. Gross domestic product per capita averages only $1,600, as compared with $3,400 per person in China. In spite of its huge population and great size, India's economy is about the same size as that of the Netherlands.

There is almost no social safety net to help widows, orphans, the homeless, or the armies of unemployed. At night the streets of India's cities become giant dormitories. Open sewers are often the only places where people can wash their clothes and bathe. For most people, everyday life is a harrowing struggle to feed large families, tend to sick relatives, scrounge up an adequate dowry for unmarried female children, and simply to move around in the frightful urban congestion and foul pollution of India's cities and towns. Child labor and near slavery are common in India and Pakistan. In January 1999, foreign rights groups even discovered fifty thousand enslaved Pakistani industrial laborers who were chained to their cots at night to prevent escapes.

These punishing economic and social stresses produce constant explosions of communal violence. Frustration, anger, misery, and despair combine into a volatile mixture of barely repressed rage that often focuses on various minority groups, usually Muslims, but also Sikhs, and more rarely India's Christians, who account for only 2.3 percent of the population. The great Gandhi considered India's unrelenting communal violence to be the nation's worst scourge.

While Indian governments have struggled to damp down communal hatreds, many local politicians, national leaders, and gangster chiefs have incited anti-Muslim riots as a way of diverting public attention from genuine problems, or gaining political support. In recent years, the nationalist BJP has whipped up anti-Muslim feeling and on many occasions incited riots, including one notorious disturbance in which a small mosque at Ayodhya, said to be the birthplace of the Hindu god Rama, was demolished. After the assassination of Indira Gandhi by her own Sikh bodyguards, Congress Party politicians encouraged enraged Hindus to massacre some five thousand Sikhs.

The endless vitriolic conflict with neighboring Islamic Pakistan has also made India's Muslims a constant target of Hindu nationalist wrath. Yet in spite of Hindu suspicions about potential Muslim disloyalty, spying, and sabotage, there have in fact been remarkably few cases of Muslim Indians betraying their nation for the benefit of Pakistan. To the contrary, Muslim Indians have always held prominent positions in the Congress Party and in the upper ranks of Indian society and the arts. Nevertheless, whenever trouble with Pakistan brews, India's Muslims become a lightning rod for nationalist passions and pent-up social tensions.

The phenomenon of economic and social distress leading to communal violence is not confined to India. Pakistan is racked by the same curse, particularly in strife-torn Sind province, where descendants of immigrants from India, known as *mohajirs*, are locked in a state of virtual civil war with native Sindis. In 1998, more than eight hundred people were killed in Karachi alone in such communal violence, while the Western world fretted about a handful of sectarian killings in Northern Ireland.

Farther north, another near civil war has erupted in Punjab between Shia and Sunni Muslims. Both civil conflicts are said to be fueled by agents of India's intelligence service, RAW, in revenge for Pakistan's covert assistance to Muslim secessionists in Indian-ruled Kashmir and modest support of Sikh independence groups in Indian Punjab. Farther north still, on Pakistan's lawless Northwest Frontier, bands of local tribesmen frequently fight pitched battles with heavy weapons. One night, in the mountains between Islamabad to Gilgit, the car I was traveling in came under rifle fire. "Don't worry," said my driver, comfortingly, "they are just local, misguided tribesmen who think all other Pakistanis are heretical Muslims. They are only shooting at us to defend Islam."

India's Muslims live in constant terror of riots and massacres, a huge minority of frightened people swamped in a sea of more than 800 million hostile Hindus. A pig's head thrown into a Muslim home, a cow's tongue thrown into a Hindu home, a minor traffic accident, or even a squabble over the price of lentils in the bazaar can ignite the kind of sudden, bloody riot between Hindus and Muslims that often results in destruction of entire neighborhoods. A favorite method of killing people during such riots is to douse them in kerosene and set them alight.

In the mid-1940s India's Muslim League, led by Mohammed Ali Jinnah, campaigned for the founding of a homeland and refuge for India's Muslims. The result was the founding in 1947 of the Islamic Republic of Pakistan, composed of chunks of western India and Bengal in which Muslims predominated. Divided, and separated into East and West, Pakistan was fated to fail as a unitary state, but at the time of its birth, Muslims hailed the new nation as a beacon of Islam and a haven for the persecuted faithful in India. Most Indians strongly opposed the creation of Pakistan, but Nehru and his Congress allies reluctantly agreed to the sundering of their newborn, and just united nation, under intense pressure from Great Britain and the Muslim League. Some Indian Muslims also opposed the creation of Pakistan, fearing it would invite even more persecution, and make them a distrusted minority in their own land, vulnerable to accusations of dual loyalty, just as a minority of anti-Zionist American Jews opposed the creation of Israel.

Pakistan, to which millions of Muslims fled, was in effect an Islamic Israel, created to secure the future of a persecuted, endangered people. But like Israelis, Pakistanis have never been able to decide whether they should have a secular state, or a theocracy based on religious law. Jinnah, however, wanted and got a secular state that has managed to sputter on for half a century, though dismembered by India and riven by dangerous religious, tribal, and regional dissension that persist to this day. Hopes that Pakistan would become a model nation guided by the Islamic precepts of Koranic law, social justice, and civic virtue, governmental honesty, and Muslim brotherhood were quickly dashed. Pakistan turned out to be a clone of corrupt, venal, feudal India, but without India's proudest accomplishment, a rough, deeply flawed, but still functioning democracy, which had endured since 1947.

Both India and Pakistan are composite nations stitched together from a welter of states, regions, and tribes. Many Indians and Pakistanis feel little allegiance to the state. The primary unit of loyalty is the extended family, the village, the tribe or caste, and the region. As the

Trinidad-Indian writer V.S. Naipaul pointed out many years ago in his incisive study of India, *An Area of Darkness*, there is almost no sense of community on the subcontinent. The idea of the common good, of helping others who are not relatives, is largely foreign. In India and Pakistan the overriding rule is every man for himself. This national self-ishness ensures that both countries lack social cooperation, a common sense of purpose, or a notion of political compromise for the good of the state. Mao believed that China suffered from the same selfish, family-centered atomism, and sought to force national consciousness and civic altruism upon his hitherto unruly people. His social engineering eventually produced the lunatic Red Guards, who nearly destroyed China in the name of national salvation from "feudalism" and "bourgeois values."

For the past half-century, Pakistan has been ruled by a succession of military regimes interspersed with inept, profoundly corrupt civilian governments. Far from blossoming into a just Islamic state, Pakistan remained a feudal society, in which powerful land barons who paid no taxes ruled like medieval nawabs, buying and selling venal politicians like so many bags of Basmati rice. The military was the only Pakistani institution that managed to avoid being fouled in the national swamp of corruption and chicanery, or that succeeded in holding popular respect in a country steeped in poisonous cynicism. Pakistan's ablest, most effective post-independence leaders, Marshal Ayoub Khan and General Zia ul-Haq, both came from the army. The fiery Zulfikar Ali Bhutto was a traditional feudal baron who advocated extreme and unrealistic populist policies that enthralled the ignorant masses, but led the nation into bankruptcy and eventually brought on a military coup. Bhutto's daughter, Benazir, who was much idolized by the Western media, was twice ousted from office for gross incompetence, and is now under criminal indictment for rampant corruption and malfeasance.

The threat of invasion by seven-times-larger India is the dominant feature of Pakistani psychology, which is in turn an extension of India's Muslim minority's original fear of being swamped by a sea of hostile Hindus. Pakistan is a long, thin, strategically vulnerable nation, stretched along the narrow valley of the Indus River, which could be overrun by Indian armies in a matter of days. Nearly every Pakistani believes India has never, and will never, accept the 1947 partition, and is determined to reunite the entire subcontinent by military force, re-creating the old British Indian Raj. India's relentless military buildup, incessant threats by Indian nationalists to "crush Pakistan," and Indira Gandhi's invasion—or "liberation," as Indians call it—of East Pakistan in 1971 are proof positive, in Pakistani eyes, of India's lethal intent to exterminate the irksome and offensive Muslim state.

For many Indians, the very existence of Pakistan is both a military threat and a daily reminder of past national humiliations. Hindu nationalists warn that India faces strategic encirclement by a coalition of hostile states—namely China and its close allies, Pakistan and Burma. "Pakistan," as one Hindu chauvinist puts it, "is a dagger thrust at the heart of India." Or: "The Muslims and China are conspiring to destroy India." Such alarms reflect the persistent inferiority complex many Indians still harbor when it comes to the military prowess of the martial races, and uncertainty about their own considerable military power. Leading Hindu strategists claim the subcontinent can never be stable until its "artificial" divisions are eliminated, an assertion that predictably raises alarms not only in Pakistan, but in Nepal, Bangladesh, and Sri Lanka as well, all of which have experienced varying degrees of Indian intervention or strong-arm tactics.

In effect, Pakistanis feel much as Israelis did in the 1960s, when the Jewish state believed it was "surrounded by a sea of hostile Arabs bent on pushing us into the sea." Neither nation understood just how powerful it really was compared with its hostile neighbors. As a result, both Israel and Pakistan secretly developed nuclear weapons as the ultimate form of national life insurance. An important difference, however, is that Pakistan's small nuclear arsenal is purely defensive, while Israel's two to four hundred nuclear weapons are clearly configured for offensive, war-fighting operations.

Fear of India among Pakistanis combines with an even more potent force, loathing of Hinduism. Islam, the passionately held credo of 140 million Pakistanis, infuses the daily life, behavior, and thinking of Muslims in a manner that Westerners, with their fading faiths and perfunctory religious observances, find difficult to comprehend. Perhaps a better comparison of the intense animosity felt between Muslim and Hindu is the former life-and-death struggle between capitalism and communism: the two ideologies could not coexist in the same physical space. They were mutually exclusive: acceptance of one system meant negation or elimination of the other.

Everything about Islam is in direct antithesis to Hinduism. The religion revealed by the Prophet Mohammed in the seventh century AD is the world's youngest major faith, and thus still virile where older religions have become jejune, meaninglessly ritualistic, or spiritually and morally exhausted. Islam is a severe desert faith of stark simplicity, whose intense observance totally fills the life of observant Muslims. In orthodox Sunni Islam there is no church and no official clergy, merely leaders of prayer. Islam sets a framework for family life, society, commerce, and conduct of government. The faith and state are inseparable, at least in traditional Islam. Each man stands alone before Allah, and must pay for his own sins or misdeeds. There is no church, to intercede or grant absolution. The main tenets of Islam are: acceptance of the one god and his last prophet Mohammed; prayer; fasting during the holy month of Ramadan; pilgrimage once in a lifetime to Mecca; defense of the faith; and payment of *zakat*, or a tithe, to help the community and the needy. In modern times, many Muslims interpret zakat to mean creation of a state welfare system and redistribution of income, notably oil income, to the needy, and Islamic polity—a concept that provokes intense alarm among the fabulously wealthy, Western-supported potentates who rule so much of the Muslim world.

The Islamic credo begins, "There is no god but Allah..." and herein lies the primary and most violent clash with Hinduism. Islam's first struggle after birth was against the pagan idolaters of Mecca and Medina, who sought to extinguish the infant Muslim community. Idol-worshiping, or adoration of multiple gods, is the worst of abominations to Muslims. The first act performed by Muslim forces as they swept out of Arabia in the late seventh century was to destroy all idols in their path. So intense is Islam's prohibition of idolatry that the artistic portrayal of the human figure is almost unknown in the Islamic art of the Arab world, though it does occur in Shia Iran, India, and Muslim South Asia.

Hinduism is the very opposite of austere Islam. Hindus worship a busy, crowded pantheon of gods, goddesses, animals, and even inanimate objects, all of which can assume different incarnations, forms, and natures. Over several millennia, Hinduism has mutated from the fairly simple faith of India's Aryan invaders into a dizzying collection of schools, sects, cults, and offshoots. Like Islam, Hinduism seeks to impose strictures and guidance on everyday life and the conduct of human affairs. Like Buddhism, it teaches that reality is merely illusion, and truth can be achieved only through meditation and enlightenment. But Hinduism is far more relaxed, flexible, and amorphous than Islam or Buddhism, and subject to varied personal interpretation.

Traditional Brahmin-Hindu belief holds that all forms visible on this Earth are merely emanations of the sole eternal Entity, like drops of water from a sea, or sparks from a fire. Animate and inanimate objects—humans, fleas, elephants, or mountains—are all part of the upward movement of progressive steps of the infinite evolution of the supreme Entity's being. Man, who is divided into classes or castes as part of the upward progression of life, is the highest earthly emanation of this process.

Hindus hope that through the long, painful cycle of death and rebirth to eventually gain absorption by the universal spirit of Brahma. While the principal Hindu trinity remains Brahma, Shiva, and Vishnu, who represent creation, destruction, and preservation, over the centuries worship and adoration of the myriad lesser expressions of the supreme Entity have grown up. Mythology, superstition, sorcery, and idolatry have widely displaced higher religious thought, particularly among the uneducated. As a result, Hinduism often appears to be a faith in which form has completely supplanted content.

While Islam still retains some of its *force vitale*, Hinduism has tended to fall into rote and superstition, a decline that modern Hindu fundamentalists and reformers seek to reverse by reinvigorating the early warrior nature of their ancient Aryan faith through Hindutva, and purifying it of the accumulated dross of centuries of misinterpretation, idolatry, and corruption.

For a Muslim, there can be fewer more horrifying experiences than entering a gaudily decorated, richly ornate Hindu temple. Naked *sadhus*, or holy men, perform bizarre contortions before its portals. Inside are collections of candle-lit idols of every color, shape, and size: green multi-headed gods; black, many-armed goddesses; man-eating ogres; animal gods; deities, half man, half animal; devil gods; pungent incense; and, everywhere, worshipers praying to their favored idol.

"I respect many Hindus," one Indian Muslim told me, "but how can I take seriously a senior civil servant who leaves his office, goes home, lights incense, and worships an idol of a blue monkey? How, I ask you? Who can respect a religion that worships sacred rats, and even has a rat god?"

Many Westerners find Hinduism just as bizarre and off-putting. The Hindu belief that the great life force takes many shapes, or *avatars*, and myriad expressions, that the idols they worship are merely points on which to focus faith and prayer, or a temporary shape the gods have chosen to come down to Earth, is too alien for most nonbelievers. So, too, the concept of reincarnation, in which a soul can progress from insect to nirvana over many, many lifetimes.

Caste, a bedrock of the Hindu faith, is also anathema to egalitarian Islam, which teaches that all men, no matter their birth or race, are equal before the one god. So, too, is belief in reincarnation, which Muslims see as absurd and blasphemous.

Muslims consider Christians and Jews as "peoples of the book," sharing such prophets as Jesus, Moses, and Abraham. In fact, Islam considers itself the direct, lineal extension of Judaism and Christianity, at least in their early form, though it rejects belief in the virgin birth of Jesus. Mohammed was simply the last and most important prophet who was sent to once again reveal God's word to the peoples of the book, who had strayed from the path of righteousness.

But Muslims have no spiritual links at all to Hinduism, only abiding scorn and, more often than not, loathing or contempt. Hindus return the favor by dismissing their Muslim neighbors as violent, primitive, oversexed, and untrustworthy religious fanatics, worshiping a fierce, grim deity, unwelcome alien interlopers from the distant, backward Mideast, who would do well to pack their bags and return to Arabia.

A much cherished mantra of Western liberals holds that misunderstanding is the root cause of international tensions and war. If people only understood each other, goes this roseate credo, they would be able to peacefully settle whatever disputes arise. "We're all alike, just separated by a wall of fear and confusion." Such Panglossian thinkers need only voyage to South Asia to see the folly of such nonsense. Indians and Pakistanis are two peas in a pod. Hindu and Muslim have intermingled for centuries, often in the same villages or towns; they understand one another all too well, and easily anticipate their foe's thinking and reactions. Deep mutual comprehension has bred deep distrust rather than enlightenment. Arabs and Israelis are the same. So, too, the Greeks and Turks of Cyprus. For men of profound ill will, to know your enemy is to truly distrust him.

Ironically, north Indians and Pakistanis of Punjab, that nation's most populous province, are ethnically almost identical, save by religious profession. North Indians and most Pakistanis have much more in common culturally and linguistically than do Indians of the north with their Dravidian southern co-citizens, who speak languages like Telugu, Tamil, and Kannada, which are unrelated to the northern tongues of Hindi, Punjabi, and Urdu. A north Indian can easily converse with a Pakistani Punjabi in Hindi or Punjabi, while he must usually employ English, India's lingua franca, to communicate with a fellow Indian citizen from Tamil Nadu or Karnataka. The grand ethnic divide on the Indian subcontinent is north-south rather than east-west. The governor of Karnataka once proudly showed me a large rubber stamp he kept on his desk. "Whenever those bloody paper wallahs in Delhi send me a letter in Hindi, I stamp 'English correspondence only' on it, and send the damned thing back!"

Northern Indians and Punjabi Pakistanis are part of the same ethnic family. Like all families, their members need deliver only a few key words or gestures to ignite immediate irritation or instant rage in their relatives. Indians and Pakistanis have turned goading one another in ways both great and petty into a virtual art form. One-upmanship between the two old foes is a national sport that rivals cricket. Probably the most famous and admired example occurred in the late 1980s, when India and Pakistan were on the edge of war, and India had concentrated some 300,000 troops on the Pakistani border under the code name "Operation Brass Tacks." Just when war seemed imminent, in a dazzling *beau geste*, Pakistan's leader, President Zia ul-Haq, suddenly flew to New Delhi to attend a cricket match to which he had been invited before the crisis. The Indian government, still trumpeting claims of an imminent Pakistani attack, was left looking extremely foolish and abashed. The crisis quickly defused. The lusty Indian media had a field day heaping ridicule on the red-faced politicians in Delhi.

The media on either side never miss an opportunity to pour criticism, scorn, and vitriol on their neighbor, nor to deliver outrageous accusations unconnected in any possible way to reality. Much of the endless Indo-Pakistani bickering is simply silly and juvenile, but occasionally it blows up into a major crisis that inflames passions and produces dangerous crises.

After fifty-two years of acrimony India and Pakistan are no closer today than they ever were to peaceful coexistence. Endless ministerial meetings, peace conferences, and outside arbitration have produced scant results. Relations have remained so strained for half a century that inauguration of the first regular bus service between India and Pakistan, in early 1999, was hailed as a major diplomatic triumph. Perhaps it was, but a bus service seems a pretty pathetic result of so many decades of sustained diplomatic attempts to improve relations, and make Pakistan and India act like normal, well-behaved neighbors.

So long as neither side in this historic conflict possessed nuclear weapons, the ever-present threat of a major war between the two Asian powers was strictly a regional concern. The end of the Cold War and collapse of the USSR eliminated the risk of possible Soviet and American involvement in an Indo-Pakistani conflict, as was nearly the case during the 1971 war. But the deployment of nuclear bombs and missiles by both sides has now made their dangerous feud a matter of the most urgent international concern.

The terrifying threat of mutually assured destruction should have forced nuclear-armed India and Pakistan into the kind of stalemate experienced by the U.S. and USSR during the Cold War, a tense, armed truce in which the two superpowers took great pains to avoid a direct clash. But the U.S. and Soviet Union had ample surveillance and early warning systems, which would have afforded them a few hours, or at least minutes, of analysis and consideration before igniting a nuclear war. Mobile and submarine-launched missiles gave the U.S. and USSR counter-force nuclear capability that even after a surprise nuclear attack would still deliver a devastating riposte. Counterforce capability made it unlikely that a sudden nuclear attack could decapitate America's or the Soviet Union's deterrent forces and national command authority. And fortunately, there was no common border between the U.S. and the Soviet Union. After the big scare of the 1962 Cuban missile crisis, both antagonists sensibly elected to confine their struggle to proxy wars in remote places. The superpowers took great pains to avoid potentially dangerous incidents or provocative military exercises along the inner German border.

India and Pakistan, which share a 1,000-mile (1,600-km) border, enjoy no such luxury. Their vulnerable nuclear arsenals must remain on hair-trigger alert, lest they be destroyed by a decapitating, surprise attack. Trigger-happiness is a constant feature of Indo-Pakistani relations. As previously noted, a major incursion by either side in Kashmir, or spreading of combat operations south from Siachen, could ignite a major war between the two nations that could quickly escalate into a nuclear exchange.

It would take only three nuclear weapons to destroy most of Pakistan; eight to destroy northern and central India. Besides the millions of deaths and casualties a nuclear exchange would produce, radioactive dust from the explosions would circle the globe, contaminating the major groundwater sources of as much as a third of the world's population on the Indian subcontinent and China. Ensuing famines would kill further tens of millions.

Pakistan's chronic political instability is another constant danger. Half a century after its creation, the strife-racked nation holds together by fraying threads. Sind, Pakistan's southern province on the Arabian Sea, is convulsed by civil war; Shias and Sunni Muslims are slaughtering one another in Punjab; Baluchistan goes its own eccentric tribal way. The Northwest Frontier is a no-man's-land; the disputed Northern Territories are lost in geopolitical limbo. Pakistan's civilian government barely governs, the nation teeters on the edge of bankruptcy, and politics is little more than tribal warfare. Corruption is all-engulfing. The generals are uncertain whether to watch Pakistan slip into chaos, or seize power and then be stuck running a fractious nation that has more often than not defied most past efforts to govern it, and ruined the careers or ended the lives of many of those who attempted to do so.

A Pakistan coming apart at its seams, or rent by civil war, might well tempt India to intervene, as Delhi did during the civil war in former East Pakistan. The civil war in Sind bears some disturbing similarities to strife-torn East Pakistan in 1970. Once again, India might decide to seize this opportunity to lop off another large part of its embattled enemy.

In such a dire event, Afghans might also be tempted to proclaim their long-sought "Pushtunistan," detaching the Northwest Frontier and joining it to southern Afghanistan. Iran, too, could be drawn into the fray, either to annex Baluchistan, or to defend Pakistan against India. It should be recalled that Iran began development of nuclear weapons under the Shah, in part out of fear of India's infant nuclear program. Iran's government may have changed, but the dangerous geopolitical realities of the region remain the same. Iran sees itself, somewhat contradictorily, as both a self-appointed defender of Islamic Pakistan against *kufir* India, and a forceful rival of Pakistan for influence in Baluchistan, Afghanistan, and Central Asia.

Nor can we totally discount the possibility that India might also splinter, though the possibility of such a dramatic geopolitical event seems much more remote than the potential breakup of Pakistan. While India may appear monolithic to outsiders, this immense nation of two hundred languages and major dialects is an unstable quilt of regions, races, and religions that holds together more by inertia than a sense of common interest. Strong secessionist movements operate in Kashmir, Punjab, Assam, and the eastern tribal states along the Burma border. The ongoing insurrection by Sri Lanka's Tamil minority could spread to the populous Tamil regions of southern India, producing calls for a united Tamil state. The existing Indian state of Tamil Nadu, for example, has 57 million citizens, making it about the same size as Italy, in terms of population. Many parts of Dravidian India chafe under what is seen as unfair domination of the union government by Hindi-speakers of the north.

We are entering an age of geopolitical dissolution. The nationalism and concentration that characterized the nineteenth century have peaked and are now beginning to recede under the pressure of rising regionalism and ethnic separatism. Modern telecommunications have sharply lessened the need for centralized governments. Complex modern states are more effectively administered politically and economically at the regional or local level. In North America, the power of Washington and Ottawa is steadily declining as states and provinces assert control over their own affairs.

The collapse of the Soviet Union was the most dramatic example of this trend toward devolution. India and China, both nuclear powers, are also potentially susceptible to centrifugal forces, driven by economic crisis, regionalism, or civil war between competing political factions. India and Pakistan are only half a century old as united, centrally governed nations. The fragility of these nuclear-armed nations, which make up a third of humanity, should not be underestimated.

Lowering the level of mutual hatred and mistrust in South Asia may take generations. Cultural-religious animosity may never disappear. Even so, possession of nuclear, chemical, and perhaps biological weapons by India and Pakistan now mandates decisive international action to begin reducing tensions between the two enemies.

Kashmir, and to a lesser degree, Siachen, are the two obvious flashpoints that could ignite a war. In spite of the enormous difficulties involved, the world community must press India and Pakistan into a gradual settlement of Kashmir. Once the Kashmir dispute is demilitarized, Siachen will no longer be of strategic value to either side. India's ruling circles must accept—and be seen to accept—that the chimera of reabsorbing Pakistan into a Greater India has been abandoned. The two sides will then be able to set about reducing their grotesquely oversized armed forces. Confidence-building measures along the border, and between the two military establishments, will substantially lessen the threat of accidental war.

Watching two of the world's poorer nations, in which most citizens are malnourished and illiterate, spend huge amounts on arms is truly to observe an act of collective madness. India's defense budget consumes nearly 3.4 percent of GDP, and this official figure does not include its secret nuclear weapons program, which very likely *at least* doubles the actual figure. Pakistan, with a much smaller GDP, spends over 5 percent, but, again, when nuclear arms are taken into account, the real figure is likely closer to 10 percent. Almost 40 percent of all Pakistani government spending goes to defense. By comparison, the United States, with a huge strategic nuclear arsenal and forces deployed around the world, spends 3.4 percent of GDP on defense.

Better living conditions and more education would do much to lessen the irrational hatreds and communal tensions on the subcontinent, but the money to achieve these goals is being poured into the arms race. India has embarked on a long-term program to dominate the Indian Ocean by deploying aircraft carriers and nuclear submarines, some armed with nuclear-tipped cruise missiles. At the same time, India is pouring billions of dollars into intermediate and long-range nuclear missiles and military satellites.

Pakistan, outnumbered, outgunned, and left far behind in the military technology race, strains every sinew and courts bankruptcy just to remain far behind in this accelerating Asian arms marathon. As Pakistan's ability to challenge India recedes, Hindu nationalists have adopted a new tack by claiming India's arms buildup is necessitated by the growing threat to India from China. It has been estimated that if

India and Pakistan would end their arms race, the funds saved and reinvested in national development would double their annual rates of growth, India to 10 percent and Pakistan to 6 percent.

Tragically, but inevitably, politicians on both sides of the ceasefire line keep stoking Indo-Pakistani animosity and mutual fear as a handy way of diverting their citizens from the failure of either nation to resolve the scourge of massive poverty and illiteracy. Like politicians in Greece and Turkey, whenever the economy takes a serious nose-dive, they begin beating the war drums and inflaming the always explosive passions of the illiterate masses. Pampered military establishments in India and Pakistan have little interest in seeing funding diverted to social programs, yet another doleful example of the subcontinent's pervasive I'm-all-right-Jack mentality. For the military and civilian élites on both sides, constant purchases of arms provide a ceaseless flow of secret commissions, bribes, and payoffs.

Seemingly insoluble conflicts *can* be resolved. Observing the Indo-Pakistani conflict, the equally long struggle between Jews and Arabs, and the irrational animosity between Greeks and Turks, one can easily become convinced that there are struggles that are fated never to end. Yet when confronted by such determined pessimism I always refer to the titanic, historic clash between Germans and French that so shaped the course and conduct of the bloody twentieth century. Few, fifty years ago, could possibly have imagined that one day Europe's two great warrior tribes, Teutons and Gauls, would cast aside their arms and embrace.

I have seen two miracles in my lifetime. The first was on the nightmarish French battlefield at Verdun, where in 1916 a million men died, or were seriously wounded, in an area that could barely hold two of New York's Central Park. There, on a cold, rainswept fall day, the president of France, François Mitterrand, and the German chancellor, Helmut Kohl, stood before the Ossuaire, Verdun's grim bone repository, held hands, and solemnly pledged that forever hence Frenchmen and Germans were brothers and comrades-in-arms who would never fight again.

The second miracle occurred as I was driving with a friend from Germany into France on one of our annual expeditions to explore the magnificent World War II forts of the Maginot Line. We motored across a bridge outside Rastatt that spanned the Rhine, the historic border between the two old foes. There was no customs post; not even a single policeman monitoring the frontier crossing. We stopped on the French side, stunned. After two titanic wars that caused the deaths of millions of Frenchmen and Germans, after enormously costly battles for this river frontier, and over the fiercely contested provinces of Alsace-Lorraine—the Kashmir of Europe—after all the slaughter, herculean effort, nationalist passions, and killing for this most fought-over of borders, nothing at all remained. A century of Franco-German hatred that brought three wars had completely vanished, to be replaced by the mundane normality of everyday European traffic. There was no watch on the Rhine, only small towns in France twinned to small towns in Germany, exchanging their children for summer holidays, to learn one another's language and be taught mutual admiration and respect.

Wise postwar German and French statesmen fashioned this miracle, but it probably could not have happened without the outside influence of the United States, under whose aegis Europe's old enemies finally found trust and cooperation.

A few years later I sat in Moscow, drinking vodka with two former colonels of the Soviet KGB, swapping our Cold War adventures. After some hours of levity, we stopped, looked at one another, and said, at virtually the same moment, "How could we ever have been so crazy as to think of going to war with each other."

A few days later, I discovered that my driver, a delightful man named Gennady, had served as a Red Army lieutenant colonel with the Communist forces fighting in Angola. I told him I'd been on the opposite side as an observer and a journalist, with their foe, the UNITA rebel army. I asked Gennady where he had served.

"At Cuito and Mavinga," he replied. "I was there, too," I exclaimed. In a remarkable coincidence, it turned out we had both been in the front lines during the battle of Mavinga, at precisely the same time, trading rocket fire at each other's positions. "Gennady!" I cried. "Eric!" he cried. We fell into each other's arms, kissing Russian-style, two old warriors and comrades-in-arms, albeit on opposite sides. Such is the madness of war, at least on the personal level.

I recount these anecdotes to show that peace can come where none thought it possible. One day India and Pakistan may find a way to be rid of the demons that haunt them, to reach a compromise over their territorial disputes, and to realize what the Germans and French have learned, that borders are one of our stupidest and certainly most pernicious inventions. Instead of "Death to the enemy," we should all be crying, "Death to all borders."

Of course, that all depends on the will on both sides to end their long feud. Today, there appears little inclination to do so. In Pakistan, Islamic fundamentalists, who are steadily gaining power as the corrupt traditional parties founder, call for renewed confrontation with India. Across the border, India's chauvinists and Hindu fundamentalists continue demanding their nation's new nuclear muscle be used to intimidate Pakistan and even China. For now, ill will rules supreme on the troubled, volatile subcontinent.

• • •

High up on the Siachen Glacier, the wind picked up force. Whirling snow devils, white cousins of the vortices that spiral in the deserts of the Mideast, rose from the steep slopes around us. My nostrils contracted in the cold, dry air. Heat and cold assailed me at the same time. I struggled to comprehend the vastness of the panoramic vista before my eyes. Many hundreds of miles to the south, across impassable mountain ranges, lay northern India and Delhi. North of us, across more mountains and glaciers, the remotest part of China. To the west, Afghanistan; to the northeast, Tibet. We were in a vast, empty, vertiginous nowhere, which had somehow become the epicenter of all the conflicting border claims of the nations that surrounded the Siachen Glacier.

I wondered how large this region would be if it were flattened out: perhaps, I mused, the size of France. It seemed utterly impossible that these mountains had once, in eons past, been beneath the sea, as the geologists tell us. Battling over this desolation reminded me of what had been said of the war that began in 1998 between Ethiopia and Eritrea over their barren, almost uninhabited border regions. "Two bald men fighting over a comb."

A Pakistani officer and I drank mugs of hot chai in a forward position, looking for movement on the Indian side. There was an occasional flash of metal, nothing more. This was to be a peaceful day on the world's highest battlefield. Both sides would devote the day's struggle to combating cold, altitude, and, the soldier's curse everywhere, and in every war: boredom.

"Could there ever be peace between India and Pakistan?" I asked the captain.

He thought for a while, sipping his steaming tea. Then he shrugged. "I don't know, Mr. Eric, we have been fighting the Indians all our lives. I'm afraid our children will also end up fighting them... maybe even for this miserable place."

"But don't you think some sort of settlement could be possible over Kashmir and Siachen?" I pressed him.

"How can you settle something that two men want so badly?" he asked. "It's like two men fighting over one woman. One will get her, the other will not."

The struggle over Siachen had gone on for more than ten years. According to the Hindu newspaper, operations at Siachen were costing India $400 million annually. By my estimate, Pakistan spends about half of that. The difference in cost is mainly due to India's need to extensively employ helicopters for resupply and reinforcement. The human cost of the conflict is about one thousand dead, and ten thousand wounded or injured each year in combat and accidents, or from altitude sickness. There was nothing at all to suggest that this bizarre, sterile conflict could end anytime soon. The two old foes would continue battling, each hoping to ensure the other did not gain control of this icy hell.

• • •

The descent from Siachen and return to Islamabad were as long and arduous as the ascent. I was suffering from advanced exhaustion, serious dehydration, the beginning of altitude sickness, an ear infection, and a twisted back. Two of my ribs were cracked. I was sunburned, bruised everywhere, contused, and unimaginably filthy. But I was filled with the most profound and passionate elation. I had just lived an adventure that very few others on this Earth would ever share.

I had been to war at the top of the world.

PART FOUR

The Roof of

the World

15
The Forbidden Kingdom

ndia's nuclear tests in May 1998, Pakistan's swift riposte, and the violent upsurge in fighting in Ladakh from May to July 1999 alerted the world to their increasingly dangerous confrontation in South Asia. Meanwhile, barely noticed, another potential conflict is building up to the east in the Himalayas along the Roof of the World.

Two nuclear-armed superpowers, China and India, are locked in a growing strategic rivalry for regional mastery whose outcome will shake not only Asia, but the rest of the world.

Three potentially explosive flashpoints between India and China are clearly evident: strategic Tibet, at the midpoint of their long, disputed Himalayan border; isolated, remote Burma; and the waters of the eastern Indian Ocean.

Of these three, Tibet is the most immediate and volatile flash-point, and the very epicenter of the looming clash between the colliding ambitions of Asia's two giants. When this collision will occur remains uncertain, though a reasonable estimate is sometime within the coming ten or fifteen years.

What is certain, however, is that the inevitable geopolitical rivalry between India and China, who have already fought one war during the past forty years, is steadily escalating. The first superpower conflict of the twenty-first century could erupt along the disputed 2,486-mile (4,000-kilometer) India-China border, as Asia's colossi vie to dominate the world's most populous region.

To see first-hand the epicenter of this coming conflict, I decided to make the long, arduous voyage to the Forbidden Kingdom of Tibet.

• • •

Light. Waves of shimmering light assault the eyes and stun the senses. Such was my first impression after landing on the Tibetan plateau: light, and the pure, cold, bone-dry air.

The second sensation was of having alighted on a different planet, one whose atmosphere and gravity resemble Earth's in many ways, yet are unfathomably different. Then I felt myself on a huge, mysterious island, floating high in the ether, somewhere above the Earth.

There are only three ways to reach Tibet: by supposedly regular but in fact quite erratic flights from Chengdu, the largest city in western China; scheduled, but frequently undependable flights from Katmandu, Nepal; or, for the truly intrepid traveler, a magnificent road journey up the "Friendship Highway," a long, exhausting undertaking suitable only for those wholly indifferent to time, squalid conditions, breakdowns, or avalanches, and well inured to miserable rations, evil toilets, and innumerable bureaucratic impediments.

In spite of my long experience in the mountains, I unwisely chose the Chengdu gateway, a decision that would later cost me dearly. I was already in China on other business, and due thereafter to fly to Japan. I thus did not want to waste time on a 2,200-mile (3,539-km) detour through Nepal.

The roughly rectangular region extending east from Chengdu to Tibet, and south to the borders of Chinese Yunnan, Laos, Burma, and Indian Assam, is one of the least-known, most topographically difficult parts of the globe. Mighty Asian rivers that rise on the Tibetan Plateau—such as the Brahmaputra, Salween, Mekong, Yangtze, and Red rivers—surge down like the extended fingers of an open hand from their sources at the top of the world, carving and clawing impossibly deep gorges and steep, narrow valleys into the mountains. East-west communications across this maze of rushing rivers, narrow defiles, and heavily forested or jungle-covered slopes is almost impossible, as the Allies and Japanese discovered during World War II.

The primitive tribespeople of this sparsely inhabited region are isolated and unfamiliar even to their neighbors. The writ of distant governments does not extend into this frontier region.

Flying due west from Chengdu aboard a Chinese airliner, I marveled at the utter wildness of the landscape below, a vista so fascinating I forgot my usual nervousness aboard mechanically questionable Chinese aircraft. Tiny villages, blackened plots of land from slash-and-burn farming, and the occasional poppy field clung to the terraced sides of precipitous cliffs. Torrential brown rivers surged south and east through steep gorges, carrying infusions of rich alluvial soil down from Tibet to nourish the fields of Southeast Asia. No bridges or roads marred this near pristine wilderness.

After an hour, low-lying clouds obscured the land below. We flew onward at 39,000 feet (11,887 m) over a flat sea of unbroken gray and white. Then, thirty or forty minutes later, I looked out the airliner's window and suddenly beheld a scene of the most stunning, incomparable grandeur I had ever encountered in a lifetime of travel around the globe.

Before us, an unbroken line of titanic, snow-capped peaks thrust up from the sea of clouds that completely hid their bases. They extended in perfect linear formation from east to west, as far as the eye could see. Each mountain towered majestically alone, separated by many leagues from its neighbors, enormous tors of ice and snow that thrust their jagged peaks into what seemed like the very top of the clear, azure sky, their near vertical sides glowing in the powerful morning sunlight with shifting hues of gold, russet, and bronze.

We had reached the great wall of the Himalayas, the world's highest and longest range of mountains, which begins in China and sweeps ever westward in an immense arc across the north of Burma, Nepal, and India. At Ladakh and Kashmir, the Himalayas then merge with their ranges, the Zanskar, Karakoram, and, far to the west in Afghanistan, the sinister Hindu Kush.

Breathtaking is too weak a word to describe the spectacle that lay before us. Seeing those great Himalayan peaks thrusting up from a sea of low cloud, glowing like beacons in the morning sun, was without question the closest I had ever come to having a religious experience. I was awestruck. In years past, I had spent much time in the Himalayas, but never before had I seen them from so high a vantage, so fully arrayed in all their glory. Each golden peak looked like an ancient god, standing fixed and immobile, surveying the lower world beneath his adamantine feet. I suddenly understood why the peoples of the Himalayas worshiped these towering mountains as sacred objects, or even deities. Here, for certain, was Valhalla, home of the gods.

The great wall of the Himalayas separates the Indian subcontinent from Central Asia, effectively isolating one from the other. Here the heavy clouds from the south break against the mountainsides and pour out their burden of rain onto the slopes, where much of it joins huge rivers and their many tributaries, and returns south to India and Southeast Asia.

To the north, Tibet, Ladakh, and much of Central Asia is a vast, arid wasteland, suitable only for the most meager subsistence agriculture and grazing. As a result, the populations of these sere, dusty lands has always remained small, and usually nomadic. Water is the mother of civilization.

Imagine Tibet as a great island set in a sea of high mountains. The Himalayas, crowned by the 29,028-foot (8,848-m) Mt. Everest, form the southern side of the Tibetan plateau. Its western flank is delineated by the Karakorams, Ladakh, and disputed Kashmir, and its north by the Kunlun Shan and various tributary ranges (*shan* means "mountain" in Chinese), beyond which lie the empty wastes of the Takla Makan desert. Tibet's eastern border is slightly less mountainous, though its passage is rendered extremely difficult by broad, turbulent rivers and parallel lines of mountains and deep gorges. A few perilous passes in the region of Khamb, and farther north, at Lake Koko Nor, afford limited access to the Tibetan plateau by the old trading route to western China. To the southeast lie the impassable jungle-covered mountains of Yunnan and Burma.

Behind this rampart of crags lies the lofty plateau of Tibet, twice the size of France, roughly 1,500 miles (2,400 km) in breadth and 500 miles (800 km) in width, at an average elevation of 15,000 feet (4,572 m), or 3 miles (5 km) above sea level, the highest nation on Earth. Contrary to popular belief, Tibet is not exclusively a land of crags. Most of Tibet consists of barren, undulating plateau, dotted with innumerable tarns, or glacial mountain lakes, often ringed by deposits of mineral salts. Mountains soar up from this table land to altitudes of 16,000 to 25,000 feet (4,877 to 7,620 m). Tibet was long known to China as "the western treasure house." Beneath its soil lie important deposits of gold, copper, gemstones, and radioactive ores.

The northern portion of Tibet, Chang Tang, is a sweeping plain of rocks, glacial moraines, and salt flats, occasionally cut by glacier-fed rivers, assaulted by snow and bitter cold in winter, and by intense heat and dust storms in the summer months. This is the land of Tibet's nomadic herders, who drive their flocks of brown, wooly yaks between small oases, or search for water on the higher slopes of the mountains.

Central and southern Tibet, with the wonderfully named province U, are somewhat less dry, though more mountainous, as they rise to meet the crests of the Himalayas. In the lower, and thus richer, eastern region of Tibet, the province of Amdo is renowned for its forested mountains and scenic beauty; the province of Khamb for its rich pastures, and fierce, nomadic warriors. Since most of Tibet is above the tree line, all wood used in building must be laboriously dragged up from Nepal, northern India, or Amdo and Khamb.

Like many mountain lands, notably Switzerland, or Canada's British Columbia, Tibet's contorted topography, with its mountain-sheltered small valleys and lakes, produces a remarkable variety of micro-climates. Sun-drenched valleys, where temperatures rise in summer to 91° F (33° C), lie just beneath gelid peaks whose snows never melt, even in July and August. Arid wastelands suddenly give way to fertile fields of barley, oats, and wheat. Green pastures bloom magically in the desert after short summer sprinkles of rain. Tiny patches of verdant land nestle at the feet of towering mountains of snow and ice. Unexpected oases dot the Tibetan plateau, which far from being a land of eternal snow, is actually a vast, cold desert at the very top of the world.

Like so much else about the "Abode of Snows" or "Hermit Kingdom," there is widespread uncertainty and debate over the borders of Tibet. There seem to be three distinct Tibets: geographic, political, and ethnic Tibet, each of which has different frontiers. Simply put, few, apart from Tibet's Chinese occupiers, are certain of where Tibet actually begins or ends, or even how many Tibetans exist.

According to most Western specialists, Britain's imperial cartographers, and Tibetans themselves, geographic Tibet extends from Kashmir, in the west, to the eastern edge of the great plateau that ends 60 miles (100 km) from Chengdu, and close to the Chinese frontier outpost city of Xining in the extreme northeast. These are the lands traditionally considered part of Tibet, from its early history until the modern era.

Political Tibet, roughly 500,000 square miles (1,295,000 sq km) in size, is the current, truncated, Chinese-ruled "Tibet Autonomous Province," an entity largely rejected by the people of Tibet but generally accepted by the outside world, including India and the United States. After seizing Tibet in 1950, China carved away almost half of geographic Tibet, appending a third of its territory to Szechuan, and creating from the remainder a new province, Xinghai.

Ethnic Tibet spans a far larger territory. Peoples of Mongol-Tibetan stock inhabit not only geographic Tibet but also Ladakh, Baltistan, bits of Kashmir, Bhutan, Sikkim, Assam, parts of Nepal, and the Chinese province of Sinkiang. The peoples of Chinese Inner Mongolia have close ethnic, cultural, and religious kinship to Tibet. At no time, however, did past Tibetan governments in Lhasa ever exercise control over more than half of the total population of ethnic Tibet.

No one is quite sure how many ethnic Tibetans there actually are today. Western experts maintain that no reliable census figures for Tibet exist. They dismiss Chinese census counts as unreliable or purposely distorted. The most commonly accepted total number of ethnic Tibetans is about seven million people.

Today, there are an estimated 2.5 million Tibetans within Chinese-ruled Tibet proper, and perhaps an equal number in the neighboring regions annexed by China. In other words, more ethnic Tibetans may live outside modern Tibet than within its borders. China has purposely obscured Tibetan population figures in order to undermine nationalist aspirations, and mask the large numbers of Han Chinese immigrants—perhaps as many as 2.5 million in total—brought in since 1950 to solidify Beijing's grasp on the country. China claims that according to its first national census in 1953, there were only one million Tibetans, a figure that by 1990, according to the fourth national census, had reached 2,196,000.

In the capital, Lhasa, Han Chinese now considerably outnumber ethnic Tibetans.

• • •

My second impression of Tibet, after my eyes had grown accustomed to the searing waves of light, was a sweeping panorama of immensity and stark beauty: broad, flat, dun-colored stretches of arid land; deep blue, motionless lakes interspersed with rugged hills; and, in the far distance, soaring, snow-capped mountains. A cold, relentless wind blows across this barren landscape, raising sheets of dust that linger in the air like low-lying clouds. Only the sound of the wind, and the occasional cry of blackbirds, breaks the overwhelming silence of this pristine wilderness.

On the way from Gonggar airport, which is a two-hour drive east of mountain-ringed Lhasa, I asked my driver to stop our Chinese jeep before a high wall of rock set next to a lake. On its surfaces was carved an enormous group of Buddhas, painted in vermilion, light blue, topaz, and gold. As I stood admiring this monument and its perfect reflection in the still waters of the lake, a sense of elation came over me. I took out my camera to take a picture, suddenly lost my balance, and almost fell over backward. I did not know it at the time, but this was the first ominous portent of high-altitude sickness. The relatively rapid, 9,000-foot (2,743-m) ascent from Chengdu to Tibet was beginning to affect my body.

Entering Lhasa, Tibet's temporal and spiritual capital, produced an electric thrill for even a jaded traveler like myself. Here, at last, was the heart of the Forbidden Kingdom; the ultimate goal of pilgrims, adventure-seekers, and professional voyagers alike.

The capital extends along the Kyi Chu River, set in an elongated, bowl-shaped valley, surrounded by 15,000-foot (4,572-m) mountains and rugged brown hills. Turning a sharp corner one suddenly beholds, atop a steep hill, the great Potola Palace, which entirely dominates the city below. This enormous, flat-roofed, white and red structure, with backward-curving white and red walls, was completed in 1694 under the Fifth Dalai Lama. It rises more than 400 feet (121 m), about thirteen stories, and contains a bewildering maze of corridors, secret passages, and some thousand rooms. The almost half-mile- (1 km-) long Potola is both the Vatican City of Buddhism and the seat of Tibet's government, a warren of dark, low-ceilinged assembly halls, chapels, libraries, schools, reliquaries, offices temporal and spiritual, and a monastery.

Much of the dark interior is decorated with hundreds of statues of Buddha and various deities, ornately carved and gilded wood, murals, frescoes, rich silk wall hangings, colorful Tibetan carpets, and endless shelves filled with religious scrolls and sacred texts. Dungeons and huge storerooms occupy the lowest levels, reminders that the Potola was as much a functioning palace and seat of government as a religious center—rather as if Rome's Vatican and nearby Castello St. Angelo had been combined into one enormous edifice.

I stood gazing at the Potola, my senses overloaded by its immensity, majesty, and soaring architecture. Its external design was harmonious yet complex, imposing yet functional. I had the impression of looking at a sort of gigantic, spiritual power plant.

Pilgrims came from all over Tibet to worship the Dalai Lama, their Divine Protector, often taking a year or more to perform the journey to the Potola. In the final stage of their adoration, begun outside Lhasa, pilgrims would crawl forward the final miles on their bellies, praying as they went.

Though moved by the ancient dignity and exotic richness of the Potola, as I walked its dark, narrow corridors, redolent of hundreds of smoking yak-butter candles, I also had a strong sense of eeriness and lurking evil. In the flickering light, shadows played on the walls and tapestries, giving them life and movement. The omnipresent darkness, the statues of fierce, glowering gods, the sound of distant chanting, lent a rather sinister aura to this palace of arcane mysteries and intrigue. Red-robed monks moved silently along the corridors, or clustered about objects of particular veneration, intoning prayers and making obeisances.

I decided that high altitude and persistent cold must induce a sense of lugubriousness and melancholy that promotes the worship of angry, ferocious, unforgiving deities who punish more often than they reward. Here was none of the warm, flower-bedecked beauty of Italian or French country churches, or the charming Buddhist wats of Thailand and Burma. This was the home of the thunder gods and evil spirits of the Himalayas, who were to be feared and placated.

Yet these dark feelings quickly vanished once I left the glowering devil-demons and angry deities inside the Potola and Tsuglakhang. Outside in the bright sunlight, central Lhasa's market was bustling, packed with colorful throngs of shoppers, monks, Muslim butchers, Chinese traders, pilgrims, and nomadic tribesmen. It would be difficult to discover a gentler, more amiable faith than Tibetan Buddhism.

In his epic first sermon, Gautama Buddha promulgated the Four Noble Truths that form the core of Buddhism: sorrow is the universal condition of mankind; the cause of sorrow is desire; sorrow only ends when desire ends; desire can be eliminated by following the path of enlightenment. Once all desire is expunged, man no longer desires life, and passes, in a state of enlightenment, to "nirvana," or pure being. Followers of the Noble Path must practice nonviolence and moderate asceticism, reject selfishness, and refrain from taking human or animal life. In its early stages, Buddhism was a faith without gods, and almost agnostic in nature.

In Tibet, the Mahayana sect blended the classic Buddhist teachings of self-denial, compassion, contemplation, and monasticism with important elements of Tibet's earlier shamanistic Mongol faith, including ancient rituals, assorted deities, evil mountain spirits, multi-form gods, and totem worship.

The result is an extremely elaborate, ritualistic, complex faith, which emphasizes the doing of good deeds, avoidance of evil thinking or acts, profound introspection, constant religious observance, and, perhaps most important, nonviolence. Tibetans believe man exists on a middle level, above the lower realm of eternal suffering, but well below the ultimate nirvana attained by the Buddha. Through a process of reincarnation, people rise slowly upward or fall, depending on their accumulated good or bad deeds (their "karma").

The first Dalai Lama, Gerdun Truppa, appeared as a child in 1419. After his death he was recognized by popular acclaim as the true incarnation of the Living Buddha. The office of Panchen Lama, subordinate to the Dalai Lama in a teacher-student relationship, but still a considerable power, was established during the same era. According to Tibetan belief, each subsequent Dalai Lama has been the direct reincarnation of the line begun by the First Dalai Lama, five centuries ago. The current incarnation, the Fourteenth Dalai Lama, born Tenzin Gyatso, was discovered through the traditional arcane process of divination and ritual after the death of his predecessor in 1933.

Ominously, not long before the Thirteenth Dalai Lama died, he made a chilling prophecy: "Unless we now learn how to protect our land, the Dalai Lama, and the Panchen Lama, the Father and the Son, the upholders of the Buddhist faith, the gracious Incarnations, all will go under and disappear and leave not a trace behind...." The child who succeeded him would inherit this fearsome divination.

• • •

I walked about Lhasa's central market, idling my way from stall to stall, taking photos and appearing every inch the average tourist. The shoppers and strollers in the streets wore a mixture of colorful Tibetan native wear and shabby Chinese clothing; the common universal uniform of blue jeans and sneakers one sees from Omaha to Osaka was pleasingly absent. I noted, however, a rank, pungent odor that seemed to permeate everything, a cloying mixture of rancid yak butter and unwashed, sweaty bodies. Tibetans, it is said, wash only three times in their lives: at birth, on their nuptials, and at death. Like other peoples of the Himalayas and Andes, Tibetans rarely have the luxury of hot water for bathing. So everyone smells, a fact that only outsiders seem to find unpleasant. Perhaps we Westerners have grown too sensitive, or too devoted to sterility. I recalled Napoleon's famous message to Josephine upon his return from the Russian campaign: "Arriving in three days. Don't wash!"

Foreign tourists made the Chinese edgy, but their dollars were badly needed by the People's Republic, which charged visitors piratical prices for supervised tours of Tibet. I managed to leave my guides, on the pretext of shopping for souvenirs. After two hours of sightseeing, and dodging into temples, I was reasonably certain agents of the Chinese security police were not following me.

Lhasa looked normal, but to my eyes, trained to watchfulness in a score of nasty Communist or Third World dictatorships, the signs of repression were evident. Large numbers of uniformed and plainclothes Chinese police kept discreet watch on the Tibetan population. Police checkpoints guarded many important intersections. Hidden up back alleys, squads of riot police waited for trouble. My reconnaissance around the capital showed that three regular divisions of the Chinese People's Liberation Army were based just outside Lhasa in a rough circle, ready to intervene on short notice. Military checkpoints carefully monitored traffic in and out of the capital.

Following instructions I had received before coming to Tibet, I entered a small, shabby store selling curios and trinkets. In the tiny back room I met with two Tibetan men, who seemed extremely nervous and wary. While a third kept watch outside, they related to me in broken English how the Chinese were relentlessly destroying Tibet's religion and culture, as well as importing large numbers of Han immigrants in a massive effort to make Tibetans a carefully controlled minority in their own country. One of the men had been in the Lao Gai, the fearsome Chinese gulag that is spoken of only in whispers wherever one goes in China.

There is an underground resistance movement across Tibet, but it is badly fragmented, disorganized, and frequently penetrated by Chinese agents. Lacking arms or foreign support, Tibetan nationalists are compelled to adopt a policy of sullen, passive resistance until the day, however distant, that a miracle occurs, and China's iron grip is somehow broken, or at least relaxed. It had happened before in Tibet's long history, I was told, and, with patience, would happen again.

I returned, after much diversionary walking, to my hotel, a low, modern structure that seemed quite out of place in Lhasa. My head was throbbing with pain, and my laboring lungs could not seem to get enough air. My nose became clogged. A sharp metallic taste filled my mouth. The thought of eating repelled me. Deny it as I might, I knew my body was experiencing the adverse effects of altitude. Having undergone a bout of altitude illness in Cuzco, Peru, I knew what to do. I decided to take to my bed and rest, the recommended treatment for oxygen deprivation.

As the night wore on, the pain in my head grew steadily more intense. My body began to ache. I tossed about, listless, enervated, and increasingly miserable. I called the front desk, asking for oxygen. There was none, but I was told to call room service and ask for an "oxygen pillow." Ten minutes later, I was presented with a swollen brown rubber bladder, from which a clamped tube protruded. I loosened the clamp and sucked greedily on the tube for air. What issued from this strange device may have been oxygen, or it may only have been thin air; whatever it was, the emergency pillow did nothing at all to lessen the painful throbbing in my head. Three more pillows, procured from room service, made no difference.

I spent a night of torment. By morning, however, I felt slightly better and decided to continue exploring Lhasa, albeit with painful slowness and frequent stops to gasp for air. My guides insisted on taking me to the famed Nordulingka, the Dalai Lama's former summer palace built on the banks of the river. Grudgingly, I went.

The wood and masonry palace was as delicate and lovely as the Potola was grim and intimidating. One easily understands why the youthful Dalai Lama preferred to pass his hours here, often in the company of his foreign companion and mentor, the Austrian adventurer Heinrich Harreer, as far as possible from the intrigues and stultifying rituals of the oppressive Potola.

Every room of the sprawling Nordulingka was filled with religious statues, tapestries, and scrolls. The by now familiar palace guard of scowling Buddhas and savage protector deities lined the long, dark corridors. I was finally shown into a modest-sized room with a narrow bed, writing table and lamp, and two hard chairs. This, I was informed, was the private bedroom of the "imperialist, reactionary stooge, the former Dalai Lama."

I was at once filled by a sense of shame and embarrassment at intruding uninvited into the vacated personal quarters of so august a figure.

More to the point, I had once met and conversed at length with the Dalai Lama, a fact that made my discomfort all the more acute.

My encounter with the Living Buddha occurred in Canada three years previously, when he was giving a lecture on Tibet. The Dalai Lama was a gentle, mild-looking man who radiated kindness and warmth. The audience of wealthy donors had come to hear His Holiness explain the meaning of life. Instead, the Dalai Lama delivered a long discourse on the history of the Indian-Chinese border dispute that left his listeners dazed and uncomprehending. During the question period, I asked him a number of questions about his views on the border question.

After the talk, the Dalai Lama came over to talk to me. We fell into a long discussion on the details of the McMahon Line, a subject that clearly fascinated him and about which he was exceptionally well informed. The Living Buddha demonstrated an incisive grasp of Asian geopolitics and the growing strains between India and China. My heart instantly warmed to this highly intelligent man, who is often—and wrongly—depicted as an unworldly mystic. He also left me with a very personal message, whose simple, profound meaning I would not discover until I had voyaged to Tibet and stood in his personal quarters in the summer palace.

16
India Awakes

China's concern over the loyalty of its "new Tibetan brothers" was well-founded. On the busy streets of Lhasa, Tibetans would shyly approach me, bow, and whisper, "Please, a picture of the Dalai Lama." All photographs or paintings of the Tibetan leader were banned as "subversive" by the Chinese police. Even possession of a photo can lead to beatings, prison, or even the Lao Gai, the vast gulag created by China in the wastes of Quinghai Province, where the average sentence for political deviation, real or imagined, was fifteen to twenty years' hard labor on subsistence rations. Yet it was plainly evident that Tibetans yearned passionately for the return of their spiritual leader, and sorely chafed under the harsh Chinese "liberation."

This point was amply demonstrated to me by a violent riot that erupted before my eyes in downtown Lhasa. Chinese police had tried to seize a picture of the Dalai Lama from a seller of hides. He had resisted; a mêlée erupted, as passersby sought to prevent his arrest. In a few minutes, the streets of central Lhasa were filled with demonstrators hurling curses at their occupiers, and attacking Chinese-owned shops.

Truckloads of Chinese riot police and heavily armed troops suddenly appeared, sealing the main intersections and cordoning off the downtown area. Tibetan demonstrators were beaten with rubber truncheons and tear-gassed. More troops took up positions on the outer roads ringing the capital. I was stopped by security police, searched, and forced to return to my hotel, for my "protection against bandits and troublemakers," I was helpfully informed. More riots had erupted, I later learned, in Shigatse, Tibet's second city.

Chinese authorities would subsequently denounce the riots as the work of "splittists, feudal elements, and foreign agents." Clearly, Tibet's liberation was not progressing satisfactorily, in spite of four decades of socialist re-education and ideological purification, Chinese euphemisms for brute force, terror, intimidation, and ceaseless propaganda.

Beijing's insistence that Tibet has been an integral part of the Chinese nation for more than 1,500 years is historically unfounded.

Trade links have existed between western China and Tibet for the past two millennia, but China had no political influence, and thus no valid historic claim over the region of ethnic Tibet, until the late thirteenth century. In 1280 the Mongol ruler of China, Kublai Khan, developed an interest in Tibet and its religion. Mongols and Tibetans shared the same ethnic roots and shamanistic beliefs. A delegation of Tibetan lamas of the Sakya order was invited to the Mongol imperial court. Kublai Khan was so impressed by the wisdom of the Tibetan lamas, he immediately converted to their faith, and ordered his followers to do the same. In a matter of a few years, the mighty Mongol Empire adopted Tibetan Buddhism as its state religion. In doing so, the Mongols assumed the role of protectors of their new Vatican, Tibet.

The vast Mongol empire proved ephemeral, disintegrating and vanishing in the fourteenth century. Rebellion erupted across China, producing the powerful Ming dynasty. The Ming rulers continued the spiritual liaison between China and Tibet, which came to be known as the teacher-ruler or priest-patron relationship. Tibetans paid nominal obeisance to the Chinese emperors who, in turn, granted Tibet's religious leaders a unique position in matters spiritual, and complete temporal autonomy over Tibet.

The priest-patron relationship between the Chinese emperors and Tibet mirrored China's traditional feudal policy toward the vassal regimes around its borders, whose rulers were granted full autonomy—in exchange for obedience and payment of annual tribute. This unique relationship would continue as a principal theme of China's foreign policy right down to the end of the twentieth century, when Beijing would "teach a lesson" to neighboring states that failed to comply with the will of China's rulers.

This very Asian relationship continued when the First Dalai Lama returned to Tibet in the fifteenth century, unifying thenceforth the powers of church and state under his unquestioned rule, and lessening the danger that China might gain control of Tibet by playing off its many political or religious factions against the others. Whereas before Tibet had had many respected priests and wise men, it now had a pope, of resplendent spiritual power and majesty.

China's Manchu dynasty replaced the moribund Ming rulers in the seventeenth century. The Manchus reasserted China's nominal suzerainty over Tibet, which in turn continued to pay token tribute to

Imperial China. In 1720, a Manchu army marched up into Tibet, but soon departed. In fact, until the twentieth century, China had only sporadic physical control of the remote, far western regions of Tibet and Turkestan to which it laid claim. The best a steadily weakening China could achieve was a few ineffectual military expeditions into the region, and the occasional stationing of a handful of imperial officials, known as *ambans* in Lhasa.

Tibet remained happily isolated from the outside world, thanks to its mountain remoteness, until the dawn of the twentieth century, when various imperial powers suddenly took an interest in the lost kingdom, which had until then escaped their predatory designs. The British grew concerned that the relentless southward expansion by the Russian Empire into Central Asia might penetrate Tibet, as well as Afghanistan, thus threatening the borders of British India. There were rumors of Russian agents operating in Tibet. Besides, British interest in the Himalayas was growing: in 1890 the British Raj detached the ancient Buddhist kingdom of Sikkim from Tibet and made it a protectorate.

Seizing the initiative, the British viceroy of India, Lord Curzon, who had described Tibet as an "anachronism," dispatched a three-thousand-man expeditionary force to Lhasa in 1904 to assure Britain's strategic, political, and commercial interests in the kingdom. The expedition succeeded in making the arduous ascent to Tibet, battling Tibetan tribesmen along the way. On August 4, 1904, the British marched into the Vatican City of Central Asia, forever ending Tibet's splendid isolation. Before withdrawing, the expeditionary force imposed a trade treaty on Tibet, which, as was the case with all such imperial pacts, was really designed to open the way to British political influence over Tibet. A direct diplomatic link had been established between Great Britain and Tibet.

The British incursion greatly alarmed the Manchu court. China's anxiety was deepened by Lord Curzon's curt dismissal of China's claim to Tibet as "fiction." In 1909, the Manchus dispatched an army to reassert their claims to Tibet. The Chinese force marched up into Tibet from Chengdu, deposed the Dalai Lama the next year, and occupied Lhasa in the face of stout and prolonged Tibetan military opposition. In 1911, however, the decayed Manchu dynasty was overthrown by Sun Yat-sen. Revolution swept over China, forcing the Chinese garrison in Tibet to withdraw. Strongly encouraged by the British, Tibet declared independence from China in 1913.

These events finally led to an important conclave in 1914 at the Indian hill station of Simla. The Thirteenth Dalai Lama sought British support for full Tibetan political independence. Britain and Tibet signed the accord, which recognized Tibetan independence, and guaranteed British imperial interests in Tibet. China's nominal suzerainty over the kingdom was acknowledged as a face-saving gesture for China, but the new Chinese Republic refused to sign the Simla Agreement. Britain, distracted by events in Europe, soon lost interest in both Tibet and the alleged Russian threat to the Raj. Tibet slipped back happily into obscurity. The Thirteenth Dalai Lama reaffirmed that Tibet, now freed of Chinese occupation, was fully independent of China, but his declaration attracted neither recognition nor attention from the great powers, who were by then absorbed by the looming threat of a world war. Nevertheless, Tibet was *de facto*, and to all intents and purposes *de jure*, independent, and would remain so for the next thirty-seven years.

• • •

On October 7, 1950, China's First and Second Field Armies, totaling eighty thousand soldiers, crossed the upper Yangtze River and invaded Tibet. Late in the previous year, Chinese military forces had slowly infiltrated Tibet's extreme eastern provinces after Beijing Radio had announced that the "renegade" provinces of Tibet, Taiwan, and Hainan would be reunited with the motherland.

Resistance by Tibet's tiny army and bands of Khampa tribesmen was quickly crushed. Beijing Radio proclaimed Chinese troops had entered Tibet to liberate it from "imperialist oppression." Tibet's frantic appeals for help to the United Nations, India, Britain, and the United States were ignored, or rebuffed with diplomatic evasions. No nation was about to challenge the new People's Republic of China, which had some ten million men under arms, over the fate of an obscure mountain kingdom lost in the Himalayas.

India, the most immediately concerned power, closed its eyes to the invasion. Nehru was preoccupied by Kashmir and Pakistan; he cited the vague 1914 Simla Agreement—which China had never signed—as a legal basis for Beijing's claim that Tibet was, in fact, a part of China, and a strictly internal matter. It was a fateful decision India would live to regret.

Tibet was forced in 1951 to sign a treaty confirming Chinese rule over the nation. The young Fourteenth Dalai Lama saw his nation suddenly turned into a province of Mao's revolutionary China. Chinese troops, police, and settlers poured into "liberated" Tibet.

At first, the Chinese promised Tibet full autonomy, religious freedom, and the preservation of its traditions and customs. The Chinese earnestly attempted to convince Tibetans that communism was a superior way of life, which would free them from superstition and feudalism. When this effort failed dismally, China's occupation forces began a severe crackdown, jailing thousands of "reactionaries" and "wreckers." Increased repression, and forced collectivization of agriculture, led to the outbreak of a major rebellion across Tibet in 1959. China poured troops into Tibet and ruthlessly crushed the uprising, killing nearly 100,000 Tibetans. A similar number of Tibetans, and their beloved god-king the Dalai Lama, fled to exile in northern India.

In the early 1960s, the U.S. Central Intelligence Agency began a top-secret operation to form, train, and equip Tibetan exiles in India into anti-Chinese guerrilla bands. In 1998, the Dalai Lama's administration in India for the first time acknowledged receiving $1.7 million a year during the 1960s from the CIA, as well as an annual personal subsidy for the Dalai Lama of $180,000, but this is merely a fraction of the total funds expended by the U.S. to support the Tibetan resistance.

The CIA organized regular airdrops of weapons and supplies to bands of Khampa warriors fighting Chinese occupation in eastern Tibet. India, by then finally aroused to the Chinese threat, joined the effort, directing its foreign intelligence agency, the Research and Analysis Wing (RAW), to cooperate with the CIA in supporting Tibetan resistance forces. This was one of only a few known instances when the normally adversarial CIA and RAW worked together. It was even a rarer example of cooperation, albeit chilly and very limited, between RAW and Pakistani intelligence; the latter was aiding the U.S. in the effort to supply Tibetan rebels. Bases for Tibetan guerrillas were established in the Indian protectorate of Sikkim and in Nepal, which was equally concerned by the looming Chinese threat.

The 1962 border war between China and India finally spurred

Delhi's decision to undermine Chinese rule of Tibet. China was caught in a dilemma. Beijing's official propaganda position was that Tibetans welcomed Chinese "liberation" and were joyously participating in the modernization of their nation. China could not thus openly admit that Tibet seethed with rebellion. Nor could China publicly accuse India of trying to undermine its hold on the kingdom, since Tibetans were supposedly reveling in the joys of Chinese occupation.

Tibetan resistance spread across the nation, tying down over 250,000 Chinese troops in counter-guerrilla operations. Unable to crush Tibetan resistance or stop infiltration from guerrilla bases in Nepal and Sikkim, Chairman Mao finally took decisive action. In the late 1960s, China threatened to invade Sikkim and Nepal unless the rebel bases were closed and guerrilla forces disarmed. At the same time, the U.S. and China were beginning secret negotiations, through Pakistan, aimed at establishing an entente against the Soviet Union.

Secretary of State Henry Kissinger decided opening the door to Beijing was worth far more than wresting Tibet from Chinese control: all aid to Tibetan resistance would cease forthwith. As a result of combined pressure from the U.S. and China, India and Nepal abruptly abandoned the Tibetan resistance and arrested its leaders. Tibetan guerrilla units that were not encircled and destroyed by the Chinese PLA were disbanded and imprisoned by Nepal. The betrayal of Tibet was complete.

A second enormous disaster, Mao's Great Cultural Revolution, fell upon Tibet, inflicting untold suffering. Much of Tibet's religious and lay leadership, "bourgeois elements," and its small group of intellectuals were executed or thrown into the Lao Gai.

Armies of Red Guards rampaged across Tibet, destroying vestiges of "feudal culture and superstition." In a barbarous act of cultural genocide, more than six thousand monasteries were razed, their precious art and literary treasures either looted or burned.

The West largely ignored this campaign of terror and vandalism, just as it did the similar, and equally egregious, destruction by Mao's Red Guards of China's own cultural and artistic treasures. The Great Cultural Revolution marked one of history's worst cultural disasters, akin to the barbarian invasions of the Roman Empire, or the destruction of Islamic civilization by the Mongols. Many Western intellectuals and leftists, and much of the media, closed their eyes to the barbaric madness that swept over China, loudly extolling the "social progress" brought by the Chinese communists. Only a few, notably the courageous Belgian writer and art historian Simon Lys, denounced the monstrous criminal acts of Mao and his demented mobs of Red Guards.

During the same dark period, China continued to pour Han Chinese settlers into Tibet, to the point where they eventually came to outnumber native Tibetans by at least one million. China also pursued this policy of strategic demographic inundation in Sinkiang, Inner Mongolia, and Manchuria.

Chinese propaganda made much of the fact that "liberation" had brought Tibet badly needed modernization, and redistribution of land. China constructed roads, bridges, hospitals, and schools in Tibet, where none had existed before. Feudal serfdom was ended, only to be replaced by the more draconian servitude of Communist collective farming. Although much of the infrastructure in Tibet was designed primarily for the benefit of the military and Chinese settler population, China did drag parts of Tibet into the semi-modern age and improve the standard of living of many Tibetans—but at a fearsome price Tibetans were clearly unwilling to pay.

By the 1970s, China had firmly cemented its strategic control of Tibet. All-weather military roads crossed the country, enabling Chinese troops to move quickly into Tibet from Sichuan, and to all key points along the long border with India. The PLA built a score of new airbases on the plateau, which for the first time put much of northern India within range of Chinese warplanes. Medium-range missiles capable of striking Delhi, Calcutta, and Bombay were emplaced, for the first time, in Tibet. China also rapidly developed its new nuclear testing center at Lanzhou, on Tibet's northeast border.

Over the past two decades, India and China conducted sporadic negotiations over their border disputes, and announced various plans to lessen mutual tensions, including annual meetings at the minister- ial level. India remained preoccupied by the confrontation with Pakistan, unrest in Kashmir and Punjab, and the civil war in Sri Lanka. Indian strategists had no desire to become embroiled in a two-front conflict with Pakistan and its ally, China. For its part, China was focused, under the leadership of Deng Xiaoping, on rapid economic development. China's military was denied funds for modernization. Beijing sought to downplay all regional disputes and adopt a non-confrontational foreign policy that would diminish Western fear of the Communist giant, thus affording China access to badly needed foreign investment, technology, and export markets.

By the late 1990s, China had achieved remarkable economic growth, and as a result of Deng's enormously successful reformist policies was winning grudging acceptance by the outside world as a new regional superpower. The post-Deng political succession had progressed smoothly: China was economically sound, politically stable, and, save for the always explosive Taiwan issue, generally perceived by the West as non-threatening in its foreign policy. Fears a power struggle among Deng's would-be successors might bring chaos, regional secession, or even national disintegration proved unfounded. The collective leadership under President Jiang Zemin managed a smooth, efficient, peaceful transfer of power from the Old Guard to a somewhat younger (though still old) and more forward-thinking group of party leaders who were determined to press ahead with Deng's economic reforms, while avoiding at all costs Gorbachev's loosening of Communist political controls, an act of folly, in Beijing's view, that caused the collapse of the Soviet state.

India, too, had made important, if less dramatic, economic progress. During the same period, India also succeeded in developing a substantial military-industrial base, and a world-class computing and software industry around Bangalore, India's "Silicon Valley." In effect, India was really two contrasting nations: a backward agricultural country of some 900 million; and a fairly modern, industrial-technological urban society of 100 million. Modern India and antique Mother India coexisted uncomfortably, pulled in opposite directions in a constant tug-of-war between modernists and traditionalists, and afflicted, like so many other Third World nations, by deep cultural confusion.

So, as the century drew to a close, China and India, Asia's two most populous states, once relegated to the world's lowest ranks as hopelessly backward, chaotic pauper nations, had attained a state of semi-development, internal stability, and self-respect that permitted, and even encouraged, both to look outward and reassess their relative positions in South and East Asia. It was also evident that while China had succeeded in stabilizing its population growth at 1.2 billion, India's population was still growing at a rapid rate: sometime in the first decade of the twenty-first century, India would surpass China to become the world's most populous nation.

To understand how strategic events and conflicts will develop in Asia, it is essential to examine the way its two great powers see themselves, and their rival interests, within the region.

India's view is largely shaped by its Hindu nationalist-dominated political establishment, an influential group of strategic thinkers in Delhi, the military establishment, the intelligentsia, and the nation's powerful business leaders. Since independence, India has been torn between two currents of geopolitical thought. The first, espoused by Nehru, saw India as a champion of Third-Worldism, Fabian socialism, and peaceful coexistence with its neighbors—Pakistan excepted.

Asia's problems were largely the fault of British and American imperialism, and could be resolved through negotiation, solidarity, and cooperation. India would be the moral champion and prime motive force of this new, benign, post-colonial Asian order. This thinking reached its apogee during the heady days of the 1960s, when Nehru joined with Egypt's Gamal Abdel Nasser, Indonesia's Sukarno, and Yugoslavia's Tito to proclaim the era of non-aligned nations.

India's 1962 war with China, the massive economic failure of socialist Third World nations, and Israel's stunning victory in the 1967 Arab-Israeli conflict put an end to the pretensions and dreams of the non-aligned movement. After the deaths of Nehru, Nasser, Tito, and Sukarno, the movement lost its most articulate, charismatic spokesmen and with them its moral impetus; from then on it would be fatally undermined by the inflated ambitions, empty rhetoric, and the demoralizing economic and military weakness of its leading members. Hope was replaced by disillusionment and widespread cynicism.

Indira Gandhi's rise to power profoundly altered India's geopolitical thinking. This remarkable iron-willed lady, as strong and decisive as Nehru was weak and dithering, abandoned for good his uncertain, confused policies. She was determined to see India quickly become the great power it inherently was. There would be no more silly talk about nonviolence, or foreign policy driven by high moral concerns. India, in Indira's view, had to meet its destiny as Asia's superpower, the subcontinent's unchallenged master, and overlord of the vast Indian Ocean.

This muscular strategy meant building up India's industries, military power, and nuclear capability.

In what soon came to be known as the "Indira Doctrine," Indira Gandhi and her dynastic successors, sons Sanjay and Rajiv, translated the aggressive theories then being developed in India's strategic and political think tanks into concrete policy. In 1970–71, Pakistan was confronted, defeated, and dismembered into Pakistan and Bangladesh. Nepal was warned to bow to India's will and to cease flirtation with China. Indian "peacekeeping" forces invaded Sri Lanka during that nation's civil war in a failed effort to turn the island nation into another protectorate of New Delhi. Indian paratroops were dropped on the Maldive Islands to put down a coup. Efforts were intensified to crush rebellions by Sikhs in Punjab, Muslims in Kashmir, Gurkhas in Assam, and tribal peoples in the remote eastern hill states bordering Burma and in the strategically important Andaman Islands that lie in the Indian Ocean south of Burma.

India's wobbly post-Gandhi governments were too consumed by domestic problems to follow their predecessor's aggressive world view. But when the nationalist BJP came to power at the head of a coalition, it dusted off the Indira Policy, making it the party's unofficial foreign policy. BJP militants called for the eventual reunification of the entire Indian subcontinent into Bharat Hind, or Great India. In the view of Indian nationalists, British imperialism had chopped up India, creating an unstable and unnatural group of minor states, in order to undermine independent India's power and maintain Western influence in the region. Pakistan, in particular, was seen as an agent of U.S. imperial interests in the Indian Ocean, and a tool for keeping India on the strategic defensive.

This assertive doctrine held that the entire Indian Ocean and its littoral states were an integral part of India's legitimate sphere of geopolitical interest. In effect, India's maritime sphere of dominance extended in a great pyramid, first east across the Bay of Bengal to the highly important Strait of Malacca between Indonesia, Malaysia, and Singapore, and then as far south as the western coast of Australia. Next, forming the bottom of the great triangle, it followed a straight line from Australia to the coast of East Africa and the Madagascar Channel, between Mozambique and Madagascar. Then around the Horn of Africa, and northward through East Africa, finally encompassing the

202 The Roof of the World

entire Arabian Sea, including the mouth of the oil-producing Gulf.

To assert dominion over this vast body of ocean, and project power far from its coasts, India embarked in the 1970s on a major program of naval construction, which included deployment of two aircraft carriers with their supporting task forces, submarines, a large number of surface combatants, a squadron of long-range TU-142M Bear maritime bombers, and a nuclear attack submarine leased from the Soviet Union.

The primary mission of India's growing fleet was to blockade Pakistan's coast and the port of Karachi, in time of war. Secondary but still important considerations were protecting India's maritime commerce and imports of oil coming from the Gulf or through the Strait of Malacca; monitoring Sri Lanka and the island groups of the Andamans, Nicobars, and Maldives; and keeping a weather eye on the coasts of Bangladesh and Burma. Another key unstated mission of the Indian Navy was to deter naval intervention in the Arabian Sea by the U.S. fleet in the event of a conflict with Pakistan. During the 1971 war, deployment in the Arabian Sea of a U.S. carrier battle group in support of Pakistan had caused profound alarm in Delhi, and convinced Indian naval strategists any such future American action had to be prevented.

India's maritime assertiveness provoked widespread concern among the littoral states of the Indian Ocean, and even more from the U.S. Navy, which saw a challenge to its hitherto unchallenged domination of that ocean. The strategic axis between India and the Soviet Union and Moscow's supply of enormous amounts of advanced weapons to India at bargain prices heightened American anxiety. A new war between India and Pakistan, or the spread of the war in Afghanistan, might bring the U.S. and USSR, supported by India, into a direct clash in the Indian Ocean.

The collapse of the Soviet Union allayed these fears, but in recent years, the old Delhi-Moscow entente has been largely restored. India remains Russia's leading foreign customer for arms, spare parts, and military and nuclear technology. Russia is selling India its most advanced aircraft, such as the MIG-29 and SU-30MK, conventional Kilo-class attack submarines, surface warfare systems, and technology for India's planned nuclear submarines—some of which will be armed with strategic missiles. India's and Russia's strategic interests in Central and South Asia still remain in concert, particularly with regard to

Afghanistan, their enmity to Pakistan and opposition to the spread of militant Islam, mutual concern over China, and the shared conviction that the United States has grown too powerful and aggressive as the world's sole superpower.

Pressure from the U.S. on India to cease its nuclear weapons program and on Russia to halt the export of weapons and nuclear technology to Iran have produced cries of blackmail from Moscow, and heated accusations by India of "U.S. nuclear apartheid," further pushing Delhi and Moscow into a closer embrace.

India's steady economic development, averaging over 5 percent per annum in recent years, has permitted it to continue modernization of its armed forces, the world's third largest after China and the United States. India's 980,000-man army has been transformed over the past decade by mechanization and more combat-effective, mobile formations structured around armor- and artillery-heavy strike corps designed for war against Pakistan. India now fields over 3,400 main battle tanks, the most effective being the newly acquired Russian T-90s; updated models of the Soviet T-72; and the locally developed, much troubled Arjun tank, due for introduction in 2004. The army's striking power has been substantially enhanced by the addition of self-propelled artillery to supplement its already large force of Swedish and Soviet-supplied guns.

The Indian Air Force's 772 combat planes have been supplemented with the latest Russian strike aircraft, France's excellent Mirage 2000H, and highly effective air-to-air and anti-aircraft missiles. Some of India's large fleet of older MiG-21s are being modernized, with Russian and Israeli assistance. Nevertheless, India's air force has serious problems of training, spare parts, and coordination, as well as a truly awesome record of accidents, leading Pakistanis to claim their best strategy is to defer the next war until the Indian Air Force crashes all its planes.

India's navy currently lists one aircraft carrier (the second is out of service, but due to be replaced by a new model, likely the 40,500-ton Russian "Admiral Gorshkov"), nineteen submarines, twenty-four destroyers and frigates, and an air arm with British Harrier jump jets and Soviet reconnaissance bombers. By comparison, Japan, whose GDP is eleven times as large as India's, and whose maritime commerce is greater by an entire order of magnitude, has no aircraft carriers, sixteen submarines, and fifty-seven major surface combatants. India is building its first nuclear submarine, based on technology and equipment supplied by Russia, due to be commissioned in 2004. The submarine will carry the new Sagarika sea-launched ballistic missile, also based on Russian technology, armed with a nuclear warhead. India will thus acquire a long-range nuclear-strike capability from the sea, with a very low vulnerability to enemy detection or attack, which will give Delhi a survivable reserve nuclear force that can respond even after a surprise enemy nuclear attack.

To India's 1,175,000-man armed forces must be added its large paramilitary forces, which number 1,090,000 active men. Included in this second army are such units as the Rashtriya Rifles, Indo-Tibetan Border Police, Assam Rifles (twice as many men as the entire Canadian Armed Forces), Central Reserve Police Force of 185,000 men, and state armed police numbering 400,000. Some of these units have heavy weapons, are reasonably well trained and disciplined, and must be counted as active army reserves. Other units, such as the notorious Central Reserve Police Force, which has committed extensive atrocities in Kashmir, are undisciplined thugs of little military value. While these paramilitary forces are designed for internal security, some are mobile and could be trucked to combat fronts in wartime, or at least free up army regulars from internal security duties in troubled regions of India.

India's large conventional forces have clearly been designed to fight a war of movement against their historical enemy, Pakistan. The army's most powerful mobile units, three corps with six divisions, face Pakistan. China's invasion of Tibet and the ensuing 1962 war, however, compelled the Indian defense establishment to develop a substantial mountain-warfare capability with specially trained divisions. India currently deploys, at least under its nominal order of battle, seventeen mountain divisions on the border with China and Tibet, though some have been moved to Kashmir for counter-guerrilla operations. A large, mobile reserve is maintained for rapid reaction.

The development of India's nuclear arsenal, however, has been aimed at China since the beginning. India has overwhelming conventional military superiority over Pakistan; nuclear weapons were unnecessary, and if used against neighboring Pakistan would cause enormous civilian casualties in India. Delhi's nuclear arsenal confers great-power status and diplomatic muscle; it also counters China's modest but still worrisome nuclear forces. There is some debate whether it was China or India that first began to develop nuclear weapons, though China tested and deployed nuclear warheads well ahead of India. After the 1962 war with China, India put its nuclear program into high gear, exploding a 12-kiloton nuclear device in 1974.

India adopted a two-track nuclear program using enriched uranium and reprocessed plutonium, based on technology supplied by Canada, France, the United States, and the Soviet Union.

Canada's role was of primary importance. The Canadian government sold India four 220MW pressurized heavy water reactors at give-away prices as part of its foreign aid program. Equally important, Canada supplied India with blueprints and technology for nuclear plant design and local production of components, as well as the key technology to produce and enrich nuclear fuel. In addition, Canada also trained a sizeable cadre of Indian nuclear scientists and technicians. When India conducted its first nuclear test in 1974, Canada, deeply embarrassed, cut off all nuclear transactions with India, but it was too late. The nuclear genie was out of the bottle.

France helped India build the heavy-water plants at Baroda and Tuticorin, and the fast breeder reactor at Kalpakkam (all three unsafeguarded), and trained large numbers of Indian nuclear engineers and technicians.

The unsafeguarded heavy-water plants at Nangal and Talcher were supplied by Germany, along with the strategic metals beryllium and lithium, the latter used to produce tritium, an element that boosts the power of nuclear explosions. Norway illegally sold India 26 tons of heavy water, which was diverted through Switzerland and Romania. The Swiss helped build the heavy-water plants at Baroda and Tuticorin.

The Soviet Union covertly provided India 80 tons of heavy water and a large cadre of nuclear technicians and advisors for the important Madras and Dhruva reactors. Britain supplied turbine generator pumps and sent repair technicians, Sweden special steel plates and flash x-ray devices. The United States unwittingly supplied heavy water for the Canadian Cirus reactor that produced the plutonium used in India's first nuclear device.

Today, four decades later, India has a highly developed civilian nuclear infrastructure consisting of ten major nuclear reactors, with four more due to come on line in the near future, supplying 2 percent of the nation's power requirements.

Many of these plants are under International Atomic Energy Agency safeguards, and produce only electric power. But India also has a very large military nuclear infrastructure, dedicated to the production of plutonium and uranium weapons, which operates without any international inspection or safeguards: twelve reactors, nine "research reactors" (most clustered in the Trombay complex outside Bombay), a fast-breeder reactor, six uranium-ore processing and refining plants, five nuclear-fuel fabrication plants, four reprocessing plants, and eight heavy-water plants.

According to foreign intelligence estimates, India has a stockpile of 800 kilograms of weapons-grade plutonium 239, sufficient to produce between 80 and 120 nuclear warheads. Annual production of enriched uranium-233 is estimated at 1,433 pounds (650 kg), enough for 70 to 100 nuclear warheads. Israel has reportedly been secretly helping India develop the reliability, explosive power, and miniaturization of its nuclear warheads, and supplying guidance technology for their delivery systems, the Prithvi and Agni series missiles. By the end of 1998, India was estimated to have anywhere from 10 to 100 operational nuclear warheads that could be activated within hours by insertion of nuclear cores in the weapon's high-explosive outer shells. Development of this powerful nuclear infrastructure and missile delivery systems is estimated to have cost India at least $40 billion, and could very likely reach $100 billion by 2005, a tremendous expenditure for a nation whose per capita GDP is $1,600, and which still receives substantial development and humanitarian aid from foreign donors.

The underground nuclear tests conducted by India in 1998 were designed to validate the reliability of tactical and strategic warheads for missiles, air-delivered bombs, and 155mm artillery shells. The most important part of the tests was the validating of the new nuclear warheads for the short-range Prithvi, the medium-range Agni series of missiles. Indian nuclear officials also leaked the news that they had tested the "big bomb," a thermonuclear (hydrogen) weapon. This claim is disputed by some Western nuclear analysts.

On April 11, 1999, eleven months after detonating five nuclear weapons, India staged a test of the new, solid-fuel Agni-II missile. The missile flew some 1,250 miles (2,011 km) in a mere eleven minutes and landed in the Bay of Bengal.

The brief hopes for a thaw in Indian-Pakistani relations that appeared after a much-publicized bus trip to Pakistan by India's prime minister quickly evaporated in the backblast of the Agni-II. Not to be out-rocketed by the Indians, Pakistan promptly launched its new Ghauri-II solid-fuel, mobile missile, which has a range of at least 932 miles (1,500 km), soon to be extended to 1,553 miles (2,500 km).

China, which had been watching India's nuclear and missile tests with mounting ire, made statements protesting Delhi's "provocative, unfriendly" acts. There were reports that China was moving mobile M-9 short-range, and M-11 medium-range missiles toward India's border. All of this missile-rattling raised uneasy memories of the naval race and well-publicized naval war games that led up to World War I.

Any doubt that India's Agni-II and oncoming Agni-III were designed for use against China were dispelled by India's prime minister, Atal Behari Vajpayee, who announced that India would build a "credible" nuclear deterrent. Dropping any pretense of diplomatic language or tact, in late 1998, Defense Minister George Fernandes asserted China was now India's "number one enemy."

Soon after, India formed a new National Security Council, headed by the prime minister, to review and formulate nuclear doctrine, another clear sign India was determined to use its nuclear weapons arsenal to enhance its increasingly muscular diplomacy, and if necessary for war. Pouring fuel on the fire, India's outspoken Home Secretary and BJP stalwart, L.K. Advani, warned Pakistan that in light of India's newly revealed nuclear power, it should back down over Kashmir—or else. Indian voters, however, proved considerably less truculent than the BJP's firebrands. In state elections in November 1988, they kicked the BJP out of three important states: Delhi, Rajastan (where the BJP had recently conducted nuclear tests), and the BJP stronghold of Madhya Pradesh. Though rising food prices, notably that of onions, was a major issue in the election, many Indian voters expressed dismay at the BJP's aggressive policies and nuclear scimitar-rattling. The far more moderate Congress Party, led by Sonia Gandhi, Rajiv's widow, gained many seats. Still, the damage had been done.

To no one's surprise, China denounced India's "provocations," vowing it would counter Delhi's nuclear threats by enhancing its own nuclear forces targeted on India. Beijing warned that India was igniting an Asian arms race. Long-simmering strategic tensions between India and China had finally broken out into the open.

• • •

Though hardly anyone noticed at the time, the unveiling of India's nuclear weapons provoked considerable unease in another regional power with nuclear aspirations, Iran. The late Shah Reza Pahlavi had decided in the mid-1970s to begin developing nuclear weapons to counter the threat from the Soviet Union, assure Iran's domination of the Gulf, and underline Iran's self-appointed role—in alliance with the United States—as policeman of the central Mideast. Iran began work on small test reactors, and trained a cadre of nuclear technicians in Europe and America. More important, the Shah entered into secret negotiations with Israel to purchase nuclear weapons, associated technology, and the Jericho-1 MRBM (medium-range ballistic missile). The 1979 revolution in Iran ended covert nuclear cooperation with Israel, but the new Islamic government, seeing itself surrounded by enemies, accelerated nuclear development and speeded construction of a large reactor complex at Bushir.

Iran is a geopolitical swing nation, looking both west into the Mideast and east to the Indian subcontinent. In recent decades, Tehran, whether under the Shah or the mullahs of the Islamic Republic, has seen itself as a defender of Muslim Pakistan and a key force in the newly independent states of Central Asia. India's nuclear program, and its evident great-power aspirations, considerably worried Iran. The long war with Iraq, and intelligence reports that Baghdad was striving to develop nuclear weapons with secret financial aid from Iran's bitter foe Saudi Arabia, convinced Tehran to accelerate its nascent nuclear program.

A former director general of Pakistani intelligence told me that, in the late 1980s, Iran offered to underwrite Pakistan's total defense budget for ten years if Islamabad would supply nuclear weapons to Iran. Pakistan refused outright. This forced Iran to follow a slower, more arduous program of nuclear development by covertly acquiring bits and pieces of nuclear technology from abroad.

There seems little doubt Iran will eventually acquire nuclear warheads for its Shahab series of MRBMS, which are currently being tested. Any major Indian invasion of Pakistan, or military intervention in Afghanistan, could very well draw in Iranian forces, raising the danger of nuclear confrontation between Delhi and Tehran.

17
The Clash of Titans

I t has long been clear to Indian strategists that their nation and China will one day come into open confrontation; the only question is when. Economic growth has permitted both states to upgrade and modernize their conventional and nuclear forces. At some point in the early twenty-first century, the two powers will be locked in a fierce rivalry for mastery of South Asia and its important resources. China, the Indians believe, will not sit back and allow an ever-strengthening India to assert its domination of the region without a struggle.

In the Indian view, China's long-term strategy is to surround and isolate India in a sort of gigantic version of the Japanese board game Goh. China's land strategy is based on two nations, Pakistan and Burma. Pakistan and China have been close allies since the early 1970s: Beijing is Pakistan's principal supplier of weapons, some nuclear technology, and diplomatic support. The Karakoram Highway over the mountains from northern Pakistan to Chinese Sinkiang, the sole land link between the two nations, is China's only opening to the west. In the event of war, India fears, China would move large numbers of troops over the highway into Kashmir, threatening Ladakh and India's northern regions.

Burma, now known officially as Myanmar, is the second prong of China's grand anti-Indian strategy. This isolated, little-known nation of 49.5 million dominates India's eastern flank. During World War II, Burma was called "the back door to India" by both the British and the Japanese, who battled ferociously in its thick jungles and mountains. For the past three decades, China has steadily increased its political, military, and economic influence in Burma. The military regime in Rangoon (Yangon), boycotted and shunned by the outside world because of its deplorable human rights record, has turned increasingly to China, and to a lesser degree, to Japan, for support.

A complex series of rebellions by Shan, Karens, and Kachin ethnic minorities has kept Burma in a prolonged state of civil war for the past forty years. In addition to ethnic rebels, powerful opium armies operate in Burma's wild interior, including the descendants of two Chinese

Nationalist divisions that were pushed into Burma from Yunnan in 1949, and then subsequently armed and supplied for many years by CIA airdrops.

Though impoverished, chronically unstable, and riven by ethnic strife, Burma is potentially one of South Asia's richest nations, with huge stores of precious teak and other hardwood timber, gemstones, strategic minerals, fertile land, and, most important, extensive, largely unexploited oil reserves. As a result, Burma receives the attentions of its two powerful neighbors, India and China, who covet both its natural riches and strategic position.

In my view, Burma is destined to join Tibet as a major flash-point between India and China during the first decade of the twenty-first century. The collapse of Burma's ruling military junta, which until recently was known by the wonderfully sinister Orwellian acronym SLORC (State Law and Order Reconstruction Council), could very likely result in the country dissolving into a chaotic civil war between army units, political supporters of opposition leader Aung San Suu Kyi, and the nation's various ethnic armies. This, in turn, could provoke Indian or Chinese military intervention, and a direct clash between the two powers. Stationing of Chinese ground forces or naval units in Burma would also very likely spark a major conflict.

To the west of Burma, India's remote, little-known northeast region has been in a state of almost constant insurgency since independence in 1947. A mountainous, forested region of 98,000 sq. mi. (254,000 square kilometers), with poor roads and scant communications, the states of the northeast are often called the Seven Sisters. They comprise Arunachal Pradesh—formerly the Northeast Frontier Agency—Assam, Meghalaya, Manipur, Mizoram, Nagaland, and Tripura, with a combined population of some 32 million people.

This region is highly strategic and extremely sensitive: it is bounded on the north by China and on the southeast by Burma, and connected to the rest of India only through the narrow Siliguri corridor in the state of West Bengal. To its west lies Bhutan; to the southeast, Bangladesh.

Often termed an "ethnic reactor," the region contains a bewildering collection of five different racial groups, hundreds of tribes—110 in Arunachal Pradesh alone—and three main religions: Hinduism, Christianity, and Buddhism. For the past half-century, major insurgencies and secessionist movements have flared in Nagaland, Mizoram, Manipur, and Assam, fueled by immigration from neighboring parts of India. The best-organized and most dangerous rebel groups, in the view of Indian security authorities, are the National Socialist Council of Nagaland and the United Liberation Front of Assam, both of which are seeking to establish independent states.

Most of the tribal groups are Christians, except for those of Arunachal Pradesh, and the leadership of the various insurgent groups is predominantly Christian as well. Christian missionaries have long played a key role in supporting and financing the tribal insurgents, just as they have in southern Sudan. The Hindu fundamentalists of the BJP see a sinister plot by international Christian organizations to detach the tribal states from India.

Indian authorities have long accused China, Pakistan, Burma, and Bangladesh of supplying arms, training, and secure bases to the different rebel groups. China and Pakistan have given the insurgents substantial covert support, and continue to do so; Burma and Bangladesh offer passive assistance by allowing rebel units to cross their porous borders. If relations between Delhi and Beijing worsen, it seems likely China will squeeze India by stirring the pot in the northeast, or even actively supporting uprisings there from Burma, where Chinese influence is rising rapidly.

Tribal peoples make up about 8 percent of India's population. Many of the tribes of the hill states are ethnically linked to those of neighboring Burma. These hill states, and rebellious Assam, make up the long salient of India's vulnerable northeast frontier, which is threatened by Chinese forces in Tibet. In the event of another Indian-Chinese war, Chinese forces striking south from Tibet through Bhutan could cut off eastern India. If Chinese armies were stationed in Burma, they could push east through the hill states into Bangladesh, threatening Calcutta, and India's most populous states, Bihar and Uttar Pradesh.

Most worrisome to India, though, is the steady increase of Chinese military power on the Tibetan Plateau, which confronts India with the specter of simultaneously facing serious strategic threats on its western, northern, and eastern borders. This fear has led Indian strategists and politicians to warn that India was being "surrounded" by a hostile coalition of forces directed and armed by China.

By the early 1990s, China had deployed 500,000 soldiers, a quarter of its standing army, on the Tibetan Plateau, half of them based on the border between India and Tibet, half in central Tibet. Four additional Chinese armies, each the equivalent of a 60,000-man army corps, were based in Sinkiang and the Chengdu military district, able to support operations from Tibet against India by delivering flanking attacks or providing follow-on reinforcements.

China is reducing its three-million-strong armed forces by 20 percent, with 400,000 men transferred from the army to the paramilitary police. Troop strength in Tibet is also being somewhat reduced. The objective of this massive reduction is to divert funds into modernization and better equipment. China's 8,800 tanks are largely obsolete or obsolescent; it needs to acquire modern artillery and self-propelled guns. The navy is being upgraded into a true blue-water arm. China's huge, 3,566-combat-plane air force is totally obsolete: it has only 40 modern, Russian-supplied SU-27 fighters, and 200 J-8s, an upgraded version of the old MIG-21. The remainder are 1950s- and 1960s-vintage warplanes, with short range, poor engines, and primitive avionics.

As a result of this modernization program, China's armies in Tibet are improving their firepower, communications, and mobility, in spite of the decrease in sheer numbers. In addition, China's western armies received, along with those facing Taiwan, some of the newest and most advanced arms and equipment. The collapse in 1991 of China's former principal threat, the Soviet Union, allowed China not only to reduce the size of its armies, but to redeploy some of its most effective units from the Soviet border to the south and west, including the 149th division of the 13th Group Army, specialized in mountain warfare, to Chengdu, and the 62nd division of the 21st Group Army, configured for mobile desert warfare, to Lanzhou, covering China's Central Asian region north of Tibet. New combined arms divisions with enhanced offensive power are being deployed to western and southern regions.

Ever since occupying Tibet in 1950, the PLA has worked feverishly to build networks of all-weather roads, crisscrossing the kingdom and linking it to the Chengdu military region and to Sinkiang. Two other major roads lead to Pakistan and Nepal respectively. The new road system allowed China to move large military formations swiftly along the entire length of the Indian border, affording Chinese generals the ability to concentrate mutually supporting armies almost anywhere along the frontier. A chain of permanent bases, many with huge underground storage sites and heavy fixed fortifications, linked to rear echelons by good roads, has been extended like a new Great Wall along the length of the border with India.

The militarization of Tibet presented India with serious strategic and tactical problems. China quite literally commands the high ground from the 14,000-foot (4,267-km) Tibetan Plateau. The PLA's forward positions are located at the very crest of the plateau; Indian positions are located, in many cases, below them. In the event of war, Indian troops must advance uphill to attack Chinese positions firing down on them. India's topographical disadvantage was piquantly summed up by the late Zhou Enlai, who once quipped that if China wanted to destroy India, it need only march 100 million of its citizens to the southern edge of the Tibetan Plateau, and wash India away by ordering them to urinate downhill.

This serious tactical disadvantage is compounded by the chain of intelligence-gathering stations established by China along the plateau's southern edge, which allow China to monitor Indian air space, electronic communications and troop movements south of the Himalayas. Israel enjoys a precisely identical intelligence advantage from another plateau, the Golan Heights, which it seized from Syria in 1967. Israeli ELINT antennas atop Golan can monitor and track every Syrian warplane that takes off from southern air bases from the moment they start their engines. It is a simple matter for them to observe major Syrian troop movements and intercept most of the communications issuing from Damascus.

China has constructed fourteen major air bases on the Tibetan Plateau, and a score of tactical airstrips. These bases give the Chinese air force unquestioned domination of Tibet's air space, the forward edge of battle in the event of war, and the capability, for the first time, to fly sustained combat operations over India's north and strike all India's northern cities, including Delhi, Bombay, and Calcutta. Chinese electronic intelligence atop the plateau, looking down from a height of 14,000 to 15,000 feet (4,267 to 4,572 m), also confers an important advantage of combat information and battle management in any air war, in part compensating for the technological inferiority of China's aircraft against India's far more modern air arm.

But of all China's military emplacements on the Plateau, by far the most alarming to India is an extensive series of missile bases and nuclear installations. At least half China's force of around fifty CSS-2 and CSS-5 MRBMS are based in Tibet, as well as a sizeable number of shorter-range tactical missiles, all carrying nuclear warheads. In addition, China moved its principal nuclear test and development facility from Lop Nor, in Sinkiang, to Nagchuka, 165 miles (265 km) north of Lhasa. India's heartland and many of its major cities are now in range of Chinese missiles.

Water is another issue of major concern to Indian strategists. South Asia's largest rivers flow down from the Tibetan plateau. The headwaters of India's most important rivers and principal source of the groundwater that nourishes the subcontinent, including the Ganges, Brahmaputra, Indus, Chenab, Ravi, Yamuna, Gandak, and Saptakosi, to name but a few, rise in Tibet. China thus has gained a death-grip over India's main supply of water. India's strategists have long worried that China may at some point dam, divert, or interdict its vital water supplies.

To some, such concerns may seem far-fetched. But they are very real. Egypt has long made clear that any attempt by Ethiopia or Sudan to substantially divert upstream waters of the Nile will be a *casus belli*. India has looked with growing concern as Turkey's massive Ataturk hydroelectric scheme in eastern Anatolia has steadily dammed the headwaters of the Tigris and Euphrates Rivers, depriving Syria and Iraq of 50 percent of their downstream water, those nations' major source of irrigation. Israel has maintained occupation of southern Lebanon and Golan in part because they contain vital headwaters for the Jordan, Litani, and Yarmuk Rivers.

Development of naval power by China and India presents another looming source of conflict between the two Asian rivals. Until the 1980s China's large, but obsolescent, fleets, comprising 63 submarines, 53 large surface combatants, and 747 patrol vessels, was a strictly brown-water force, able to defend only China's immediate coastal region, and even then not very effectively. In recent years, however, China has embarked on a major program to build a true blue-water navy, capable of projecting power far beyond its coasts. China has introduced modern surface combatants of the Russian Sovremenny class, equipped with SS-N-22 long-range, antiship missiles, and the new Luda-class destroyers. It has also upgraded its naval aviation arm, and is struggling to build a fleet of nuclear-powered attack submarines to augment its sizeable number of conventional diesel subs. These new offensive warships are primarily designed to counter U.S. carrier battle groups, but they would be equally effective against the Indian fleet. Beijing is also said to be considering acquisition of a large aircraft carrier.

While China's naval forces remain primarily tasked for operations in the Pacific, South China Sea, and the waters around Taiwan, units of the South Sea fleet have begun operating off Vietnam, in support of China's claim to the disputed Spratly Islands, and in the waters between Malaysia, Singapore, and Indonesia, near the mouth of the strategic Strait of Malacca. The Chinese navy has made occasional patrols west of Malacca into the Andaman Sea, and port visits to China's ally, Burma. India now worries China's growing navy may begin regular patrols in the Bay of Bengal. As a result, India is rapidly expanding its naval presence in the region, forming a fourth naval command in 1998 at Port Blair in the strategic Andaman and Nicobar Islands that extend due south from the coast of Burma.

Oil is a principal factor behind these growing naval tensions. The rapidly developing economies of India and China will need to import increasing amounts of petroleum. China's domestic reserves may be exhausted within the next five years, and India's oil reserves are modest. As a result, the two rival powers will come into direct competition for foreign oil, the principal sources being Indonesia, Malaysia, Burma, and the Gulf. India is determined to develop naval forces capable of ensuring its flow of oil from Southeast Asia and the Gulf; the Indians fear that, in any war with China, the Chinese navy could quickly interdict oil shipments from Indonesia, Malaysia and, by submarine blockade, from the Gulf. China, of course, is equally concerned that its oil imports from Southeast Asia could be interdicted, just as effectively, by Indian naval action.

Navies remain, even in our modern age, the primary tool of power projection and geopolitical influence, as America's long naval presence in the Pacific clearly demonstrates. Now that China and India are bent on expanding their geostrategic interests in Asia, it appears inevitable that naval rivalry between the two antagonists will become increasingly important and active.

Some Indian analysts even fear that the Chinese navy and the U.S. Fifth and Seventh Fleets might combine forces at some future date, perhaps during a conflict with Pakistan, to threaten their coast from both the Bay of Bengal and the Arabian Sea. In the summer of 1998, India's Defense Minister, George Fernandes, underlined these concerns by publicly warning that China and the U.S. had embarked on a strategic alliance against India.

Amid all these alarms, Tibet continues to be the focus of Indian fears of encirclement and, eventually, attempts by China to destabilize and then splinter the Indian Union. The breakup of India would leave China the unchallenged master of Asia, much as the collapse of the Soviet Union eliminated any threat to Western Europe and the U.S.-dominated Mideast. Japan, though the object of constant Chinese suspicion, is not deemed likely in the foreseeable future to become an aggressive military power, though it will compete vigorously for oil.

Pakistan's long-range strategy is to encourage, whenever possible, the internal weakening of India, which Islamabad hopes will one day lead to the fragmentation of its huge foe. India is convinced China and Pakistan are colluding in this grand strategy, whose first steps would be encouragement of rebellion in India's eastern hills states, Kashmir, among Sikhs in Punjab, Gurkhas in Assam, and unrest among the large Tibetan refugee population in northern India clustered around the exiled Dalai Lama. Unrest or open rebellion in India's unstable border regions could encourage direct intervention of Chinese troops based in Tibet, or infiltration of Chinese-directed "volunteers" across India's frontiers.

If a major head-to-head clash ever comes between China and India, Indian strategists are convinced it will eventually be played out along the Tibetan border. For India, Chinese-ruled Tibet looms ominously over their nation, a mighty redoubt in the clouds, bristling with enemy armies, ready to sally forth and pour onto the open plains of northern India like a second Mogul invasion.

18
China Under Siege

China's strategic appreciation of its growing rivalry with India is, of course, starkly different. Beijing's official policy is that it has no territorial or hegemonistic ambitions in Asia, other than reunification of Taiwan to the mainland. But, in reality, Chinese strategists are keenly aware that the steady growth of their nation's power will accentuate already existing economic and strategic rivalry with India.

The two powers are already competing in Asian markets in the export of low- and medium-tech arms, electronics, and cheap consumer goods. Both vie to attract foreign investment.

The principal focus of rivalry, however, will be geopolitical. China may harbor no territorial designs on Southeast Asia, but it certainly intends to extend its political and military influence across the region that China has regarded, for the past three thousand years, as its natural sphere of geopolitical power. Burma and Pakistan, two important Chinese allies, are seen as gravely threatened by India. Some Chinese strategists also believe India has long-term designs on Indonesia's oil, and on the vast resources of the newly independent states of Central Asia.

China has worried since the 1960s about the strategic alliance between India and the Soviet Union (and now Russia). The massive arming of India by the Soviet Union/Russia convinced China that Moscow was forging an anti-Chinese axis designed to contain China's ambitions.

After the collapse of the Soviet Union in 1991, the threat to China of a Moscow-Delhi axis appeared to sharply diminish. Economic chaos in Russia delayed, or even shut off, the supply of tens of thousands of spare parts for India's arsenal of Soviet weapons and industrial equipment. Russia would no longer sell India arms or military material at concessionary "fraternal" prices, nor continue the former system whereby India paid for Soviet arms in soft rupees through "clearing accounts" and barter.

However, in the latter part of the 1990s, Russia resumed arms sales to India at an ever-accelerating pace. India was again allowed to pay for this equipment with a combination of hard currency, barter, and rupees. The Indian Air Force particularly benefited from restoration of military ties with Moscow by acquiring advanced model Sukhoi-30MKs and MiG29s, upgraded Russian avionics for its warplanes, new radars, missiles, and naval armaments. As in the 1970s and '80s, Russia and India resumed close cooperation in defense projects, and, most worrying to China, strategic coordination.

In effect, the Moscow-Delhi axis had been reborn. Its prime objectives were containing China's growing power, domination of South and Central Asia, containment of Islamic political-religious movements that threatened both Indian and Russian regional interests, and joint resistance to American power in Asia.

The particular aims of the renewed entente were first, defeating the Islamic movement in Afghanistan, thwarting Pakistan's influence there, and fashioning a pro-Russian, pro-Indian government in Kabul; second, limiting the expansion of Chinese influence into Burma, Indochina, and their neighboring waters; third, reducing U.S. strategic influence and ability to move in the Indian Ocean and along its littoral. By combining their strategic interests, Russia and India aimed to counterbalance both China's growing power and the still dominant influence of the United States.

China watched uneasily as the Moscow-Delhi axis was restored, well aware that the entente could blossom into a full-grown military alliance. Russia's grave weakness in its Pacific far east would in part be offset by the new threat posed by India to China's southern flank.

India, it is feared, might join Russia in a future conflict against China, or even with the United States, if Taiwan ever sparks an American-Chinese conflict in the Pacific.

Just as India believes it is being surrounded by a hostile coalition of neighboring states, so, too, does China. Military strategists in China have long been concerned over the threat scenario of a multi-front war that would pit against them India in the west, Vietnam in the south, Taiwan in the center, and possibly Japan, the Koreas, or Russia in the north—a coalition that would considerably outnumber China's forces in troops and weapons. China has long suspected the Japanese, in league with the United States, of financing the armed forces of their hostile neighbors.

After Taiwan, China's most important military concern centers on its far western regions of Tibet and Sinkiang. These two provinces comprise a third of China's total land mass, though only a small fraction of its population. China's hold over these far-western regions, separated by 1,000 miles (1,600 km), mountains, broad rivers, and poor communications from the Chinese heartland, has always been tenuous, and constantly challenged.

Full Chinese control of Tibet was not established until 1950. Sinkiang, which lies to the north of Tibet, is a problem of almost equal complexity. It did not come under Beijing's unquestioned rule until the last century, though China had maintained trading posts and military garrisons in the region for many centuries.

Until the twentieth century, Sinkiang was known as Eastern Turkestan, an enormous sweep of steppeland inhabited by nomadic and settled Turkic peoples, extending from the Great Wall of China to the shores of the Caspian Sea. This region had once been the heartland of the great Mongol Empire. In the eighteenth and nineteenth centuries, the Russian and Chinese empires began expanding south and west, respectively. Russia conquered Western Turkestan, today the former Soviet Central Asia; China reasserted historic claims to the remainder, Eastern Turkestan.

The Muslim peoples of Turkestan thus fell under Russian and Chinese rule, though uprisings were frequent and bloody, continuing in Soviet Central Asia and in Chinese Turkestan right down to the 1930s.

As in Tibet, China moved millions of settlers into Sinkiang in a campaign to turn its native Muslims into a minority in their own land. Beijing has established major military bases and garrisons across Sinkiang, supported by armies of police and security agents. Resentment of the harsh Chinese rule has simmered among the Turkic peoples of Sinkiang for the past half-century. While China's brutal repression of Tibet sparked worldwide outrage, its similarly cruel actions in Sinkiang have received almost no publicity, even in the Muslim world. There is no Hollywood to publicize and romanticize the plight of Turkestani Muslims, and no Muslim version of the Dalai Lama to champion and personify their obscure cause.

Sinkiang's largest native ethnic group, Uighurs, have been particularly resistant to Chinese rule. Emboldened and encouraged by the

Islamic victory in Afghanistan and the struggle for independence by Kashmiri Muslims, Uighurs have in recent years demonstrated, rioted, and even formed a number of guerrilla and underground urban resistance groups. In 1998, there were a number of bombings of Chinese targets in Sinkiang's cities. Chinese authorities reacted by arresting thousands of Muslims, and executing scores. The PLA rushed troops and paramilitary police reinforcements to Sinkiang.

According to a 1999 Amnesty International report, the first major study about Sinkiang by an international human rights organization, Chinese authorities have executed 190 Uighurs since 1997 for "subversion" or "terrorism" after summary trials; another 30 were awaiting execution. According to Amnesty International, Uighur prisoners were routinely tortured into signing confessions.

Beijing quickly proposed an anti-Islamic-fundamentalist alliance to the Central Asian states of Tajikistan, Kyrgyzstan, Uzbekistan, and Kazakhstan, designed to isolate the Islamic revolt in Sinkiang, and prevent movement of Muslim rebels and arms across the region's borders. In spite of the newfound semi-independence of these Central Asian states, their dictatorial rulers remain, without exception, old-line Communists. The main opposition to these post-Communist leaders comes from internal Islamic resistance forces and, to a somewhat lesser degree, from the Islamic Taliban movement in Afghanistan. Central Asia's Communist rulers had already formed a regional, anti-Islamic alliance, strongly backed by Russian arms, money, advisors, and troops, to oppose the spread of political Islam within their states, and to intervene in Afghanistan in support of the anti-Taliban Northern Alliance. This alliance was quick to lend China discreet aid in isolating Uighur rebels in Sinkiang.

China fears, with good reason, that growing Muslim unrest will flare into open revolt, thus weakening its hold on Sinkiang and, indirectly, on Tibet. India, which has its own long-term ambitions in Central Asia, has been confused by these developments. On one hand, Delhi would like to undermine China's presence in Central Asia; but, on the other, it is loath to support Islamic forces, whom it actively opposes in Afghanistan and Kashmir.

China and India are in dispute over yet another contentious issue in the Himalayas: the mountain kingdoms of Nepal, Bhutan, and Sikkim.

Nepal, an overpopulated nation of 23 million, occupies a highly strategic position along the Indo-Chinese Himalayan border. Consequently, India has long had designs on Nepal, regarding it as a natural sphere of influence, if not an integral part of India, as some Hindu nationalists claim. China, by contrast, has generally viewed Nepal as a useful buffer state and strategic salient that curbs Indian ambitions in the Himalayas, and renders more difficult India's defense of its northern mountain border. In time of war, China would quickly occupy Nepal in order to benefit from its mountain passes and roads that lead south to debouch on the plains of northern India.

Nepal, led by its constitutional monarch, King Birendra (who has occupied the throne since 1972), has played a deft diplomatic game between India and China for the past half-century, alternately flirting with one side, then the other. India has taken alarm and protested to India over China's building of military roads up to the Nepalese border. India has repeatedly warned Nepal over its economic and transit links with China, once going so far as to impose a trade blockade that almost wrecked Nepal's economy.

Intelligence agents from both sides are active in Nepal. In addition, Nepal is politically unsettled: a rebellion or coup against its monarchy could trigger internal chaos, inviting direct intervention by Indian or Chinese troops, or covert support of warring factions. A growing Maoist rebel movement in Nepal might request aid from China. There is also an increasingly potent Gurkha nationalist movement, made up of the 2.5 to 3 million ethnic Nepalese living outside Nepal, that seeks to detach Indian Assam, and possibly parts of Bhutan, to create a Greater Gurkha nation, or "Gurkhaland," which adds a further dimension of danger and uncertainty to this troubled equation.

The Nepalese are keenly aware their nation exists at the pleasure of India and could share the fate of their neighboring mountain kingdoms. The Indian Army occupied Sikkim in 1970 without a shot; the tiny mountain state was forthwith annexed to India. In 1975, Sikkim became a state within the Indian union. India's seizure of Sikkim closely resembled China's invasion of Tibet in terms of its questionable legality, though certainly not in brutality, yet this act provoked no protest, and attracted barely any attention, in the outside world, save a brief wave of media sympathy in the U.S. for its attractive American-born Queen Hope, the Grace Kelly of the Himalayas. Hardly anyone had ever heard of Sikkim, and those few who had were hard-pressed to find it on the map.

Farther east in the Himalayas, India made the formerly independent little kingdom of Bhutan, which had been an independent monarchy for 1,300 years, into another protectorate, also without international objection. Though taking no action, China has never formally accepted India's annexation of Sikkim or Bhutan, and could make an issue of it at a time of Beijing's choosing.

Thus, four long-independent Buddhist Himalayan kingdoms—Tibet, Ladakh, Sikkim, and Bhutan—were absorbed by their powerful neighbors, India and China. Though the religion and culture of the latter three were no less rich and distinctive than that of Tibet, the outside world paid scant notice to the annexation of the other "little Tibets."

Chinese military intelligence believes India is as intent on fragmenting China's close ally, Pakistan, as Pakistan is on fragmenting India. Though Beijing has adopted a policy of studied vagueness on how it would react to a major Indian invasion of Pakistan, it is likely China would make a powerful military demonstration on India's northern border, or, if Pakistan appeared close to collapse, might intervene massively in the war.

The main threat from India, the Chinese believe, is directed against Tibet. India would be only too happy to remove the danger to its northern border, and break its perceived encirclement, by either destabilizing or, even better, ousting the Chinese from Tibet, and then from Sinkiang. A direct Indian military assault on Tibet would be exceptionally difficult, very costly, and most likely a failure. India's most effective strategy, therefore, would be to undermine China's hold on Tibet through subversion, covert action, and infiltration.

There is little doubt ethnic Tibetans, who are now only half of Tibet's total population, would welcome liberation from their Chinese "liberators," and joyously receive home the exiled Dalai Lama. But after the long, bloody guerrilla war in the 1960s against Chinese rule, Tibetans see no possibility of mounting a successful revolt. The Tibetan resistance has been abandoned by the U.S., and denied bases and sanctuary by India and Nepal. Without outside aid, a rebellion against China's huge occupation forces would fail almost from the start.

But as tensions continue to grow between India and China, it is likely India will be increasingly tempted to mount a campaign of destabilization against Tibet, particularly if China increases its so far modest efforts to stir up unrest in India's eastern hill states, or if China provides aid to the Kashmiri rebels. The large Tibetan exile community in northern India provides an excellent pool of manpower from which to form guerrilla bands, and the means through which to organize an underground movement inside Tibet. India's intelligence service, RAW, has for the past three decades maintained top-secret special military units composed of Tibetan exiles whose mission is to act as scouts and commandos in the event of war with China, or to form the nucleus of a Tibetan liberation army that would spearhead an Indian invasion of Tibet.

China also remains sensitive to the dangerous possibility that India and the U.S. might cooperate to undermine its hold on Tibet. Beijing has watched uneasily as American investment has flowed into India, and particularly into its high-tech sector. Gradual deterioration of uneasy relations between Washington and Beijing, a new crisis over Taiwan, or a growing conviction in U.S. foreign and military policy circles that China constitutes a strategic threat to U.S. interests, or to North America, could put the two superpowers on a collision course.

Washington and Delhi understand that the quickest, most effective way to throw China onto the strategic defensive is by stirring up resistance in Tibet. All of China's rulers have been preoccupied by the threat of regionalism and secession movements. As was the case in Imperial Russia, and later the Soviet Union, the greatest part of Beijing's energies are devoted inwardly to simply holding together and governing its huge, sprawling nation. Throughout Chinese history, regional independence movements and warlordism have broken out whenever the center has grown weak, through decay or factional in-fighting.

At the very heart of these strategic concerns lies China's deep, historic fear of being weakened, then dismembered by hostile outside powers. Memories are still vivid of the nineteenth century and the early twentieth century, when the Western imperial powers Russia and Japan fell like rapacious wolves on the decaying Manchu Empire and tore away its vulnerable border regions. In the current Chinese view, if Tibet is somehow detached from China, Sinkiang will follow, then Hainan, Inner Mongolia, possibly even Manchuria. China's south, traditionally resistant to domination by the Mandarin-speaking north, is already being tugged away from Beijing's orbit by powerful financial interests from Singapore and other overseas Chinese. Szechuan is as populous as Germany and France combined, and could easily stand alone as an independent, prosperous nation. Russia has never given up its ambition to dominate resource-rich Manchuria. A declaration of independence by Taiwan could begin the unraveling of united China.

The most recent example of such lurking centrifugal forces occurred during the Great Cultural Revolution, which began in the fall of 1965. Mao's internal revolution plunged China into anarchy and chaos as civil war raged between a dizzying assortment of political, military, and regional factions. China came very close to national dissolution at the very time when the Soviet Union was considering a pre-emptive invasion of northern China and, very likely, Sinkiang. It took a military coup, followed by intervention of the PLA, to end the national madness unleashed by the Cultural Revolution, crush the notorious Gang of Four, and reunify badly fractured China under the moderate regime of Deng Xiaoping.

The collapse of the ruling Chinese Communist Party, followed by strife between warring factions in Beijing, could gravely weaken the center, unleashing regional forces and so destabilizing the nation. China's current leadership is convinced that America's grand strategy in the western Pacific is to gradually undermine the Communist Party's hold on power, while keeping China isolated and surrounded by a coalition of hostile neighbors. Washington is employing the human rights issue, Beijing believes, as its main tool to undermine the régime. At the same time, the U.S. continues to use South Korea, Japan, Taiwan, Singapore, Thailand, and now, it is feared, India, as a great outer wall to surround and contain China, or even to threaten China's vulnerable peripheral regions. The U.S. Seventh Fleet continues to patrol off China's long coast, providing the final link in the chain of hostile forces surrounding China.

• • •

I left my hotel in Lhasa at 4 A.M. for the long drive to the airport. An hour later, the first rays of the rising sun edged the mountains around us with borders of gold and red. I once again marveled at the flatness of Tibet's central plains, juxtaposed against distant walls of snow-capped mountains. We halted briefly in front of a Buddhist *stupa*, or shrine, where I said a brief, silent prayer for the people of Tibet.

My head pulsed with pain. I sat in the cold, barren departure lounge, desperately clutching my ticket, seized by waves of panic. I might be stuck there for hours. The flight might be canceled or wildly overbooked—normal occurrences in China. One never knows in Third World nations when dignitaries will commandeer a scheduled flight or appropriate seats, leaving unfortunate ordinary travelers marooned, sometimes for days. I knew time was running out: I would likely become comatose soon if I did not get down to a lower altitude.

When, after what seemed an eternity of anguish, boarding was finally announced, an unruly mob of passengers stormed the plane. I staggered onto the tarmac, reeling and dizzy, then painfully struggled up the stairs into the long Boeing 757. As I prepared to sit in my seat, I noticed it held a pool of thick, malodorous vomit from a previous passenger. I looked about for another place: there was none. A vicious little Chinese stewardess, clearly a former Red Guards officer, told me to get off the plane if I did not like my assigned seat. Gritting my teeth, and trying to keep my stomach calm, I sat down in the yellow muck and buckled up.

Once again, the dawn view of Tibet's soaring mountains was overwhelmingly beautiful. Sitting in the pool of vomit while beholding one of this Earth's most sublime panoramas seemed a curiously apt metaphor for my journey to the roof of the world.

Two and a half hours later we arrived at the welcome lower altitude of Chengdu. The next day, I flew to Hong Kong. My head had stopped aching and I could again breathe normally. However, for the next seven months, I suffered a nasty series of mysterious upper respiratory disorders, alternately misdiagnosed as bronchitis, allergies, or "airway disease," that I was later to learn were caused by the lingering effects of altitude sickness.

A medical specialist warned that, having once been stricken by severe altitude sickness, I would be highly susceptible to recurrences if I again went above 6,000 feet (1,829 m). To my dismay, I was later to learn he was correct. A passionate lover of mountains, I was henceforth doomed to the lowlands. I would see no more wars at the top of the world.

It was unlikely I would ever return—Tibet was lost to me, and I mourned. But how much worse it must be for Tibetans, who have lost their homeland; they are exiles, perhaps forever, victims of a remorseless modern industrial world they wanted no part of, yet could not, in the end, escape.

19

The Fate of Asia

China's hold on Tibet is total and, at least for the present, unquestioned. But the real question for Tibetans, Indians, and, indeed, most Asians, is who will end up in power in Beijing. In the first quarter of the twenty-first century, the fate of a full third of the globe's population will be determined, or at least significantly influenced by political, economic, and military developments in the People's Republic of China.

The China we see today is clearly a nation and society in transition, but a transition to what? The answer remains unclear, just as it does in post-Communist Russia. Two "old" Chinas have been left behind in the nation's headlong plunge into Asian capitalism: traditional Confucian China, often described as more a civilization than a nation-state; and Mao's tyrannical Communist China, one of history's more bizarre and disastrous experiments in social engineering.

When future historians look back on our times, they may well conclude that the greatest Chinese revolutionary leader of the twentieth century was not Sun Yat-sen or Mao Tse-tung, but the diminutive, underestimated Deng Xiaoping.

Deng's revolution, which began soon after Mao's death in 1976, and is still under way, was not at first appreciated by the West because it was bloodless, low-key, and gradual. There were no mobs of rampaging demonstrators, no factions fighting in the streets, no political executions or mass movements of people. Aside from the trial and jailing of the widely detested Gang of Four, to outsiders Deng's revolution appeared boring, even humdrum.

But of course, it was anything but that. The brilliant Deng pursued the deconstruction of the Communist system and its moribund ideology with exquisite subtlety, consummate skill, and ruthless determination. Who was better placed to destroy communism in all but name than a communist titan and veteran of Mao's revolution?

In only a decade, Deng transformed China from a totalitarian into an authoritarian state, reducing by an entire order of magnitude government and party control. Great revolutionary Deng also released the deep materialism and commercialism of the mainland Chinese that had been long pent up beneath a veneer of Maoist altruism and dedication to the state. The slogan "Get rich quick" quickly replaced "The East is Red." If 55 million offshore Chinese could constitute the world's sixth richest economy, imagine, say Deng's supporters, what 1.1 billion mainlanders could do when freed from the fetters of socialism.

Soon after Deng Xiaoping consolidated power in 1977–78, he made a strategic decision to concentrate the force of his new revolution on building China's economic base and modernizing his nation as quickly as possible. Deng correctly judged that in the modern world, economic and industrial power was the necessary prerequisite to development of military strength and great power status. China "must grow wealthy and strong," Deng exhorted, repeating a slogan used by Japan's Meiji modernizers in the late nineteenth century.

During Mao's rule, China had relied on the vast numbers of its armed forces and regional defense units to produce a veritable nation at arms. China's 4.3-million-man armed forces were configured, during the period spanning the 1960–80s, first to prevent the invasion of China by Taiwan, likely backed by the United States, and then, as relations with the Soviet Union steadily worsened, to be able to resist a massive Soviet invasion of Northern China. The deficiency of the People's Liberation Army in all classes of modern weaponry was to be compensated for by a huge field army of 175 divisions, supported by a lightly armed but enormous 20-million-man militia, designed to defend every city, town, and factory. A small nuclear force would assure China had at least a minimal strategic deterrent capability.

China's brief but bloody 1979 border war with Vietnam came as a nasty shock to the new Chinese leadership. Deng became convinced the USSR was attempting to strategically encircle China, using Vietnam to threaten its southern flank. The ill-defined Vietnamese-Chinese border; Hanoi's intervention in Cambodia and defeat of Beijing's ally, the Khmer Rouge; the expulsion by Vietnam of large numbers of ethnic Chinese; and a growing territorial dispute over the Spratly Islands in the South China Sea, all served as *casus belli*. China decided to "teach Vietnam a lesson," as it had taught India one in 1962.

In February 1979, China attacked northern North Vietnam with 100,000 soldiers. The combat-hardened Vietnamese army defended its border positions with skill and tenacity. Chinese forces soon became bogged down, and suffered significant problems of command and control, logistics, and tactical maneuver. In some places, Chinese troops were routed by the better-armed, more mobile Vietnamese. After a month of inconclusive fighting, China declared a ceasefire and withdrew its troops to the antebellum border. China had done precisely the same thing at the end of the 1962 border war with India. The difference, of course, was that in 1962 China was victorious, while in 1979 its army had been fought to a humiliating standstill by the hated Vietnamese, whom the Chinese considered a barbarian people.

Official Chinese losses were 26,000 killed and 37,000 wounded; Vietnamese losses were roughly equal. These were high numbers of casualties for a war that lasted only one month. Unofficial reports, however, put Chinese casualties at double that figure. PLA troops, attacking in poorly coordinated and insufficiently supported human wave assaults, were mowed down by the entrenched Vietnamese. This bloody reversal made it clear that China badly needed to modernize its armed forces, and their tactics, logistics and equipment.

To achieve this goal, Deng almost immediately embarked on a highly successful diplomatic campaign to improve relations with Moscow and Washington. China could not wage a two-front war: it would have to either rearm or modernize its economy. It could not afford to do both. Deng wisely chose to divert funds from the powerful PLA into rapid economic development, and to foster creation of a rudimentary free market. The result was stunning double-digit growth that transformed China in fifteen years from a pauper nation into a semi-developed industrial power, in which per capita gross domestic product soared from around $400 to $3,000. Deng had accomplished what Mao had not: a true Great Leap Forward.

Predictions in the early 1990s that China's ebullient economy would become the world's largest by 2010 now seem overly optimistic. By the late 1990s, China's growth had slowed, though it still remained robust. China was faced by rising unemployment, said to number 200 million people, industrial over-capacity, and growing financial strains.

The bold decision by Deng's successor, Jiang Zemin, to completely desocialize the economy by privatizing money-losing government-owned industries, which still employed the majority of Chinese workers, was a perilous gamble whose outcome remains uncertain. So, too, is China's ability to withstand the ongoing aftershocks of the

Asian financial earthquake. China's finances are shaky at best, and barely holding up under the multiple strains of modernization, privatization, a shaky banking system, and lack of capital. Still, China's collective leadership shows no sign of slowing what is by all measures one of modern history's most daring and heroic economic and social adventures.

Deng also made the profoundly important strategic decision to liberalize China's economy before tampering with its authoritarian political structure. In his view, Mikhail Gorbachev and his band of reformers had made a catastrophic error by liberalizing Soviet politics without first freeing and modernizing the economy. As the well-meaning Gorbachev was later to ruefully admit, Russians judged the success of his revolution not by the freedoms it brought, but ultimately by the lack of consumer goods and the nation's excruciating economic sickness and social dislocations.

China was determined to avoid Gorbachev's errors, which caused the fall of the Communist party from power, the collapse of the Soviet empire, grave military weakness, social unrest, and economic penury that ended up transforming once-mighty Russia into a replica of the dying Ottoman Empire, the new Sick Man of Europe. China's economy was like a runaway locomotive. Without a firm hand on the controls of power, China's leadership concluded, their nation would derail and crash like the wrecked Soviet Union. In fact, after the Tiananmen uprising, Deng told Singapore's prime minister, Lee Kuan Yew, "If 200,000 students have to be shot, shoot them, because the alternative is China in chaos for another 100 years." Yew, who understood China better than most Asian leaders, believed China needed another thirty to fifty years before it was ready for democracy.

Deng's grand strategy to steadily build China's economic power required amicable relations with the United States, Asia, and Russia to allow China to develop its main engine of growth—export industries—and reduce defense spending. Once China had attained economic strength, according to Deng's plan, it would be in a position to begin developing military capability commensurate with its new status as a world superpower. However, China would not likely reach this stage until 2010 at the earliest, and, if the economy slowed down, perhaps even later.

The outside world watched China's economic miracle with a

combination of awe, lust, and fear. China offered an enormous market for Western and Asian goods of all sorts. But it also presented a new commercial rival, a fact seized upon by Western unions that feared the loss of jobs at home to cheaper Chinese imports. Whereas few Westerners had cared about human rights in China during the era of Mao—or, indeed, before the Communists—a great hue and cry erupted in the West over this issue.

Many Western intellectuals, socialists, and opinion-makers seemed unable to forgive Deng and his successors for undoing Mao's Communist system, which in the past they had so often lauded as "progressive" and "humane." It was rather as if Che Guevara had gone to work for General Motors. Western leftists and liberals, feeling deeply betrayed, took their wrath out on China by making the Tiananmen Square uprising and the repression of Tibet into international *causes célèbres*, and demanding that trade sanctions be imposed on Beijing over its poor record on human rights.

China's leadership repeatedly insisted it had no territorial designs or major disputes with China's neighbors, save, of course, the long-running problem of "renegade" Taiwan. Over that problem, China alternated between threats, bluster, and offers of cooperation. There was also the still simmering territorial dispute over the Spratly Islands and their surrounding waters, beneath which oil was believed to lie. In fact, China even went so far as to resolve, through diplomacy, the single most dangerous territorial question, its disputed borders along the Amur and Ussuri Rivers with Russia, which had almost led to full-scale war with the Soviet Union in the 1960s. Two other less important Chinese territorial claims, on Kyrgyzstan and Tajikistan, were barely mentioned.

In spite of China's peace offensive, America's foreign-policy and military establishment still harbored deep doubts of Beijing's sincerity. Many conservatives were convinced a future military confrontation between the two great Pacific powers was inevitable. The relentless growth of China's power clearly threatened America's ability to project strategic influence onto the north Asian mainland, and it was clear that it would inevitably challenge the long, unquestioned U.S. domination of the western Pacific and its tributary seas. The loss of the vital U.S. naval base at Subic Bay in the Philippines was another major blow to U.S. strategic power. The Pacific would no longer be an American lake.

The growth of anti-Chinese feeling among American conservatives and liberals rekindled fears in Beijing that the United States was bent on a long-term strategy to destabilize China, keep it militarily weak, and contain China through a process of strategic encirclement. America's policy of studied ambiguity over Taiwan and the vociferous independence movement on the island raised constant alarms in Beijing. In mid-1999, the enormous furor in the United States over the alleged theft by Chinese intelligence of the crown jewels of American nuclear weapons technology, and the accidental bombing of the Chinese embassy in Belgrade by U.S. warplanes further poisoned already worsening relations.

At the same time, U.S. military planners became convinced China was developing the capacity to challenge the Seventh Fleet by acquiring long-range aircraft, new submarines, and surface warships armed with powerful, Mach 2 SSN-22 antiship missiles capable of sinking aircraft carriers.

The sudden emergence of India as a powerful nuclear-armed regional rival to China sharply increased Beijing's sense of being surrounded and threatened. So, too, did Japan's cautious attempts to begin flexing its considerable military muscle by patrolling beyond the Sea of Japan, taking a more active role in providing logistical support to U.S. forces in South Korea, and sending Japanese troops on UN missions. Beijing sought to keep Japan on the psychological defensive by issuing loud warnings against the rebirth of "Japanese militarism."

As the twentieth century ended, the course China would follow in the coming decade remained unclear. Rapid economic liberalization and development of modern communications would eventually diminish the political power and pervasive control mechanisms of the Chinese Communist Party. Once the party's iron grip on every aspect of people's lives was loosened, or even broken, it might be swept away by a flood of newfound pluralism. China had already permitted democratic elections at the rural village level in the late 1990s; this process was judged successful and might serve as a model in the future for nationwide free elections.

The Chinese Communist Party was also suffering from the same generational problems that led to the downfall of its sister parties in the USSR and Eastern Europe. Chinese revere age more than any other people, but it was also evident that the new generation of young, boisterous, capitalist Chinese had almost nothing in common with the elderly Communist grandees who still held the reins of power in their arthritic hands.

At some point within the first decade of the twenty-first century, when Mao, Deng, and the Long March have become remote historical memories, a generational revolution is likely to occur in China that will consign its wizened party apparatchiks to the dustbin of history. The new generation of leadership may not, as Westerners earnestly hope, be young democrats. The forces of Western-style democracy in China are weak and small in number. China, it must be recalled, has never enjoyed anything even approaching democracy during its five thousand years of history. The nature of Chinese society, philosophy, government, and experience is resolutely authoritarian: ideally, the Chinese prefer a powerful ruler whose actions are somewhat circumscribed by custom, the advice of a consultative élite, and the exercise of sound judgement and wisdom.

While a flowering of Western-style democracy in China cannot be excluded, it is much more likely that China will follow the successful example of authoritarian Singapore. Nearly every Chinese citizen, no matter how lowly, knows the old adage that whenever the government is weak, the nation begins to fray at the edges and secessionist forces rise.

The 1920s and 1930s era of civil war, regionalism, and warlordism is a stark reminder of how quickly China can splinter if not ruled by an iron hand. Few non-Chinese comprehend the sharp linguistic differences in China, a nation with at least ten different languages beside the dominant tongue, Mandarin. Or the regional and ethnic differences between the Mandarin-speaking north and the Cantonese-speaking south.

To outsiders, China may look monolithic, but beneath its smooth surface, deep fissures exist that could quickly open if the central government weakens. The forces of political devolution currently sweeping the globe, weakening the power and raison d'être of highly centralized governments, will eventually smite China, a nation that has been fragmented as often as not during its long history. This natural political development could be accelerated by the future appearance of a weak democratic or pluralistic government in Beijing—a latter-day version, for example, of the Kerensky regime in post-Czarist Russia—that would lack the power or stomach to keep China together.

The inherent fragility of the Chinese state will tend to produce popular pressure for regimes capable of maintaining national unity and order. Just as hyperinflation during the Weimar Republic seared the memories of all Germans, engendering an intense national aversion to debt or even the slightest sign of inflation, an aversion that persists to our day, so China's bitter experiences during the nineteenth and twentieth centuries—the Opium Wars; colonial rapine and national humiliation; civil war; the somber era of warlords, corruption, and banditry—have created a psychological demand for strong, even heavy-handed governments that put national power and cohesion before human rights and democratic politics.

As far as the West is concerned, its Asian interests may be better served by an authoritarian regime in Beijing—like the current one—than by the kind of half-formed, strife-ridden, mutant democracy that we now see in Russia, in which no one is really in charge, and where various rival factions wage tribal warfare to plunder the nation's wealth. China could easily go the way of post-Communist Russia, but with an even greater danger of regionalism and secession.

A splintering China could tempt Russia to seize Manchuria and Xinjiang, Vietnam to grab border regions in Yunnan and Guangzhou, and, of course, India to seize Tibet and the South Xinjiang–Aksai Chin region. In short, China has good reason to fear a return to the nineteenth century, when the Celestial Empire was torn apart by foreign powers.

So China is more likely to continue under authoritarian government than to veer toward some form of pluralistic system. In spite of this tendency, the old days of totalitarian thought control in China are fast waning. The coming decades are likely to bring an explosion of freer expression, criticism, and even a certain amount of government-tolerated dissent. China will undergo fierce social pressures caused by the dismantling of state-owned industry, which will result in growing unemployment, dislocation of tens of millions of workers, and growing demands for increasingly scarce resources. Some dissent will have to be tolerated as a safety valve. Whatever form China's future governments assume, they will all end up riding on the back of an economic and political tiger.

How, then, will this ongoing revolution affect China's policies toward its neighbors and the other superpowers?

As presently constituted, China appears to have no major out-standing territorial claims or ambitions save reunification with Taiwan, the relatively minor though still potentially dangerous question of the Spratly Islands, and the dangerous issue of the still disputed border with India in the Karakorams and Himalayas. In effect, China reached the extent of its territorial ambitions in the 1950s when it annexed Tibet and Aksai Chin.

But China's sense of borders has historically been rather fuzzy, par-ticularly in the remote, little-known western regions of Sinkiang and Tibet. China's emperors were content for thousands of years to exercise domination, rather than outright rule, over the vast lands beyond the ethnic Han heartland of central and coastal China. So long as the states around China's distant, vaguely defined borders paid homage and trib-ute to the emperor, they were left pretty much to their own devices. The many peoples beyond China's frontiers were regarded as irksome barbarians to be kept as far as possible from the imperial realm. When these barbarians failed to deliver their annual tribute, or had the audac-ity to raid the edges of the Han heartland, the emperors would dispatch large armies to punish the miscreants. These punitive expeditions almost always withdrew after finishing their work, leaving behind occasional garrisons to watch the troublesome nomads and hill peoples on the imperial borders. China's thousand-year relations with Tibet followed this pattern of benign neglect and occasional demonstrations of control—at least until 1950.

It is important to understand this historical policy of hard inner borders and soft outer borders, because China's modern leadership has acted in much the same manner as the emperors of centuries past. Mao sent 500,000 "volunteers" to Korea when he feared the United States might defeat his North Korean satraps, or even threaten Manchuria. Once the threat had passed, the expeditionary armies were withdrawn from the Korean Peninsula.

During the Vietnam War, China dispatched 320,000 troops to aid its Vietnamese allies in their war against the United States. In 1962, Mao sent 80,000 soldiers to drive the Indian Army from Ladakh and the eastern Himalayas. After routing the Indians, and "teaching India a lesson," the Chinese troops abruptly withdrew. In 1979 a Chinese expeditionary force punished North Vietnam for "disobedience," then withdrew. Chinese naval forces were similarly dispatched in the late

1970s to briefly chastise Vietnamese and Filipino forces claiming the Spratly Islands.

China's modern leaders, like the emperors, expect their neighbors to accept Beijing's paramount role in Asia and show proper deference to China's will. Until India's emergence as a nascent world power, the only Asian nation that had defied the will of Beijing was Japan, a nation and people whom China regarded with a combination of disdain, hatred, and fear. China's inimical relations with Japan and frequent outbursts against Tokyo may be viewed as similar to the fury the United States shows toward recalcitrant Arab nations—branded by Washington as "rogue states"—who defy the Pax Americana in the Mideast. China, too, has its own Pax Sinica in Asia and intends to enforce its great-power aspirations in the region.

China appears intent on enforcing its geopolitical will over eastern Asia in the traditional manner for the next two decades at least. Korea, whether united or divided, is expected to show deference to Beijing and refrain from serving as a base for the United States or Japan to threaten Manchuria. Both Koreas have clearly accepted this role. Troublesome Vietnam has yet to be brought to heel, but will likely become the focus of Chinese pressure. The smaller "dragon" states of South Asia know the rules in dealing with Beijing, and have no choice but to comply.

As previously described, China is making a significant effort to extend its influence into mineral-rich Burma, both for economic reasons and, even more important, to create a buffer between its sphere of influence in Indochina and the growing power of India. China is also deeply concerned by what it views as India's long-term designs on Tibet, and the instability of Sinkiang. After Taiwan, the most probable areas of future Chinese military operations are against Vietnam, and against India in Burma and Tibet.

China has also made clear it considers the waters of the South China Sea to be wholly within its geopolitical sphere of influence, a claim that is challenged by the United States and its Asian allies. A naval confrontation in these contested waters or in the Taiwan Strait is possible within the next decade between the U.S. Seventh Fleet and the rapidly enlarging Chinese navy.

The steady growth of China's geopolitical power must inevitably bring it into contest in eastern Asia with that of the United States, and to a lesser degree with Japan. But such regional rivalry does not necessarily mean global strategic conflict between the U.S. and China, as many anti-Chinese alarmists in America have been claiming.

Until recently, China has had only a bare-bones long-range nuclear strike force: an estimated seven DF-5 (CSS-4) single-warhead, liquid-fueled ICBM with a range of 8,000 miles (13,000 km) that are capable of reaching the continental United States, and twelve unreliable CSS-N-3 missiles aboard China's sole nuclear missile submarine, which has experienced severe technical difficulties and may not be seaworthy. The rest of China's nuclear arsenal consists of about 100 medium-range missiles and some 150 gravity nuclear weapons delivered by obsolete H-6 bombers.

This is not a force that could even begin to pose a threat to the United States. China is, however, working on a new generation of mobile, solid-fueled missiles, notably the 5,000-mile (8,000-km) three-stage DF-31 and DF-41, the latter of which is still under development; both likely equipped with multiple independently targeted vehicles re-entry warheads (MIRVS) based on technology allegedly purloined from the U.S.

These modern ICBM will have the capability to strike much of the United States. Their ability to be transported by trucks or by rail means greatly increased survivability. U.S. intelligence estimates the DF-31 will be deployed in small numbers by the year 2002 or 2003. Still, China is years away from possessing significant nuclear-war-fighting potential. Though theft of U.S. MIRV technology and plans for the miniaturized W-88 nuclear warhead have greatly aided and accelerated China's strategic weapons programs, there seems little doubt China would have eventually developed such systems on its own

China's medium-range nuclear arsenal, notably the new 1,864-mile (3,000-km) DF-21 and growing numbers of conventionally armed tactical missiles, does pose a growing threat to China's neighbors, such as Vietnam, South Korea, Taiwan, and Russia, as well as a major danger to the small island nations of Japan and Taiwan. Both are extremely vulnerable to nuclear blackmail, bombardment by conventional missiles, and maritime blockade. Japan, Taiwan, and South Korea are all considering adopting a U.S. theater anti-missile defense system.

India has made clear it considers itself particularly menaced by China's missile force, and claims it is deploying the 1,554-mile- (2,500-

km-) range Agni-II and -III medium-range ballistic missiles to counter the growing Chinese threat. In turn, India's Agni series missiles, which can strike all of China's most important cities and industrial centers, have provoked deep concern in Beijing, and sparked an arms race between the two Asian powers. Technologically, the Indian-made Agni-II appears superior to Chinese missiles in terms of accuracy, reliability, speed of launch, and mobility. Both India and China have by now mastered the art of miniaturizing nuclear warheads, China thanks to espionage, and India thanks to covert assistance over many years from Israel, which itself purloined U.S. nuclear technology and *materiel*.

China's slow but steady development of its conventional power is of far less concern to the United States, though a source of concern in Asia. China's somewhat numerically reduced army has great defensive power, but its lack of sufficient armor, transport, self-propelled artillery, and modern communications severely limits its ability to move or maneuver. The Chinese air force has only forty-six modern SU-27 and is developing the F-10 fighter, the latter based on U.S. technology sold to China by Israel, which had originally been destined for the Lavi fighter program. However, China has at least a dozen other tactical fighter projects under development, and is trying to acquire airborne early warning aircraft similar to the U.S. AWACS system. Growing Russian technical assistance is playing an important role in modernizing China's air force.

In short, China's armed forces may be huge in numbers, but they remain obsolescent, immobile, and without the precision arms and instant communications that make modern fighting forces increasingly lethal. China's ground forces are capable of threatening Taiwan, Russia's Pacific region, northern Vietnam, Indochina, and, most important, India's northern and eastern borders. But beyond these places, China has no real strategic clout or reach, and cannot be expected to have any until well into the twenty-first century.

Attempts by American conservatives to paint China as a second Soviet Union are overblown. China lacks the strategic or conventional military power of the old Soviet Union, and is only a force to be reckoned with in its immediate neighborhood. In fact, unlike the Soviets, with their theory of internationalist duty, China has never shown much interest in events beyond those in its strategic backyard. But there, China expects and demands unquestioned obedience.

It seems inevitable that as China's economic, military, and political power grows, that of the United States—hitherto Asia's greatest power—must decline. A militarily weak China allowed the U.S. to dominate the Sea of Japan and South China Sea, and when necessary to project power on the Asian mainland. The U.S. Navy will no longer enjoy this freedom of movement or action after China has managed to develop its military capabilities.

Shrinking U.S. defense budgets and heavy strain on inadequate military forces are compelling Washington to re-evaluate its traditional policy of forward deployment in the Pacific. U.S. military forces have reached a breaking point: though one-third smaller than they were at the end of the Cold War, they are being tasked with almost 50 percent more overseas operations, producing troop exhaustion, falling morale, and deterioration of equipment. The long, sterile conflict with Iraq, followed by the war against Serbia, severely depleted U.S. military capability and sustainability. Washington's efforts to hector Japan into assuming more responsibility for Asian security—meaning maintenance of the status quo—have repeatedly failed.

As U.S. power in Asia recedes, that of China must advance apace. China's neighbors have already recognized this fact and are shaping their policies accordingly. American decision-makers have yet to come to the realization that in Asia their power and authority will no longer be absolute: Washington will have to begin learning to be more accommodating in its relations with China, and more accepting of the fact that Beijing will increasingly make its will felt in Asia. In other words, the U.S. must eventually accept that China has a legitimate, recognized sphere of influence in eastern Asia.

Old powers always find it difficult to adjust to dealing with arriviste powers; the process is often marked by tension and the danger of open conflict, as in the emergence of Germany at the end of the nineteenth century, and Japan a few decades later. This is a perilous time that demands the highest diplomatic skills.

Even so, aside from Taiwan and the South China Sea's resources, there are no other major disputes that are likely to put Beijing and Washington on a collision course. Those who advocate the containment of China must face the fact that China has always more or less contained itself. In China's view, the United States and Russia are no longer its primary strategic threat: this role is now occupied by India.

Nor do China and the U.S. share any major geopolitical or historical disputes, such as are found in the Mideast or Balkans. Even the most ardent American Sinophobes find it difficult to cite specific examples of how China threatens U.S. security or international interests. In fact, China and the U.S. have much more in common than most great powers: growing trade and technological exchange, a history of American concern for China and widespread respect for its splendid culture, and a mutual degree of personal comfort and ease that neither finds with other nations, such as Japan or Russia.

The same, however, cannot be said for China's immediate neighbors, Japan, Russia, and India. The balance and nature of relations between Japan and China as yet remain to be decided: will Japan be a junior partner to China and accept Beijing's strategic diktat in Asia? Will a more muscular and self-assertive Japan eventually challenge China for regional leadership? Or will Japan remain, like the Great Britain of Asia, sheltered under America's security umbrella, unwilling and unable to intervene in the region's strategic affairs?

China's future relations with Russia promise to be more contentious. Russians and Chinese harbor deep racial hatred for one another, and share a legacy of historical animosity and fear. When I asked senior officers of Chinese military intelligence in the mid-1980s how long it would take the People's Liberation Army to conquer the Soviet Union's Pacific provinces, their terse reply was "Two weeks." Most Russian military planners are convinced that one day China will either attack their vulnerable far east, which has only 25 million people, or swamp the resource-rich region with hordes of Chinese settlers.

The Chinese, for their part, have long feared a Russian attack on industrial Manchuria. It is worth noting that Russo-Japanese rivalry over the riches of Manchuria sparked the twentieth century's first significant conflict, the 1904 Russo-Japanese War. Manchuria could well figure in a future conflict of the twenty-first century.

This Asian strategic *tour d'horizon* brings us back to India, which today is the only Asian power that appears determined to actively contest China's self-appointed domination of the region. India and China are on a geopolitical collision course in the Himalayas, in strategic Burma, and over the waters of the eastern end of the Indian Ocean. These two Asian giants now regard one another as the primary strategic and commercial threat; they have embarked on a nuclear arms race and are preparing their ground forces to fight in the Himalayas. Each sees itself as the rightful master of Asia.

If China's history is any guide to its future actions, whatever leadership emerges in Beijing over the next decade—whether younger, "reformed" Communists of the East European mode, democrats, a military junta, or an authoritarian clique—they may be tempted, as Mao was in 1962, to "teach a lesson" to increasingly self-assertive India. The Indians have made plain they will not be routed a second time, and intend to return any Chinese "lesson" in kind.

According to a 1997 U.S. Defense Department study, cited by the former CIA director James Woolsey, China will continue to build its military power "to the point where it can engage and defeat any potential enemy" in East Asia, and it is developing the capability to fight short-duration, high-intensity wars in the region. In other words, to teach more lessons.

Woolsey went on to make a fascinating point: when India and China reach South Korea's current level of per capita energy use, likely within the next thirty years, their combined demand for oil will amount to 120 million barrels daily. At present, the entire globe consumes 60 to 70 millions barrels of oil each day.

To meet such huge demands, India may be drawn to Iran and the Gulf, while China may look south to Indonesia, Indochina, and the South China Sea. Both superpowers will compete to dominate the vast but so far unexploited oil and gas reserves of unstable Central Asia, at a time when Russia will be seeking to reassert its influence over the former Soviet republics of its "near abroad."

Some Indian strategists are already speaking of the need for Delhi to "assure future sources of Mideast oil" and to dominate the sea lanes over which the oil must travel. Australia protested to Delhi over increasing Indian naval activity in the eastern Indian Ocean as long as a decade ago. Opening of a new Indian naval base in the Andaman islands at Port Blair signals that Delhi also has its eyes on Indonesia and Malaysia.

The lines of a future major conflict in Asia are thus being clearly drawn. Irresistible geopolitical forces are at work, as Asia's two continental giants, India and China, slowly and relentlessly grind against one another like the massive tectonic plates of eons past, whose mighty collision shook the globe and threw up the Himalayas.

Index